" His practised hand whirls his blade and sends it straight at the bared and brawny throat before him."—[See p. 281.]

SPECIAL LIMITED EDITION

BETWEEN THE LINES

A Story of the War

BY

CAPTAIN CHARLES KING, U.S.A.
AUTHOR OF "A WAR-TIME WOOING" ETC.

ILLUSTRATED

NEW YORK
B. W. DODGE & COMPANY
PUBLISHERS

BETWEEN THE LINES.

I.

SHADING her eyes with a slender white hand, a young girl stood gazing eastward over a broad and beautiful landscape. The sun was fast sinking behind the wooded heights at her back, and throwing long shadows over the green carpet of the lawn. It was a picturesque old place, that Virginia homestead. The house was large, two storied, with broad central hallway and heavy wings; dull red brick showing here and there through the thick veil of vines; a wide and sheltered piazza with white wooden railing and chubby balusters; a broad flight of steps leading down to the circular driveway, and flanked by white buttresses ornamented with big florid vases of the same material and ponderous pattern as the sturdy little squat balusters that supported the railing. No plants or flowers blooming in the vases to-day, and this not the only evidence of a neglect that was perhaps inevitable. The drive itself was furrowed here and there with gullies made by recent rains. The line of demarcation between flower-bed and lawn had long since become blurred in the encroachments of the thick grass or swifter creeping plants. Poultry, too, had taken advantage of the re-

1

laxation of domestic discipline, and were making themselves at home ; the hens "dusting" in various concavi-
ties of the roadway, scooped out, unrebuked, by their
busy claws, while two or three blear-eyed chanticleers
were paying court in grandiose style, as though conscious of the fact that, as natives of Virginia, a degree
of dignity and suavity of mien must be observed which
should distinguish them from the "dunghills" of com-
monwealths less favored. The big gate at the front
hung heavily on its rusting hinges, and no sign of
wheel track marked the drive. The fence, too, that
showed here and there through the hedge of rose-
bushes, was lacking a paling in more places than one,
and the old Newfoundland, that had just come lazily
in from a scout in the red roadway beyond, had availed
himself of one of these openings in preference to the
broader one where the path led through the gateway.

But the trees were beautiful in their graceful shape
and luxuriant foliage; the air was soft and still and
clear; the sunshine warm and radiant, and the view
from the piazza one that no man could look upon and
forget. The old house stood on the eastern slope of a
range of heavily wooded heights. Eastward the woods
and fields fell away almost abruptly for a hundred
yards or so, and then, like the *falda* of the western
Sierras, glided into almost imperceptible gradations as
they joined the general contours of the surface that
stretched in alternate field and forest until bounded by
the distant heights along the horizon. All across this
twenty-mile-wide valley the shadows of the silvery
clouds were slowly sailing. Northward it narrowed,

and was flanked by bolder heights and sharper curves. The woods were darker too, and the little farmhouses peeping out here and there in the sunshine were brighter by contrast.   Southward, three or four miles away, was a dusty high-road, with what looked like a railway embankment alongside, leading through open country to a little patch of houses perhaps eight or nine miles to the southeast.   There it joined another high-road, broad and dusty too, for great clouds of reddish-tinted mist were rising high and betraying its line of direction even after it was lost in the thick woods beyond the hamlet.

It seemed to bear straight away over intervening swell and shallow, dipping here and there into the bed of some little stream, until it reached the upland slope far to the east, and found its terminus in the clump of white houses that glistened in the sunshine on the distant heights of Centreville.   The white, gleaming dots upon the dark background were plainly visible to the naked eye here at Hopeville.

Beyond the first hamlet the ground began to rise towards the southeast, and a great bare plain could be dimly seen through rifts in the dust clouds that rose from the highway—a plain that was overhung by a pall of smoke rising from the unseen fires of a recent conflagration.

All the night before the skies had been lurid with the glare far over there above Manassas, and there had been excitement and anxiety and enthusiasm—all commingled—at the old homestead.   No one slept, for every little while there came hoof-beats along the

road and animated voices, and frequently the riders
had turned in at the open gateway, thrown themselves
from their panting steeds, exchanged a few jubilant
words with the venerable master of the house, par-
taken of the unfailing Virginia hospitality, and then,
remounting, had pushed on through the gloom. Soon
after sunrise other visitors had come, but these the old
man would not see; and the tall lieutenant in the
uniform of the Union cavalry who spurred so confidently into the yard, rode laughing away to join his
men who had halted without the hedge, and the only
one with whom he had exchanged a word was the
young girl herself. At her he looked back more than
once as his escort went clattering away, and finally he
bared his handsome head and bowed low over the
pommel of his saddle—unmistakably to her.

Brief indeed was the visit of this little scouting
party of blue jackets, but all the rest of the morning
she could see the dust clouds rising along the distant
pike, and long lines of cavalry skirmishers pushing up
towards the great gap four miles down the range.
Then there had been the booming of guns at Thoro'-
fare, and the old man's battered telescope had told
them that the fluttering guidons far to the south were
falling back before the cannon, and then that those were
the Stars and Stripes waving above the battalions of
dark infantry deploying to the support of the troopers; and a neighbor galloping by shouted that the
Yanks were "tryin' to shet off Longstreet. Might's
well try to squelch hell." And then there came the
sound of a bugle close at hand, and the negroes, with

bulging eyes, ran in to say the mountain road was just swarming with soldiers ; and surely enough the open fields a mile to the southeast were soon alive with horsemen and long gray lines pushing steadily down upon the distant ranks of blue ; and then there had been an hour of wild jubilee on the piazza, as the Union forces were seen slowly gathering in their clouds of skirmishers and slipping out from the threatened envelopment of their right flank. Slowly and stubbornly they were retiring—but retiring beyond all question—towards the little hamlet on the Warrenton pike, and as they went, so advanced and developed the long dusky lines under the red field and blue St. Andrew's cross. When five o'clock came the Union division, with its cavalry accompaniment, was far over towards the southeast ; no more gray columns were striding out from Hopeville Pass ; the brigades that threatened the Union flank had halted, gone into bivouac, and were building little fires down in the timber a mile or so away, while a whole division tramped out into the open fields in front of Thoro'fare, and the batteries trotted down and took their places in the brigade intervals as line of battle was reformed. Then the old man shut his telescope with a snap, and worn out with long hours of excitement and vigil, possibly, too, slightly overcome by the combined effects of enthusiasm and apple-jack, he was easily persuaded to go to his room for a sleep.

But his daughter remained at her post on the piazza. She would not go — for anything. The guns had ceased their thunder close at hand, but now, far over

to the eastward, the dull booming of a heavier cannonade burst upon the ear, and, levelling the glass and
fixing it upon the dark woods that lay between the
hamlet on the Warrenton pike and those distant
heights of Centreville, the girl could see heavy clouds
of mingled dust and battle-smoke rising above the
trees. She shuddered slightly as she turned away and
spoke to a young woman—a quadroon—who stood silently by: "They are fighting over there, beyond
Gainesville, terribly, Hannah. It must be Stonewall
Jackson; and yet they all said last night he was at
Manassas, and had captured everything there."

"I know that, Miss Lucy," was the answer, spoken
with a trace of the negro intonation and dialect;
"but all day long the Federals have been marching
through Gainesville. Young Marse Anderson rode
by when you were with the judge in-doors; he said
there was thousands and thousands of them, and they
was going to try and surround him before General
Lee could get there to help him. Where is Marse
Henry now, Miss Lucy?"

"God knows! With Stuart somewhere. He cannot be far away, and yet he could not be near without
coming to see us. We have not set eyes on him since
last March. Nothing but those hateful Yankee uniforms have I seen in the road until this blessed day.
Thank God for another look at the gray! Thank
God!" she repeated, fervently, as she gazed with moist-
ening eyes at the fluttering patches of color down in
the distant fields where here and there the St. Andrew's
cross waved above some battalion forming line. The

sun had sunk behind the ridge; twilight was settling down upon the valley; the little bivouac fires glimmered here and there in the timber, and far away over the intervening lowlands, far over among the dense woods to the north of Manassas, there still rumbled the thunder of those sullen guns, and one broad clearing, faintly discernible through the glass, was lighted by the lurid flash and glare of the incessant volleyings of battling hosts. It was the evening of the 28th of August, 1862, and the opening chorus of second Bull Run.

Presently the now familiar sound of hoof-beats rapidly advancing was heard upon the road without, and two horsemen in gray uniform came at the gallop to the gateway. The man in front—tall, dark, slenderly and gracefully made—threw his reins to his follower as he dismounted, and then walked, with clinking spurs and trailing scabbard, straight across the lawn to the house, an eager light in his eyes as he caught sight of the girl standing there half hidden by the vines. She, on the contrary, drew back slightly, and the sweet face that had flushed with hope and anticipation as the horsemen came in sight now paled a little as she recognized the arriving soldier.

He raised his broad-brimmed slouch hat as he sprang up the steps, and held forth his right hand. His uniform of gray with its sleeve-knots of gold was new and rich; his sash and gauntlets and belts and riding-boots all bespoke the "dandy" soldier; his face was oval, clear cut, and handsome; his eyes and hair dark; he was a most presentable fellow in every sense of the

word, and the dark eyes had a gleam of gentle reproach in them as he said:

"Have you no word of welcome for me, Lucy?"

"I *am* glad to see you, Captain Falconer," she answered, "and father will be overjoyed. You bring us
news of Henry?" she asked, eagerly, the soft violet
eyes searching his face for the first time in one quick,
sweeping glance, then falling again before the ardent
gaze in his.

"Not very late, I fear. I have not seen him since
the night before Stuart's dash on Catlett's Station—
wasn't it glorious?—but I've heard of him, only yesterday. He was carrying despatches 'cross country
to Longstreet, and the chances are he is with him or
General Lee over at Salem or White Plains this very
evening, and you'll see him early in the morning. This
is only our advance. But didn't we drive that Yankee
division back in style? You must have seen it all
from here. That is "—and he turned and looked into
the gathering darkness from the south end of the
piazza—"all except the fight close in by Thoro'fare
Gap. My squadron came within an ace of getting
two of their guns, and we did capture two prisoners—
one of them a cavalry officer."

"What was he like?" she asked, with interest.
"There was one here this morning, scouting; he
said—"

"Yes, and he was just as handsome as he could be,
Captain Falconer," interposed the quadroon girl, showing her white teeth.

It was evident that Hannah had long been a priv-

ileged character at the homestead, and also evident
that the captain totally disapproved of her remarks.
He ignored her entirely.

"This young fellow seems to be one of Buford's
cavalry. I hardly fancy he is the man to be scouting
these roads by himself. It takes nerve and pluck to
separate one's self from the main column in these
days. You never know what you may meet in this
part of Virginia." And it would seem as though the
young captain desired her to appreciate the risk he
ran in coming to see her. "I suppose the country
has been full of Yanks for months past."

"Ever since you fell back from Manassas last March;
but they rarely come up here. We are miles off the
beaten tracks, and have hardly been disturbed at all.
Captain Falconer," she said, suddenly, "I know you
want to see father, but he is sleeping now. He was
awake all last night, for of course we were wild with
delight and excitement at seeing our soldiers once
more, and hearing of Jackson's splendid march. Do
come in and let me offer you some refreshment, and
bid your orderly take the horses around to the barn.
I think old Nelse has still a little forage hidden away,
though our horses are gone. Then you shall tell me
all about what has been going on. I am wild to know.
See how dark it is growing, and yet they are still fighting over yonder. God be with us!"

"Amen to that! but I'm anxious. Jackson is all
alone in there somewhere with only some twenty-five
thousand men, and the Yanks must have a hundred
thousand all around him by this time. I begged the

general to let me take my squadron and ride over
there and find out how things were going, but he refused. He said the country was full of Yankee cavalry, but I warrant we could have got through. Tell
me about the party here this morning. Did they attempt any insolence?" and he twirled his mustache
fiercely.

"Not at all. Only this officer entered the gate.
He was very polite, and merely asked if this was
Judge Armistead's, and on my saying yes, he asked
to see him. Father declined, and sent word to him
that he could conceive of no possible reason why he
should request an interview. Hannah brought the reply, and also a mandate that I should come in at once,
for meantime we had entered into conversation."

"I thought you were a loyal Virginia girl, and hated
a Yankee."

"I am loyal to my state and to my people, Captain
Falconer, as you very well know," answered Miss
Armistead, with flashing eyes. "His remarks were
merely complimentary to the beauty of the neighborhood in general, and to old Hector there in particular.
He seemed to admire the dog more than anything
about the place."

"Even its fair young mistress?"

"Even its young mistress," she answered, flushing
with evident vexation at the tone of the inquiry.

"And did he introduce himself? I take it for
granted he made some overtures."

"He did. He begged pardon for intruding; said
his orders required him to see if the family were still

residing here, as it was known that this was the home of Captain Henry Armistead, of the —th Virginia Cavalry. I replied that I was proud to say it was; and then he startled me by saying that he had known him well three years before, and gave his name—Lieutenant Kearny, of the New Jersey Cavalry. I was so surprised at what he told me of having known Henry that I couldn't say another word. Then he rode away."

Falconer's eyes gleamed with an angry light. "I know well who he is. They were at college and in the same class, and it was that same Kearny who rode through our lines at Cedar Mountain two weeks ago and carried off Frank Pegram and Eustis as prisoners. By Heaven! my men would give their souls to catch him, and if I run across him in this campaign 'twill be his last ride in Virginia. Why, Lucy, he was your brother's guest a week at Richmond only two winters ago, and now he is an invader of the state whose hospitality he accepted. Which way did they go?"

"Down that very road; but he turned off eastward at the lane. He said he must ride in search of General McDowell. That was one of his divisions down there at the gap."

"Yes—Rickett's division, the prisoners say. But if Mr. Kearny cut 'cross country eastward, I don't envy him his reception. He must have run slap in among Jackson's people, and if so, Libby will get him, not I."

Just then there came other hoof-beats, and a panting steed galloped up the wood road and into the open gate. Another moment, and a tall young officer, also in Confederate gray, leaped from the saddle and bounded lightly up the steps. Miss Armistead started forward ; then with a joyous, half-articulate cry threw herself into the stranger's arms. For a moment they were clasped in each other's embrace ; he kissing her rippling hair and smooth white forehead ; she sobbing with excitement, relief, and gladness on his breast. At last, as she raised her tearful eyes to look at him, he inquired, " How's father ?"

" Well; sleeping just now, but he'll be wild to see you, Harry," she sobbed, still clinging to him. " Now let me go. I'll run and wake him."

Then the tall, dark soldier stepped forward from the shadows, holding forth his hand. " Welcome home, Armistead," he said.

The younger man started slightly, then, recovering himself, replied, in a tone that utterly lacked cordiality,

" Oh ! is that you, Falconer ? I hardly thought to see you here."

II.

LIEUTENANT KEARNY had indeed turned eastward on reaching the lane indicated by Miss Armistead, but it was early in the morning, and before he had marched more than a mile in that direction his attention was arrested by the sight of distant troops of horse far down towards the railway. It was a matter of but a moment's work for his escort to tear down a rail-fence or two and enable the party to make a short-cut southward across the intervening fields. In half an hour the lieutenant was in presence of the cavalry commander, and making his report; no Confederate troops were in sight from Hopeville Gap, but heavy clouds of dust were rising from the road west of Thoro'fare, and it was evident that strong forces were advancing from the direction of Salem and White Plains. The general listened attentively, was silent a moment, and then replied:

"That accords with the reports from our advance. We have a regiment and some light guns at the Gap already, but can hardly hold it against Longstreet's whole corps. Which way were you going, sir?"

"Back to find General McDowell. He sent me up from Buckland Mills last night. I reported to your adjutant-general as I passed the brigade, sir."

"He must be somewhere about Gainesville now, and I understand that the whole army is directed to concentrate on the Junction. Jackson was there last night, as I suppose you know. Look yonder!" And General Buford turned in his saddle and pointed off to the southeast, where dense clouds of black smoke were rising high in air above the well-known plateau. "Have your men had coffee, or anything to eat?"

"Nothing since supper last evening, general."

"Well, halt here awhile. Your own regiment is deployed out there at the front—just at the Gap—but my people here will give you all the coffee you want. There is no use in riding after General McDowell yet. Wait an hour or so and you'll have something to tell him."

Gladly enough Lieutenant Kearny led his little party into a grove near the road-side, and gave the order to dismount and unsaddle. Meantime the cavalry commander with his staff pushed on towards the dark pass through the rugged heights to the west. Already a brisk and rapid fire of small-arms could be heard ringing among the rocks. Then, as the rattle of carbine and rifle continued and increased, the cavalry trumpets along the pike could be heard repeating some signal from the head of the column, and the dust-covered squadrons ambling placidly by took up a jingling trot, and presently the rearmost went obliquely off the road and through the open fields to the south. Then the hoarser notes of a battery bugle were heard blaring from the rocky hill-sides, and the bang, bang of the three-inch rifles and the shriek of flying shells were added to the clamor. Kearny's eyes kindled at the sound.

"Old Buford's right!" he said to a staff-officer who had dismounted to tighten his saddle-girth. "There will be something to tell McDowell, and in less than an hour, too. Hurry up with your breakfast, men."

In much less than an hour an aide-de-camp came galloping down the road and reined in at sight of the little party of troopers already "saddled up" and standing at their horses' heads, while their chargers were busily cropping at the scant herbage.

"Is this Lieutenant Kearny?" asked the aide.

"Ay, ay. What's wanted?"

"General Buford wishes you to ride at once to General McDowell, and tell him that Longstreet's whole corps is at the Gap and deploying to attack. You can leave your escort here to rejoin their regiment, but take an orderly with you. The road is open back of you, and Stuart nowhere near. That is, so far as we know," and the aide-de-camp grinned.

"I understand," was Kearny's quiet answer. "But as I left Hopewell this morning I could see cavalry crossing the open fields over towards Sudley Springs, north of the pike. I counted at least three regiments through my glass. Who were they?"

"None of ours, you can bet—and Stuart likely enough. He was at Manassas last evening. You'll have to keep your eye peeled, young man. Good-day to you. Lord! hear those guns! If we had McDowell's whole corps here I doubt if we could hold those fellows. They know every rabbit track in those

hills, confound them !"　And with this outspoken tribute to the efficiency of the foe the aide clapped heels
to his horse's flanks and went sputtering back to the
front.

Directing the sergeant in command of the little detachment to report forthwith to the adjutant of the
regiment with the entire party, Lieutenant Kearny
mounted and trotted off towards the distant hamlet of
Gainesville.　His own horse was in prime condition, a
capital, mettlesome fellow, and he himself was an accomplished horseman.　The "mount" of his escort, on
the contrary, was jaded from the fortnight of hard
marching, scouting, and skirmishing that had followed
Cedar Mountain, and when he came to look them over
he did not see one that seemed fit for a rapid ride.　He
started, therefore, on his mission all alone.

For the first mile he met the inevitable stragglers
from the command, some of them hastening forward
to rejoin their squadrons, others lounging by the road-
side in evident disinclination to march to the sound of
the guns.　Every moment the cannonade at the Gap
seemed to increase in fierceness; but little by little, as
he rode southeastward, the wind carried the sound
away from him, and by the time he caught sight of
the roofs of Gainesville the roar had died into a faint
and almost inaudible rumble.　Far down to the south,
where lay the broad turnpike to Warrenton, he could
see the dust clouds mounting high in the sultry air, telling of marching columns that he knew to be the Union
forces hastening eastward to carry out Pope's jubilant
and hopeful order to "bag the entire crowd."　Daring

and wellnigh reckless as Jackson had ever been, never yet had he essayed so perilous a move as this, by which he had marched entirely around the right and rear of the Union army, and swept down upon their trains and supplies at Manassas. Now, separated a full day's march from Lee and Longstreet, he was known to be lurking somewhere among the dense forests north of the Junction, and Pope had launched Sigel, McDowell, Heintzelman, Reno, Phil Kearny, and Porter to hem him in, head him off, and overwhelm him before relief could possibly come. Just how many men he had, no one within the Union lines could tell. Anywhere from thirty to sixty thousand was the estimate, and the Union force was big enough to handle either number. Young Kearny's heart beat high with hope as he trotted rapidly eastward. He was an ardent patriot, an enthusiastic soldier, a born cavalryman; and all through the campaign his energy and enthusiasm had won the admiration and praise of his superiors. Just after Cedar Mountain, while in command of a troop out on picket duty, he had made a dash on a Confederate outpost while it was occupied by a reconnoitring party, and had borne off two distinguished young Virginians as prisoners, not without a sharp fight and the loss of three of his own men; but the exploit had made him famous in the cavalry brigade, and Bayard himself had ridden down to shake his hand and congratulate him. An envied man was Kearny from that day, but a popular one withal, for with high health, high spirits, and high social connections, without a care in the world, he was also a gen-

2

erous and manly comrade whom all men warmed to, and his face and form were such as women love to look upon.

He was smiling to himself as he rode along, and thinking of his odd adventure of the early morning. "Only fancy my meeting Hal Armistead's sister in such a way!" he thought. "She looked hostile enough to freeze a man, and yet how sweetly pretty. I don't think I ever saw a lovelier face. Halloa! Who comes *here*, I wonder?"

Spurring rapidly towards him, his horse covered with dashes of foam, an officer came riding at the gallop, followed by a couple of troopers. As soon as he sighted Kearny he lay back in the saddle and pulled hard at the reins, gradually bringing his charger down to a walk, and then signalling that he wished to speak. Kearny reined in as they came together, and seeing the silver leaves on the other's shoulder-strap, raised his gauntlet in salute.

"Where are you from, sir, and where are you going?" was the sharp question.

"From General Buford, with a message for General McDowell."

"Look well to your left, then, as you go. Rebel cavalry are in those woods off yonder. What news from the Gap! Is Longstreet there?"

"In force, sir—and fighting through when I left."

"Then you cannot get to the general too soon. I'll push forward. You will find him somewhere about Gainesville now, and take my advice—get off this road and go through the fields until you reach the Warrenton pike ; then turn eastward. It's a long way round, but there's danger ahead of you. Who are you, may I ask ?"

"Lieutenant Kearny, sir—New Jersey cavalry."

"Oh! I'm glad to meet you, my lad. I've heard of you before. Good-day again. I must hurry. Don't forget about those rebs over there ;" and with that the field-officer again rode on.

Kearny looked about him. Off to the south all the fields were open, though crossed in many places by the inevitable " snake " or rail fence that still remained in those sections of the state where large bodies of troops had not happened to camp. Anywhere within three miles of a martial garrison, however, the fences had long since gone as fuel. " It would not be difficult to make a way through those fields and fences," thought Kearny, " but even when I reach the Warrenton pike it will doubtless be crowded with wagons and stragglers. I'll find myself miles behind McDowell, and will have hard work to push through the crowd and catch him. No ! I'll risk it and stick to the road. It all looks safe enough off there to the left, and the colonel said I could not reach McDowell too soon."

So communing with himself, the lieutenant drew forth his watch, noted the time—8.45—and, with one look at the caps of his revolvers, he pushed ahead at a rapid lope. Off to the eastward—his left front— the ground rose and fell in graceful undulations, open clearings and cultivated fields, with here and there a little patch of forest. Cavalry could be hidden among those trees, to be sure, but the nearest groves seemed

full six hundred yards away from the high-road, and
with that much start no horse in Virginia could catch
him in a rush 'cross country. They might head him
off the beaten track, but that was the worst he anticipated. Far away towards Sudley Springs, through the
openings among the trees, he twice fancied he saw little bodies of horse ; but there was no time to unsling
his glass and rein in and look. He had ridden a full
mile since leaving the staff-officer who stopped him,
and was trotting over a rise, when, down in the shallow valley just in front, and not five hundred yards
away to the left of the road, he saw a sight that made
his heart leap up in his throat. A little knot of troopers, with broad-brimmed slouch hats and uniforms of
dusty gray, were watering their horses at a pool in
the brook that crossed the roadway from the south.
Another minute and one of them glanced up and saw
him. Before he had time to think, the whole party,
six in number, had clapped spurs to their horses and
came dashing down upon him. Kearny was no coward—he had showed the mettle of his race before now
—but he felt his nerves quiver and his heart beat like
a hammer as he gave one quick glance around him.
It was possible to whirl about and retreat along the
road until once more he found himself within the shel-
tering lines of Buford's cavalry brigade ; he might
tear down the topmost rail or two and then jump
"Ramapo" over the others, but both courses would
take him miles out of his way, and the message to
McDowell would be delayed or abandoned entirely.
Devoted soldier that he was, he reasoned with the

quickness of thought that that would never do; then, setting his teeth and gripping his revolver, he struck spurs to his charger's flanks, and, to the amaze of the attacking party, shot straight ahead down the slope and across their very front. Instantly they opened out, those who were farthest to the east veering to the left in wide circle so as to strike the road in front of him and head him off. Kearny bent low over his horse's neck and urged him to his utmost speed, and in less time than it takes to pen the line, despite the yells of "Halt," accompanied by whistling pistol-balls and a scattering volley of inelegant epithets, he whirled beyond range of those who had headed straight for the little rise, and the next instant was leaping the brook down in the shallow flats just as two of his pursuers cleared the low stone wall to his left and came dashing into the road, one in front, the other behind him. "Halt! halt!" were the yells, and then bang! bang! went both pistols, but with no apparent effect on either horse or rider. Bang! went his own trusty Colt as he flashed by the venturesome trooper who had leaped in front of him, and in another moment, as he raced up the slope on the eastern side of the brook and glanced over his shoulder, he could see that his shot had taken effect in the trooper's horse. Already he was down on his knees and his rider springing off. Reaching the crest of the gentle rise, Kearny found himself unpursued, the troopers wisely abstaining from the chase of such a runner as "Ramapo;" so his rider reined him in, and, stopping a moment, shouted back his laughing defiance at the disconcerted knot of foemen down by the brook. The wounded horse had by this time rolled over on his side, and his late rider was bending sadly over him. They looked up a moment as Kearny halted on the ridge, full five hundred yards away, but paid no further attention to him. The next moment, as he turned to resume his ride, with Gainesville and the marching columns of infantry only a mile or so ahead, he suddenly found himself joined by a tall stranger, in civilian dress, who trotted out of a little lane to the right, and who surprised him with the quiet remark,

"You ride mighty well for a Jerseyman!"

"How did you know I was a Jerseyman?" asked Kearny, suspiciously. His breath was still coming fast and his heart beating heavily.

"I've seen you before," was the reply, "and seeing you were in for a scrape here, I rode across to help you out. You didn't need it, though. That's a fine horse of yours, lieutenant."

"The horse is all right, but I want to know who you are, and how it happens a man in civilian dress is riding about here between the two armies?" was Kearny's natural inquiry.

"I am in the service, and on a mission as important as your own. You are carrying despatches, I presume?" and the stranger eyed him closely.

"Service! What service? See here, my friend, if you are in the military service you ought to know enough to prove your identity. What duty are you on?"

"Scouting," was the laconic answer. "And here's

my credentials," he added, slowly, as he lugged from an inside pocket a small flat package done up in oiled silk. "I am in the secret service, and know every inch of this country hereabouts."

"All right. I don't want your papers. I've no time. Was General McDowell in Gainesville when you left there?"

"I didn't leave there."

"Where *did* you come from, then?"

The stranger smiled.

"Never mind, lieutenant; I see you're in a hurry and want to get on. Give my respects to General McDowell when you see him, and tell him to look out for that Gap up yonder. And you take my advice: Don't you go fooling round these roads alone another time; and the next visit you pay to Judge Armistead and that pretty daughter of his, you take a powerful big escort with you, and watch out for a Captain Falconer."

And before Kearny could recover from his astonishment or ask another question, the stranger had shifted a quid of tobacco in his jaws, leaped his raw-boned horse over a low fence to the left of the road, and then went loping easily over the fields in the direction of Aldie Gap.

III.

LATE that August afternoon Lieutenant Kearny, with an officer of McDowell's staff, was seated in the shade by the Warrenton pike, their horses being held a little distance away by the aide-de-camp's orderly. A singular hush had fallen upon the scene. The broad thoroughfare was almost deserted; the clouds of dust had settled back to earth, powdering the beautiful foliage as they fell; the birds were twittering and piping among the leaves, and in the enclosure just to the west of them—the garden of a Virginia homestead —three or four hound puppies were chasing each other through the long grass and romping about the neglected flower beds, while their mother, lolling on the broad wooden piazza at the head of the flight of steps, watched them with an expression of benevolent interest that was barely proof against an overpowering sense of drowsiness. Some bees were droning about the rose bushes close at hand, and adding to the somnolent effect of the late afternoon sunshine; the air was still, and not a leaf rustled in the tree-tops. Far off to the west, towards Thoro'fare, a dull booming of distant guns could be heard from time to time. Mc-Dowell had sent a whole division of infantry to support the cavalry in barring Longstreet, while he, with his other division, after marching through Gainesville and up the pike a mile or so, had turned off into the wood roads leading towards Manassas Junction, where, at last accounts, Jackson was supposed to be.

It was just at the point where this road left the pike and meandered away through the trees that the staff-officer and Lieutenant Kearny had dismounted and were resting. The general had ordered the former to remain there to direct any stray bodies of troops that might be coming up from the southwest, and to receive reports or messages coming from the Gap. To the latter he had given instructions to wait for orders—he would probably have some word to send to General Buford. Together, therefore, the two had ridden with the corps and division commanders until they reached the fork of the roads, and then had watched the fine division, with its four full brigades, as it tramped in solid column into the winding forest aisles. Then Kearny threw himself on the turf at the foot of a tree, and with his saddle blanket for a pillow, went sound asleep, and was oblivious of all surrounding objects for three or four hours. He was aroused by a lively conversation between the staff-officer and some one who had just arrived from the west. He heard his comrade say, "You had better ride right on towards Manassas. Follow this wood road and you'll find the general ahead there somewhere. He ought to know this at once."

"What's the news?" asked Kearny, sitting up and rubbing his eyes.

"Buford and Ricketts are falling back from Thoro'-

fare. The Rebs have pushed a column through a gap farther to the north, and flanked them."

"That must be Hopeville Gap, where I was this morning. What time is it now?"

"Nearly five, and you've had quite a nap of it. It's the quietest day and the most peaceful neighborhood I've seen in a month. Not a sound of war except that dull booming off at Thoro'fare. What *can* our people be doing around Manassas, do you suppose? Surely it is time we heard of Jackson."

"I can't imagine," said Kearny, sitting up, and brushing off the dust with the cuff of his gauntlet. "One might suppose we were on a summer picnic. Have no orders come for me?"

"Nothing—nor for me. The trains are back at Gainesville, but a lot of beef cattle were sent through here two hours ago. McDowell halted the division in there on the Manassas road, and they have stacked arms and gone to cooking. A division aide brought me word that McDowell had gone on to find General Pope, and that we were to accompany the division when it moved. But it's still there. The rear brigade isn't more than half a mile from us, so I decided to stay here. I sent the horses down to water an hour ago, and got a feed for them. Aren't you hungry?"

"Not just now. Where would we get supper if I were?"

"In the woods with the division. I know everybody at headquarters, and they would gladly welcome you. Here comes one of them now. What is it, captain?" he asked, as an officer came riding hastily towards them.

"Orders just come from General McDowell. The division is to get back on the pike at once and march to Centreville. They say Reno and Kearny have driven Jackson up there, and that we've got him this time—sure. Hatch's brigade is just filing out on the pike now, up at Pageland Lane, just east of here—you can see them from the rise yonder—and Gibbon's follows. Good-bye. I must hurry back to the general."

In a moment Kearny and his friend were in saddle and trotting eastward up the pike. At the crest of the "rise" just referred to they came in sight of a sweep of road leading straight away through a slight depression and over another crest a mile distant. Over this second ridge the head of a long, compact, blue column was trudging, the setting sun throwing heavy shadows across them where the trees hung close to the roadway on the northern side, and flashing from the barrels of their Springfields at every opening. Putting spurs to their horses and taking advantage of the little "dirt roads" that wound among the trees on the south side of the paved highway, the two officers speedily reached the head of column—the senior riding up to and entering into conversation with the brigade commander, the junior taking his place among a group of the staff in their rear. In this order they passed the division general and his staff, who had halted under the trees to watch the return of the brigades to the pike; in this order, too, they slowly ascended a gentle slope of the road, passing on their left a dense grove of large trees, and on their right a thick and impenetrable wilderness of forest growth and underbrush. Almost at the very crest the grove to their left abruptly ended, and there to the front opened out a broad and beautiful landscape. Far to the northeastward, the range of heights on which lay Centreville and Chantilly; midway, the beautiful, undulating valley through which wound the stream already so well known — Bull Run; half-way to the fringe of trees that marked the distant windings of the run, a road crossing the pike at right angles and disappearing among the forests a good two miles distant. Directly at the left hand, north of the pike and separated from it by the remains of a "snake" fence, an open undulating field, that rose very gently towards the north for two hundred yards, then sank in almost imperceptible slope into a long, hollow swale, and rose again in slope as gradual until it reached a line of forest spanning the fields from west to northeast a full mile away. Well over to the northeast the trees seemed to follow a mathematically regular curve around the crest of the slope, and Kearny could see the staff-officer pointing thereto and saying something about a railway embankment. Three hundred yards in front of the head of column was another little ridge over which the highway led, straight away as ever, then a long, gradual descent to a little clump of houses, where the cross-road and a brook seemed to intersect the pike at the same point. Beyond these and off to the south of the highway some heavily wooded and jagged heights, one of them shorn of

timber on the crest; beyond these, a distant high plateau, where an old brick farmhouse could be seen
perched on the summit and surrounded by a garden
and little patches of fruit-trees. The general half
turned in his saddle and pointed thither.

"Gentlemen, that is Groveton down there ahead of
us, and off beyond is the battle-field of a year ago—
Bull Run."

And now, how peaceful the scene! Over all that
broad stretch of country not a warlike object was in
view. Behind them, to be sure, came the dark, dense
columns of the Union division, swinging steadily forward through the darkening highway. Out on those
open fields all was one blaze of warm, mellow sunshine; not a moving, living object anywhere except
the buzzing swarm of insects, or lazily flitting bird
crossing from the grove to find his nest in the denser
foliage to the south. Far to the rear a regimental
band had suddenly struck up a joyous, spirited quick-
step, and the men in the leading battalion began to
chaff their musicians and urge them to "pitch in and
blow those Western fellows out." Riding to one side,
the brigade commander gazed eastward through his
field-glasses.

"Odd!" said he, "I thought certainly we should
see something of Sigel or Reynolds from here, but
there is not even a dust cloud this side of Stone
Bridge. It must be that they are all well over towards Centreville by this time, and that Jackson has
been driven before them. Certainly there isn't a soul
in sight hereabouts."

"General!" called the staff captain, suddenly. "Look off yonder; there's a battery!" and he pointed straight to the north—straight across the mile-wide undulation of open field to some dark objects that were faintly discernible at the edge of the forest. The general fixed his binocular upon them a moment, shook his head, and replied, "Only cattle," then rode forward again to the head of column. Kearny started to follow, but "Ramapo" suddenly lifted his off fore-foot and refused to budge. Dismounting quickly, the lieutenant found that he had picked up a piece of stone and that the shoe was started. It took some little time to pry out the offending flint and to tack on the loosened shoe. When he remounted, the rear of the leading brigade was just crossing the crest towards Groveton, and the head of column of the second brigade toiling up the ascent in the shade of the deep grove on the northern side. Glancing across the fields to the north, he saw a sight that made his pulses bound. The "cattle" were moving slowly out from the shadows of the distant forest in marvellous and military order—six parallel columns of twos equidistant from each other, and coming out upon the slope with a red pennon fluttering by the side of the westernmost. Repressing his impulse to shout, he sat there on his horse silently pointing out his discovery to the chief of the second brigade, a tall, slender, wiry man, with keen steel-blue eyes and soldierly face—a man who took one quick glance at the distant objects and their long shadows on the sward, and exclaimed, "Coming 'in battery,' too! Ride back, and bring

up the guns quick !" he ordered, and an aide-de-camp
whirled about and dashed for the rear of column.

Sheltered by the bank to its left, the leading regiment still trudged sturdily ahead, its gray-haired colonel sitting farmer fashion astride an easy-going old
horse. He glanced inquiringly at the general as he
passed, but the latter, up on the bank, was absorbed
in watching the distant battery. A moment more and
the head of column reached the top of the incline and
came up level with the open fields. The glistening
rifles showed above the low rail-fence, and at the same
instant Lieutenant Kearny marked the distant guns
whirling around with the precision of machinery, and
then white jets of sulphur smoke belched forth from
the opposite slope, and something came shrieking
through the skies—several somethings—and before
the report of the guns could reach them the woods
rang with the sudden crash of bursting shells, and the
air was filled with hurtling, whirring fragments of
iron. "Ha-alt ! Front ! Load at will ! — load !"
came the shrill order from the old gray-haired soldier
at the head of the leading regiment. Quick as his
word, the sets of fours had stopped and sprung into
line, facing to the left; down came the iron-shod gun-
butts with heavy thud upon the ground; swarthy,
dust-begrimed faces peered out from under the visors
with flashing eyes as hundreds of hands tore open the
heavy boxes and raised the ready cartridges to the
teeth. Not a word was spoken as eagerly they poured
the powder into the gleaming barrels; and then, how
the rammers flash in the stray gleams of sunlight and

the bullets are rammed home! Some men's hands *must* tremble a little at such times; a few drop their percussion-caps, but those who are thoughtless enough to stoop and pick them from the dust become instant targets for the rebuke of the line of file-closers. Bang! crash! go more shells bursting overhead, and whir-r-r-r come the fragments to earth. "Lie down—close to the bank!" is the next order, and in a moment the eye gazes along a perspective of dusty knapsacks and blankets. Bang! bang! again, closer overhead this time. "They're getting our range," whispers a young lieutenant to his captain. "Hi! here comes the battery!"

Up from the rear, with cracking whips and plunging steeds, cannoneers racing along beside the wheels, gun-carriages bounding over the rocky road-bed, old Battery "B" comes thundering into action, greeted with cheers by the regiments it dashes by. "This way! this way!" shouts a staff-officer, indicating a break through the rail-fence just at the crest, and there the leading gun whirls sharp to the left and goes trotting out into the open field; its caisson follows; then the next gun, and the next. "Forward into battery!" is the shouted order repeated down the column; the bugle blares its signal; the rearward teams go tugging obliquely out across the field; gun after gun gains its place upon its alignment with the blood-red guidon at the right, and long before the last one is in line the first section has opened fire and the assailing battery is answered by the resonant thunder of the "light twelve" pounders.

Meantime Kearny has galloped to the brigade commander, asking to be employed, and telling him almost in the same breath that it was across these very fields he saw cavalry moving early that morning.

"I know," replies the general. "Follow me, colonel," he calls to the commander of the second regiment in his column, halted directly in the shelter of the grove. "It's one of Stuart's cavalry batteries, and we'll nab it." Almost at double-quick the long column of eager faces and dusty blue uniforms plunges into a dark wood path that winds through the grove, following loyally the lead of their general. Louder grows the roar of the guns of the Union battery, fiercer is the shriek and crash of the Southern shells as their flight is lowered to suit the range. Four minutes' brisk jog-trot brings the general, with his little knot of staff-officers, to the northern edge of the grove, and then as they look eagerly towards the rebel guns across the lowland they are surprised to see another battery trotting out on the slopes east of the first one, and, starting up from the very bosom of the earth, springing like the warriors of Cadmus from the sown dragon's teeth, there leap into view at sound of the bugle a long line of gray skirmishers not three hundred yards away. Far to the left and right they extend, covering the whole front of that opposite forest, stretching their hostile rank midway between the warring batteries, but sheltered from their fire by the hollow in which they had been so skilfully concealed. "Forward your men, colonel. Drive back those skirmishers," is the order, and the advancing regiment

3

deploys the instant its leading files are clear of the wood. Forward they go, running into line; and 'tis full time for that slender rank of gray to fall back before these overwhelming numbers; but they do not budge. On the contrary, ping! ping! ring their rifles in obedience to a stirring peal; the color-bearer of the battalion wavers, then plunges heavily forward on his face; a corporal throws down his rifle, and, seizing the color-lance, waves the standard high in air; then, with sudden simultaneous crash, a volley of flame, smoke, and hissing lead leaps from the very bosom of the ground not five hundred yards away; a whizzing hail of bullets over the heads of the skirmishers on the low ground tears its way through the long blue line, and here and there men fall heavily forward or limp painfully out of ranks, but never an inch does the battalion yield, though in that one instant it finds itself face to face with the line of battle of a whole brigade. Up from the earth it springs, barred battle-flags and all; one instant it halts to align its gallant ranks, then forward it comes to sweep the Yankee regiment out of existence. Still no order is given; the officers look anxiously around to know the reason why, and there lies their colonel, bleeding, among the weeds. The lieutenant-colonel runs to him, gives one quick look in his senseless face, then shouts, "Commence firing!" Crash go the rifles all at once—aimed full upon the advancing line. It halts, reels, staggers an instant; down from the forest edge sweeps a second brigade in support, out from behind the batteries comes a third, and in five minutes the whole broad slope is alive with yelling ranks of gray, sweeping in perfect order down upon the slender line in front, waving over their heads in wild defiance the blood-red field and blue St. Andrew's cross.

And still, as though rooted there, with men falling thick as leaves, that one blue regiment holds its ground. Out from the grove, hurling away knapsack and blanket in their eagerness to join in the fight, two comrade battalions come tearing to the rescue, ranging themselves in line to right and left of the first. "Double-quick," was the order, but run was the response. Breathless but eager they reach their place even as the old gray-headed colonel, far down to the right, is heard advancing his men in line of battle. No waiting for orders to fire now. It is every man for himself fast as he can reach the line. Some standing, some kneeling, a very few lying down, the second brigade is there to a man, and every mother's son of them who is not yet sore stricken is fighting his best —and fighting Stonewall Jackson's whole right wing. There, halted on the opposite slopes and marvelling at what Jackson calls the "obstinate determination" of the Union men, five brigades of Confederates—the flower of the Southern force—are volleying at that one command of four Western regiments. Ewell, Taliaferro, Stark, are there. "Old Stonewall" himself, sitting on his sorrel at the edge of the woods, peers across the blazing, smoke-wreathed field from under the visor of his worn cadet cap. Half fronting to their right, the rebel batteries drive shell and case-shot down upon the thin blue line, while the gray battalions hasten forward, reinforce their foremost rank, and " double up " with their rapid fire. It is desperate, stand-up, hammer-and-tongs work, and neither side will yield an inch. The third brigade of the Union column is hastening forward in support, but they are still on the pike—full quarter of a mile away. The situation is more than trying. Hundreds of the gallant blue line have been shot down in their tracks; and now cavalry can be seen twinkling out at the left front just as the sun sinks down behind the distant mountains. " Stuart's men, of course," says the general to Kearny as he looks anxiously about him. " By Heaven! I *must* have supports on that flank; half my men are gone already." Ay, here they come —parallel columns of blue striding up from the pike. But by this time the Southern force is so strengthened from its rear brigades that once more it surges forward upon the thinned and wellnigh exhausted line. Closing in on their colors, the Union men have left huge gaps between the battalions, and, seeing these, the Southern leaders urge on their ranks. Too late, gentlemen, too late! Almost at the same instant New York and Pennsylvania have swarmed into the gaps between Indiana and Wisconsin. Their cool, fresh rifles add new uproar to the volleying; the second line of Confederates crowd up to the support of the first, and off to the right the field-officer commanding one of the hardest-fighting battalions on the line, seeing his front uncovered for a moment as the advancing brigades close up their bleeding ranks, rings out an order that is heard above the crash of musketry;

and, though astonished, his men cease firing for the
moment, and then are sent at double-quick, " changing front forward on tenth company," and in another
moment are pouring a rapid and telling fire on the
flank of the charging lines in gray. It is a glorious
move. "Look at the Seventh! Hurrah for the Seventh!" ring the cheers along the line; while the shouts
and shots and uproar seem to redouble as the Southerners are seen crumbling away under such savage
fire. Every moment it is growing darker; the distant
batteries have ceased their fire for fear of landing
shell and case-shot among their own people; but they
manage to drive a dozen rounds into the right flank of
that daring battalion before it slowly retires to its old
place in the line. The volleys grow redder and redder, the opposing ranks more and more blurred and
indistinct; little by little the fire slackens, and at last
only an occasional sputtering shot is heard; and still
those worn and bleeding lines stick to their ground,
grimly, defiantly confronting each other. Not until
black darkness settles down upon the bloody field does
either side deign to withdraw. Then, slowly and sullenly, without noise of any kind, the regimental commanders post a thin veil of skirmishers along their
fronts, and, facing their men to the rear, move them
cautiously a few hundred yards away, stack arms, and
send out details to gather up the wounded. Nearly
one half of that gallant Western brigade is killed
or maimed. Scores of favorite officers, hundreds of
brave and patriotic men, have fought their last fight;
and on the other side, where those dim lanterns are

twinkling over the field, there has been equal loss. Grim old Ewell's leg is gone; Taliaferro is wounded; a dozen field-officers are killed or placed *hors de combat*, and one daring young Virginia captain, riding about the heaping field in performance of some duty for his corps commander, comes groping beyond his lines, and the flash of a lantern reveals those gray sleeves heavily laced with gold right in among our skirmishers. He whirls about and claps spurs to his horse, disdaining the order to dismount and surrender. A shot rings out on the night air, the horse plunges, staggers, then goes prone to earth, grinding the rider's leg beneath the saddle. Before he can extricate himself from his predicament, Lieutenant Kearny has leaped from his steed and is standing over him. Two soldiers rush up with levelled bayonets, but Kearny warns them off, and orders one to hold the struggling horse by the head. In another moment the Southerner stands erect, rescued, but a prisoner of war.

The division commander, with some of his generals and a number of the staff, are gathered in a corner of the old rail-fence back of the grove, when Lieutenant Kearny appears before them with his captive. He is the first officer brought in, and there is natural curiosity to see him and hear what report he has to give of himself. The general is his examiner, and his manner is as courteous and kindly as though the soldier were one of his own command. "The fortune of war," he says, "has placed you in our hands. You are of Jackson's corps, I presume?"

"I'm not," is the answer, sullenly.

" What then ?"

" I am on the staff of General Stuart."

" How are we to account for your being here in our front with Jackson's command ?"

" You wouldn't have had to trouble yourself with such a problem, sir, if my horse had not fallen on me," is the answer.

" Where is General Stuart's command now, captain ?"

" I should decline to answer if I knew, sir, but I don't."

" We will not ask you where Jackson is," says the general, with a sad shake of the head, as he thinks of the losses sustained by his pet brigade, " but I would like to know at what you estimate his force."

The prisoner eyes his questioner a moment, then answers, " We count them at sixty thousand—or as good as that."

" Indeed ! We knew he was strong, but did not rate him quite that high. Captain," he continues, turning to his adjutant-general, " take this gentleman's name and rank, and do the hospitalities of headquarters, so far as you can. I have a despatch to write. Is this Lieutenant Kearny ?"

" Yes, general," answers the young cavalryman, saluting.

" I believe General McDowell expected to send some word back by you to your brigade commander, who is reported as out beyond Haymarket on the road to the Gap. The general has gone, however, to join General Pope, and if you prefer to return to your command to-night you can do so, and I will ask you to leave a despatch with General Ricketts as you go. He is probably somewhere along the road between Gainesville and Haymarket."

"I shall be glad to go, sir. They will not know what has become of me in the regiment."

"Very well, then. The note will be ready in a moment," and the general turns away.

His chief of staff, meantime, has offered the prisoner a drink from his flask, and it is thankfully accepted. By this time the Virginian is apparently coming to the conclusion that his treatment is much more courteous and considerate than he supposed would be the case. His answer, therefore, to the next question, though somewhat hesitating, is given in a pleasanter tone of voice.

"Your name and regiment, captain?"

"I am Captain Falconer, of the —th Virginia Cavalry."

Kearny turns sharply in mingled interest and surprise. The words of the stranger whom he had met in the morning—"Watch out for a Captain Falconer"—are suddenly brought to mind. Can it be possible that this is the man? If so, what reason is there for being especially on his guard against this by no means ill-looking Virginian?

"You stated that you were on duty with General Stuart, captain," continues the adjutant-general; "where and when did you last see him?"

"You will have to excuse me, sir," is the answer, given most courteously and with a pleasant smile. "I am sorry to have to requite your hospitality in this way, but I must decline to give any information as to my commander and his movements. You know that under like conditions you would do the same."

At this moment the division commander reappears, a folded note in his hand.

"You can probably reach Gainesville unmolested, Mr. Kearny," he says; "our fourth brigade covers the pike most of the way, but after that you must be on the alert. It is my belief that Stuart's men are scouting all the lanes and by-ways north of the road to Thoro'fare Gap."

"I know they are, general," is Kearny's answer, as he swings into saddle; "they nearly got me this morning as I was coming down from Hopeville. Good-night, sir; good-night, gentlemen;" and the lieutenant rides forth upon the crowded turnpike and heads his horse for Gainesville. He has hardly disappeared in the darkness when the Virginia captain, who has been gazing fixedly after him, turns to the adjutant-general.

"May I ask that officer's name?"

"That is Lieutenant Kearny, of the —— New Jersey Cavalry, and you are not his first prisoner, captain."

"No, by Heaven! There are men who would give their eye-teeth to know just where he is this night;" and, as though urged by an irresisible longing, he turns and looks over to the northwest—one quick glance—then, recovering himself, suddenly resumes his nonchalant mien.

"I thought so," whispers the chief of staff to a comrade. "Stuart must be in those woods in front of Patrick's brigade. No doubt he is watching every inch of the Gap road, too."

"If that be the case," is the reply, "young Kearny will have to run the gauntlet to-night."

IV.

LATE that night, threading his weary way along a road blocked with wagons and straggling troops, Lieutenant Kearny rode out westward from Gainesville in hopes of rejoining his own regiment and having a few hours' sleep before dawn. He had delivered his despatch to the division commander, and received another which he was requested to hand to General Buford, who was covering the front, so they said around the headquarters tents, out beyond Haymarket. One aide-de-camp said three miles; another said three quarters of a mile; no one seemed to know exactly, and all of the staff, having been in saddle, marching, fighting, and running about the country since early dawn, were now too sleepy and tired to lift their heads from the ground on which they lay, rolled in their dusty blankets. A field-officer, charged with the duty of looking after the grand guards and pickets, assured him that he would find the road "in the hands of our people" well out beyond Haymarket, and that Buford's patrols and videttes held it beyond them almost to the Gap. One or two divisions of Longstreet's corps were already through, he said, and bivouacked in the open fields just under the range. Stuart's people? No. He had seen or heard nothing of them. If they were

north of the pike they had all been called eastward
over towards Groveton, where all that heavy fighting
had been going on about sunset.   Could the lieutenant
tell him anything about that ?   The lieutenant could
and did.   In point of fierceness and fatality there had
been nothing, he said, from the outbreak of the war,
to equal the combat he had witnessed that evening.
Now that the excitement of battle no longer sustained
him, and the darkness of night weighed heavily upon
his wearied senses, Kearny shuddered as he thought
of those long ranks of dead and dying, facing each
other along that rolling, undulating mile of open fields
where the battle lines had stood loading and firing for
two mortal hours, until nothing but the red flash of
musketry could be seen.

"Won't you let me send a sergeant and three or
four men with you ?" asked the field-officer, as, riding
together, they finally reached the outpost.   "You will
be alone for a mile, perhaps, before you reach any of
Buford's people, and there's no telling what you may
run across along this road."

Kearny looked at the little party grouped in silence
under a patch of trees by the road-side. All seemed
weary and depressed after the long, long day of tramp
and the nervous strain of hours in line of battle. There
was something pathetic in the silence and subordina-
tion with which they awaited his reply. Two of the
men had spread their blankets under a tree, and had
apparently just been relieved as sentinels, and were
about to lie down. They knelt there looking up at
the two mounted officers, and one of them muttered a

low word of expostulation, which the sergeant promptly
rebuked.   They were infantrymen — volunteers — and
their duties were onerous enough already, thought
Kearny, without having to tramp out into the darkness and danger escorting every belated dragoon who
happened along. "No," he said. "Thank you, kindly,
major. 'Ramapo' and I pulled through here all right
to-day, and I think we can do it again. Some Reb
troopers tried to cut me off just about a mile from
here this morning, but we slipped by them. They
cannot see me at night, and we'll walk along soft as
a kitten. Won't we, old boy?"   But "Ramapo,"
though thus affectionately appealed to, did not rise
to the spirit of the occasion. With drooping head
and jaded mien he looked wistfully about in search
of possible shelter and refreshment, and did not even
prick up his ears in response to the encouraging slap
from his master's gauntlet.

"Now, good-night, sir," said Kearny, holding out his
hand, after a brief examination of his revolver cham-
bers. "These caps seem all in good shape. I feel
that I *must* get to my regiment to-night, for they are
sure to be fighting at daybreak, and they don't know
where I am.   Next thing I know they'll be reporting
me as captured, killed, or missing, and scaring my
home people to death. Thank you for coming so far
with me, and good-night again. Sergeant, keep your
ears open, and if I *am* driven back, be ready to back
them up in turn;" and, waving his hand and touching
"Ramapo" with the spur, he rode slowly away into
the darkness, leaving a silent little group behind him.

There were no trees now on either side. The fields, he knew, were bare and lying neglected. There was no one to till them if crops could be raised, and there were too many to sweep away the crop in case a struggling growth were effected. It was dark as pitch. He could not recall a night so dark in his year of campaigning. Not a vestige of moon was there, though here and there a faint twinkling star peeped through rifts in the clouds, that seemed to have been drawn like a veil over the face of the heavens, hiding from celestial eyes the woful scene of this day's bloody work. Earlier in the evening, as he rode into Gainesville, he heard the mournful plaint of the whippoorwill in the moist and misty aisles of the forest, but now a hush had fallen on the broad, beautiful valley, and not a sound disturbed the deathlike silence but the muffled tread of his charger's hoofs in the deep, dust-covered road. Such silence, following on such scenes and incidents as he had encountered through the day, is trying to nerves long set on edge. A faint whiff of night wind swept across the highway from time to time, and he turned his head, hoping to catch the sound of pawing hoof or the *p-r-r-r-r-r* of grazing horses on the south side of the track. Only Buford's men would likely be there; while, on the other hand, to the north, he knew not how many foemen to expect. Stuart's cavalry, Mosby's rangers, Turner Ashby's partisans, any of these might be scouting the fields and trotting through the wood roads above the pike and keeping up communication between Longstreet's advance brigades in front of the two gaps, and Stuart and Jackson

over there to the northeast of Gainesville.   Time and
again he reined in " Ramapo," fancying he could hear
muttered words or muffled hoof-beats over in that
direction, but after a few minutes of intent listening
would again push slowly on.   Once or twice "Ramapo's" hoofs struck some loose stone upon the road
with loud and startling click, and once this betraying
noise was accompanied by a sudden gleam like an elec-
tric spark, as flint and iron clashed together.   His sabre, too, swinging at the full length of its slings, clanked
occasionally against his spurred boot-heel, and he shoved
it between his leg and the saddle-straps to put an end
to its clamor.   So moving, he had covered perhaps half
a mile without molestation of any kind, when, far out
to his front—in the roadway, doubtless—he caught
sight of a faint and sudden flash of light that he instantly divined to be the result of just such a clash of
flint and steel as caused the spark under "Ramapo's"
forefoot but a moment before.   Horsemen ahead !
Now for the question, who are they ?   Judging by
its feeble glow, that flash must have been nearly two
hundred yards away, and as yet no sound had reached
him.   Again he halted "Ramapo" and listened, his
heart beating a little heavier.   For a few seconds all
was stillness ; then, bending forward and with hand
at his ear, he could catch the faint beat of iron-shod
hoofs upon the dusty carpet of the road.   "Ramapo"
heard it too, and began pricking up his ears, and there
was imminent danger of his bursting into a shrill neigh
by way of hailing his fellow-quadrupeds, when Kearny
leaped quickly from the saddle, caught his charger by

the nostrils, and led him to one side, down into the
ditch that just there ran along the road. It was so
dark that he could not see it at all, and both he and
his horse slid and stumbled as they groped their way.
There was an appalling rattle of his sabre as it clanked
against the stony brink, and he felt that he had splashed
into some water. This led him to the belief that he
must be down in the shallows where the brook crossed
the road. Perhaps it was here, close at hand, and
these troopers were coming down to water their horses.
If they were Buford's men, all well and good; he could
soon tell by the muttered chat that was pretty sure to
be going on. If they were the enemy—and they might
readily be, for it was just here they pushed their scouting parties in between the lines that morning—then he
must lie *perdu* until they moved away, or else steal off
to the fields on his left hand, still holding "Ramapo"
by the nose. He could not mount and ride, because
the horse would be sure to signal to his fellows, now
approaching at a rapid and audible walk, and because
the railway, with its rough ties and parallel ditches,
lay between him and the open country to the south.
No, his best plan was to hold his ground until satisfied
who these midnight raiders might be, then make himself known or crouch in hiding as they turned out to
be friends or foes.

Almost before he had succeeded in leading "Ramapo" out of the water and into a dry place where he
could not betray them by splashing, the sound of hoofs
crossing the little wooden culvert was heard; two horsemen rode like shadowy spectres between him and the

stars of the northern sky, and reined in just beyond, while the rest of the party stopped at the brook to water. These two in front were evidently the extreme advance or "outlooks" of a cavalry patrol, but in the impenetrable darkness he could form no idea of the uniforms or equipment. If they would only speak! He knew the Southern intonation so well, the soft elision of the r's, the modulation and inflections which a harsher clime seems to have exiled from the Northern tongue. He could hear the murmur of voices at the brook-side, but not a word came from these drowsing cavaliers in front. While one seemed intent on listening for any sound towards Haymarket, the other waited until he could hear the patrol once more advancing, then turned eastward, and in ghostly silence the two moved slowly away. Lost in the darkness perhaps half a minute were these pioneers, then came others in sight; muffled in cloaks or capes they seemed to be, for the night was chill, and the two whose forms were outlined in advance were talking softly with each other; the rest, perhaps half a dozen troopers, were strung out in column of twos behind their leaders, silent, and doubtless sleepy. Kearny strained his ears to catch the words that passed between the two horsemen at the head of the little troop as they came abreast of him, but the hoof-beats and the clank of steel scabbards were sufficient to render the voices indistinguishable. Suddenly one of the leaders threw up a shadowy hand, and his voice, low and muffled, was heard.

"Steady!—halt!"

Far out to the front—from the darkness in which

4

the pioneers had disappeared—some one whistled soft and clear. The patrol stood motionless in the roadway a moment, listening. No further signal came; all was silence.

"What's the matter?" finally queried a deep voice, hardly above a whisper.

"Don't know," was the muttered answer. "Corporal, just ride out yonder and see what they want."

Kearny crouched lower, and kept his iron grip on "Ramapo's" nostrils. The soft drawl, the languid intonation, the long-drawn "*yawnduh,*" were enough for him. No man of Buford's brigade sat on those spectral steeds not ten paces from the New Jersey cavalryman. Those were "Rebs," and out on one of their daring scouts along the Union lines.

Presently the corporal came trotting back. "You can see the camp-fires from where they are, lieutenant," he reported.

"Well, we *want* to see 'em. Whut 're we *hyah* faw?" is a faint imitation of the next remark that reached the attentive ears of Lieutenant Kearny. "C'mawn, men!" and the leader of the little troop would have started but for a restraining voice—a voice that startled the hiding Jerseyman almost to the verge of losing his grip on his horse's nose.

"One moment, lieutenant. Between here and their lines the fence is intact on both sides of the road. At least it was when I came across two days ago. We are now just midway between Buford's outposts and those main lines. If one of Buford's patrols should come along while we are east of this point there might be difficulty in slipping out. He has patrols in every direction to-night, and, much as I would like to pick up some courier or staff-officer with despatches, I don't want to sacrifice the whole platoon. Our nearest supports now are more than a mile away, and it is not worth while to move from here."

"I thought you wanted to get close in to their lines, Captain Armistead," said the junior.

"Not if it place us in a *cul-de-sac*. It is open to our rear now, but there's no saying how soon we may have to fight a patrol. I must have heard at least four since leaving Hopeville at dusk."

"That man Falconer go back to Thoro'fare ?" asked the junior, after a moment's silence.

"Captain Falconer left before I did," was the reply, in a somewhat distant tone. "I understood that he was to return to his squadron at once. Know him well ?" he questioned, with no lack of interest in the inquiry.

"Know him well enough to say I don't trust him," was the uncompromising answer. "Shall we stay here on the road, or lead off to one side ?"

Already, mindful of what he had heard in the morning and the peril of his present situation, Kearny was striving noiselessly to lead "Ramapo" over the soft ground until, in the darkness, he should gain the rear of the party, then he could mount and away. His cavalry instincts told him that two or three members of the platoon must be some hundred yards behind them up the road, watching for anything that might come from the west, but he believed that they would never suspect him to be other than one of their own party until he reached them, then he must trust to surprise, darkness, and "Ramapo's" heels. His arm and hand were wellnigh exhausted now from the long struggle to "gag" the excited horse. If he could only hold out a minute longer! If only there should be no stones, no stumble! If only the sabre would not clank! Ah! a plunge, a snort, a rattle of gravel down the slope, a scrambling of hoofs, a desperate leap and spring, a fierce and sudden chorus of "*Who goes there?*" "Who goes there?" "Halt!" "*Halt!*" "Head him off, men!" A sputter and crash of scores of iron-shod feet, the rattle of steel, the click of a dozen revolvers, then a flash and loud report, another, another! and "Ramapo" is plunging headlong down into the running brook, rolling heavily, crushingly, upon a prostrate and senseless rider.

There are anxious hearts in the bivouac of Buford's men when morning dawns and gallant Frank Kearny is still reported missing.

V.

ANXIOUS days were those that followed the first grapple of Pope and Jackson along the famous old Warrenton turnpike. Darkness had put an end to the initial conflict; darkness had shrouded from the watchers at Hopeville Gap all sign of the tragic scenes and weary marches of the night, but early morn found them again at their station on the piazza, the old judge with his telescope, his pale and sweet-faced daughter kneeling by his chair. Brief indeed had been the visit from devoted son and brother the evening before. He had been led to his sleeping father's side, and soon the three — father, son, and daughter — were absorbed in the joy of their reunion and engaged in eager talk. Rapidly as possible the young soldier told them of the situation of affairs, and their hope that Lee and Longstreet would be able to join hands with Jackson early on the coming day, and beat the Yankees back or cut them off from Washington. He was eager, enthusiastic, confident. Every officer and man, he said, had most implicit faith in Lee; and as for Jackson, the enthusiasm with which his "foot cavalry" followed him on the most daring flanking moves was something no words could describe. "But it looks ugly to-night," he continued, with an anxious glance eastward, where the

guns were still booming, and the distant flashes could
be seen in the gathering gloom. "The Yanks seem
to be crowding all around him, and I've got to hurry.
Stuart is on his right, and I'll doubtless meet some of
our patrols before I get half-way across." Cautioned
by his father to look out for Federal cavalry, whose
main body was known to be on the road to the lower
gap, he answered that they were simply holding the
line to Gainesville and Haymarket; the direct road
from Hopeville over to Jackson was open, and scouted
only by Stuart's men. If all went well, he said, he
would be able to see them again within a day or two,
but he felt that he must rejoin his chief that night.
When the three went out upon the dark piazza it was
found that Captain Falconer had gone.

"His father and I were such warm friends that I
hate to think of his having gone away without a word.
Lucy, child, I hope you invited him in and gave him a
welcome."

"I did, father; but Henry came just in the midst
of my words, and—surely he will understand and appreciate that we did not mean to be discourteous; he
knows we had not seen Henry since last March."

"And who was that Federal officer who rode in here
early this morning and said he knew Henry?" asked
the judge, with a frown upon his venerable face.

"Oh, yes, Harry! Think of it! A lieutenant of
cavalry who was scouting, he said, rode in and asked
to see father, who declined, and then he told me that
he knew you well—had been in college with you."

Captain Armistead was standing by his horse at

the moment, busily stowing away some packages of home-made "rations" that Hannah had brought him from the kitchen. "Old Nelse" was at the horse's head, and his portly spouse had come forth from her own dominions to see "young mars'r" on his way. On one of the lower steps were the judge and Lucy, side by side, his arm around his daughter's slender waist; her arm uplifted and bearing a lantern whose beams shone upon her sweet face and tinged the shimmering gold of her hair. The young soldier turned suddenly at her words, surprise and interest in his eyes, but the question he would ask seemed checked for the moment as he gazed up at the group before him—his father's silvered hair and noble features, his sister's graceful form and girlish beauty, all illumined by the rays of the battered old lantern, and shining forth against the black background of the vine-shrouded piazza. With the blindness of brotherhood, never until then had he realized how fair a woman she had grown to be.

"Lulie," he broke forth after brief study of her face, and hailing her by the old pet name of their childhood, "I declare you're getting to be a tearing beauty. Don't you be making eyes at any of those fellows who come up here saying they're 'scouting.' I know too much about that. There's no likelihood of your seeing any more of the Yanks; but no flirting with them, Miss Armistead, whatever you do. Who was this fellow who rode in to-day? Some of their rear-guard, I reckon."

Her face had flushed with girlish delight at her

brother's involuntary tribute. Compliments from such a source are rare in any household, and are worth their face value wherever uttered. She hardly heard the question that followed, and it was her father who answered,

"He gave his name as Kearny, of the New Jersey Cavalry."

"Frank Kearny! *Here!*" exclaimed Armistead, as though shocked and startled. He dropped the strap from his nerveless hand, and turned suddenly away, so that his face was hidden. "Are you sure he said Kearny, Lucy?" he queried, seizing again the strap and striving to buckle down the flap of the saddle-bag with fingers that bungled painfully at their work.

"I am sure he said Kearny, Harry," was her answer. "Who is he? Why should it startle you so. *Were* you at college together? Captain Falconer spoke of his having been your guest in Richmond two winters ago."

"How did he know of it? Did you tell *him* of Kearny's being here?" asked the captain, with deep anxiety in his tone.

"I did, certainly. Why, what is there about him, Harry? Why should I not speak of it?"

"No reason, really, except—this was the Federal officer who captured Pegram and Eustis down by Cedar Mountain. You heard of it, did you not, father? And we have heard ugly stories of the way they were treated—not by him, but by their guards while being sent to Washington, and the whole brigade is up in arms about it. I believe that Pope himself would not be so prized a captive as Frank Kearny. And it is true, we were chums at college, and at one time room-mates."

"I don't remember your writing of him," said his father; "that is, I remember the name, and it seems to me you used to say something of him at first—"

"We had a falling out during the senior year, father; that was the reason. It was a foolish affair, and all my fault, I suppose; but we were estranged from that time until we happened to meet at the Spotts-wood one night late in the autumn of '60. Then we shook hands, and the hatchet was buried."

"But Captain Falconer said he was your guest for a week at Richmond," interposed Miss Armistead.

"Falconer exaggerates the case if he meant to inti-mate that he was especially my guest. I introduced him at the club, and his own social qualities did the rest. We were always on courteous and pleasant terms when we met there, which may have misled Falconer; but not what we had been. There was a matter that couldn't well be explained," and he turned away again.

She was down in the roadway and at his side in an-other moment, twining her arm about his neck.

"Oh, Harry!" she whispered, "I know now. Miss Paulding, wasn't it?"

But he bent down and kissed her gently. "Hush, little sister," he murmured; "never mind the old sore. I have a lady-love now that none can rob me of, and yet the more rivals I have the better I like it. We allude to her somewhat disrespectfully at times, Miss

Armistead," he said, with resumption of the gay cavalier manner.   "She has beaux without number this
summer, and we mean to proclaim her Queen of Beauty, Chivalry, and of these Confederate States of America before another winter.   I allude to 'Old Virgin-
ny,' Miss Armistead, one of whose fairest daughters I
have now the honor to salute in parting.   God bless
you, little one!" he said, softly, tenderly, as he clasped
her in his arms.   "Pray for us and the Star of the
South to-night.   Now let me go."   She was clinging to him, looking with tearful eyes into his brave
young face.   He led her to their father's side, grasped
the old man's hand in both his one moment, then
with sudden impulse bared his head, bent and kissed
it as courtier might have kissed his sovereign's, then
sprang to his horse, swung lightly into the saddle, and
turned sharply away into the dim and shadowy vista
to the gate.   Another moment and the hoof-beats
were dying away in outer darkness.

All that next day the sullen guns were booming at
intervals over in the valley of the Run.   All the long
morning the dust-clouds rose dense and stifling over
the road to Gainesville, and through his ready glass the
old gentleman could catch occasional glimpses of the
marching columns and the red battle-flags fluttering
overhead.   All the day from time to time patrols and
scouting parties of Stuart's men went riding by, sometimes sending in an officer to ask a question or two,
or a man in search of water for the canteens.   From
one and all the same report was received: "Everything going well.   Lee and Longstreet were pushing

ahead to join Jackson and give the Yanks another
beating on the field where we thrashed them the year
before. It would all be settled by nightfall!" And
then the long afternoon wore away, and the roads
from the two gaps were cleared of troops, and the
dust began to settle back to earth, and the windows
in the little hamlet at the junction of the pikes to
gleam red in the rays of the setting sun; and then,
just as the day before, the thunder of a fierce cannonade rumbled in the distance, and the faint roar of musketry could be distinguished by the listening ear, and
the far-away forests were lighted up with a lurid battle-
glare; and then again, just as suddenly, it died away,
and another restless, anxious night succeeded. Then
came the morning of the third day, and from sunrise
to darkness the old Virginian never left his post on
the piazza. The open fields to the north of Groveton
were distinctly in view, and there through the glass
he could see the charging lines in blue, reeling back
again and again before that fire-flashing embankment.
He could see long lines in gray filing into the forest
south of the broad turnpike, and being swallowed up
in the density of the foliage. Then late in the afternoon the distant crests of Bald Hill and the plateau
back of the old Henry house blazed with musketry,
and were soon shrouded from base to peak in clouds
of sulphur-smoke; and then the little dots of red could
be seen peeping out here and there above the steadily
advancing lines in gray, and then through rifts in
the smoke they gleamed at intervals upon the slopes,
and ere long crest after crest was crowned with the

crimson, fluttering folds, and old Armistead, trembling
with enthusiasm and delight, could plainly see that the
St. Andrew's Cross was gaining everywhere ; and when
at last darkness intervened and shut the scene of triumph and victory from his tired eyes, his heart welled
up in audible prayer and thanksgiving as he clasped
his daughter in his arms.

"The Yanks are falling back behind Bull Run.
We've licked them everywhere," was the report
brought in to him late that night by a young trooper
who was riding up towards Aldie. "I saw the captain just before dark, judge. He's all right; he'd
have sent some message if he'd known I was coming.
I didn't know it myself until just afterwards, when the
colonel told me to run up and see my folks. I live
over yonder on the Leesburg road, and I'm to join
'em at Fairfax to-morrow. Oh, we ain't goin' to stop
short of Washington this time, you bet !" and the
young fellow rode away. At the gate he turned.
"Say, judge, I passed a wagon down the road a piece,
with a wounded officer they're bringing here. You
might have got a scare, fearin' 'twas Captain Armistead. 'Tisn't, though. Good-night, sir; good-night,
Miss Lucy."

"Who can it be?" asked the old man, turning anxiously into the house. "Lucy, child, tell Hannah to
get that spare room ready at the head of the stairs.
We'll have to put him there. Can it be Falconer, do
you think?"

"I cannot imagine who it is, father," she answered.
"Some one we know, undoubtedly, and some one,

probably, who has been wounded near here—though there has been no fighting around us since day before yesterday. Wait here and watch for them, and I'll go with Hannah at once."

Barely ten minutes later there rode into the gate a sergeant in the gray dress of Stuart's cavalry. Dismounting quickly, he sprang up the steps and handed the judge a note.

"Judge Armistead," he said, in low tone, "my orders from the captain were to return immediately after having handed you this, and having conducted a wounded officer to your house. Yonder comes the wagon, sir, and there are two boys with it, who, with the help of Nelse and the others here, can carry the gentleman into the house. Then they are to go back with their team and wagon. Have you any message to send, sir? I shall be with the captain by morning, unless our people march all night."

"Wait one moment, sergeant; let me glance at this note first. Let me offer you some refreshment, sir. Lucy!" he called.

"Pardon me, judge," said the trooper. "Don't open it yet. Wait until I'm out of the yard. No refreshment, thank you, sir. I must go at once."

The wagon, drawn by two venerable mules, was slowly coming through the gate as the soldier sprang again into saddle and was about to turn away.

"But, sergeant, who is the officer? Is it Captain Falconer?"

"Judge Armistead," was the answer, "I would do anything on earth for your son. He knows it, and this night has put me to the test. You ask me a question I cannot answer because I do not know. I do not *want* to know—I hope to God I never *may* know!"

And, turning sharply, he struck spurs to his horse and rode away at a rapid trot, leaving the old man and his pale-faced daughter standing there at the head of the steps, dumb with surprise.

VI.

Mid-September had come and gone. Lee, with his enthusiastic followers, had crowded the Union lines into the fortifications around Washington, then crossed the Potomac, and found himself so crippled after the desperate battling at the Antietam that he was compelled to fall back into the valley of the Shenandoah. For the time being the beautiful sweep of country between the heights of Centreville and the gaps in the Bull Run Mountains was unobscured by the dust-clouds of heavy marching columns or the smoke of thunderous battle. Heavy rains had roiled the streams and bogged the Virginia roads, but there were no guns, no heavily laden wagons, to stall at every brook or ford. A silence as of desolation had settled upon the land, for all the fields from Chantilly down to Manassas were peopled only with the dead, and every slope and pasture green was ridged with new-made graves. Over on the broad plains about the railway junction other freight-cars had appeared among the blackened ruins of those destroyed by Stuart ; but the storehouses and buildings were only charred stumps and scattered ashes now, and the white tents and rude board shelters hastily thrown together here and there were only temporary resting-places for hundreds of poor fellows whose wounds were too severe to enable them to travel. Stuart, with his bold raiders, was over near Martinsburg, in the Valley, watching for the next move of the Union force still halted on the hard-won field at Sharpsburg. Every now and then, however, little scouting columns of Virginia Cavalry came trotting over through the passes and taking a look at the Union outposts in front of Washington; then, scattering here and there through the country roads, they would disperse all over the broad valley east of the gaps, and spend a few hours in cheery visits to the homesteads from Aldie down to Warrenton, bringing joy and delight to mothers, sisters, and sweethearts, and all the time keeping wary watch and slipping away just too soon to be caught by the Union horsemen, who were sure to come marching out from Fairfax in pursuit. A strong garrison had ever to be kept up in the fortifications in front of the National Capital, and, out in advance of the earthworks, several regiments of blue-jacketed troopers picketed all the roads, occupied the neighboring villages, and, to use the army phrase, "covered the front" against surprise, and, when occasion offered, launched forth a column in chase of raiders. And so it happened that while the main bodies of both armies were gone long marches away, and the guns no longer thundered, and the volleys no longer flashed, the by-roads and the fields were often gay with the guidons of venturesome detachments of cavalry, and the soft autumnal air made merry with the ringing trumpet-calls; and one day the worn and dingy gray uniforms would ride in amid the acclamations of farmyards full of enthusiastic women, and the next the doors and windows would be banged shut at sight of the fluttering "stars and stripes," then carried in the shape of swallow-tailed pennons by every squadron of Union horse. Many a lively little skirmish, many a stirring charge and chase, did the troopers on both sides enjoy while thus having this lovely and populous section of Virginia all to themselves, and one of the regiments occupied on this genuinely "cavalry" duty was the —— New Jersey, Lieutenant Kearny's regiment ; but Lieutenant Kearny had not been seen since the first night of the battle of Second Bull Run.

Long since the reports had borne his name as "missing." Anxious and influential relations from Trenton and New York had hastened to Washington and besieged the War Department for particulars. All New Jersey—all the Union army—was in mourning just then for another, a greater Kearny, and in the shadow of the bitter disasters that had befallen the nation it seemed as though

"The black shroud of that night at Chantilly"

had indeed overspread all Union-loving hearts, and there was no hope anywhere. It was some time before even senators and representatives could bring the military powers to energetic investigation, and meantime a sorrowing mother lay wellnigh heart-broken at home. Three weeks of vigorous prodding on part of the Jerseymen resulted finally in the utter exhaustion of all information to be had on the subject, and left

5

the inquirers more puzzled, more troubled, than before.
The last seen of Mr. Kearny was late on the night of
the 28th of August, when, all alone, he set forth on
the road from Haymarket to Thoroughfare Gap in
hopes of finding his regiment. In less than half an
hour the picket at which he had parted with the field-
officer of the day was alarmed by pistol-shots faintly
audible several hundred yards out towards the west.
A few minutes later a platoon of Buford's troopers
came clattering in to inquire what it meant. They
had scouted the road and found a dead horse near the
brook, but the horse equipments were all gone, and the
assailants had probably ridden off to the northward
bearing their prisoner with them. The horse was
identified as Lieutenant Kearny's the very next morning, and it was regarded as a matter of course that he
had fallen in with some of Stuart's scouting parties
and been captured.

But, as luck would have it, two of General Stuart's
staff-officers were among the prisoners brought in to
Washington. One was Captain Falconer, of Warrenton, who courteously answered inquiries on the subject by saying he was captured by Lieutenant Kearny
himself, at the close of the fight between Jackson's
men and the Union force west of Groveton. He
could, therefore, give no information with regard to
the matter. The other officer was an assistant adjutant-general who had ridden into our lines near
Vienna in the rain and darkness that followed Jackson's dash on Chantilly. This gentleman said that
every prisoner, without exception, who had been capt-

ured on the 28th or 29th of August by any of Stuart's
men was brought before him and questioned by him.
He knew that no officer resembling the description
and photographs of Lieutenant Kearny had so appeared, and he felt equally certain that if killed by
Stuart's men in an attempt to escape capture, Mr.
Kearny's death would certainly have been reported.
It was the staff-officer's confident belief that Lieutenant Kearny had neither been killed, wounded, nor
captured by Stuart's men, and "no other Confederate
cavalry," said he, "was anywhere along that road the
night referred to." Confidentially, the Southern officer expressed to the inquirers this theory : that the
lieutenant had come suddenly upon a small party of
his own people ; that in the darkness and confusion
each had taken the other for the enemy ; that Kearny
had been shot and killed by his own comrades and
then borne off and buried by them, and the whole
matter had been concealed for fear of punishment.
The Jerseymen were still persistent. Finding that
nothing definite could be learned in this way, they
were advised to call upon a certain gentleman once
high in government circles before the war, but an
avowed sympathizer with the South in the present
conflict. It was more than half believed that he had
means of communication with the authorities at Richmond and with the army of Lee, enjoyed, perhaps, by
numbers of other residents of Baltimore and Washington, but not by the War Department of the United
States. Those were strange times, and within a week
the Jerseymen were assured that no man answering

to the name or description of Lieutenant Kearny had been or was now in the hands of the enemy. "I speak advisedly, for he is a prize they would not overlook in Virginia, where Pegram and Eustis are not forgotten." This was the report of their confidential adviser.

And so, with October close at hand, Frank Kearny's name was spoken as of one who had vanished from the face of earth, no man could tell whither, and more than one New Jersey home was filled, for his sake, with mourning and with dread anxiety. Down among the cavalry camps in front of Washington, too, they talked in low tones and "wondered" in many a chat around the evening fires what possibly could be the solution of the mystery. The regiment, of course, had been informed of the theory advanced by somebody that he had been killed in the darkness and buried in dread of punishment by his comrades of some scouting party. This, however, was promptly and indignantly denied by every officer and man on scout that night, and the most rigorous cross-examination and investigation failed to discredit their statements in the faintest degree. The affair, thanks to Kearny's prominence and popularity in the regiment, as well as to the interest kept up by this investigation, had become a *cause célèbre* in the lines in front of Washington ; and then, little by little, another story began to be hinted at.

There had been from the very outset the usual rivalry between the few cavalry commands in the Army of the Potomac, speedily followed by that devil of jealousy that seems inseparable from human nature in or out of the military service. While the —— New Jersey gloried in Kearny's soldierly exploit and in Bayard's handsome compliment at Cedar Mountain, there were not lacking men in other regiments who affected to "pooh-pooh" the whole affair, and who strove on every possible occasion to belittle the participants. For a while none of the Jerseymen did more than laugh at this, it was all so harmless and so transparent. But in the long evening chats, and in the leisure and "loafing" hours that followed the August campaign, some sneering remarks, alleged to have been made by certain officers at brigade headquarters, were brought in in that inevitably exaggerated form in which such things are always told, and a good deal of feeling began to be manifest about the camp-fires. Most of the officers of the —— New Jersey were gentlemen by birth and education ; nearly all the old families of the state were represented among them ; but the officers of a cavalry regiment in the same brigade and from an adjoining state were chosen from a very different class. That there should have been no affiliation was natural enough ; but the Jerseymen were utterly at a loss to account for the innuendoes that presently reached their ears. Finally one warm September evening there came an explosion. The adjutant had been over on some duty at the headquarters of the general commanding the defences along that front, and came back fuming with wrath.

"Gentlemen," said he, striding in among the group of officers chatting around the colonel's tent, and unceremoniously interrupting their placid talk, "I have just heard a story that reflects on the honor of the regiment, and it is time we put a stop to this sort of thing. We have stood it too long. It is my belief that we should run down the author of these lies and hold him responsible."

"What is the story?" was the eager question.

"It is about Kearny. Those fellows over in the 'Dunghill Dragoons' have never ceased to sneer at him and at us, as you know; but to-day Major Merrill, of the staff, told me that one of their officers informed him that he knew from indubitable authority that, so far from being killed or a prisoner, Frank Kearny had found a sweetheart over near Thoro'fare Gap, and was hiding under the roof of her home at this minute. I demanded the name of his informant, and he gave it to me ; he said it was a story that we ought to know, and trace to its foundation. Captain Mullane was the man; you all know who he is. Now, who will ride over to their camp with me to-night, and bring that fellow up to the scratch? By Heaven ! he must prove his words, or swallow them !"

Half a dozen young fellows were on their feet in a moment ; but the colonel's restraining voice was heard, calm yet authoritative.

"One moment, gentlemen. Resume your seats, if you please. This is no matter for impetuous or hotheaded action. Of course, if Captain Mullane were to make this statement to one of you, or to any one in your presence, I could not find fault with your knocking him down on the spot—I *might* find fault if you didn't do so—but this matter comes to us semi-officially; the division chief of staff tells it to the regimental adjutant as something we ought to know. Captain Chetwood, Mr. Stockton, order your horses and be ready to go with me; you too, Mr. Adjutant. I will look into the matter at once."

An hour later four officers of the —— New Jersey were at the camp of their comrade regiment and in conversation with its colonel. As a result of their communication Captain Mullane was sent for, and presently appeared. He started and looked uneasily around as he caught sight of the four visitors; but it was evident to all present that he had been drinking, and was just sufficiently under alcoholic influence to be ugly and truculent. In few words he was told of the story laid at his door, and asked for his authority. He stood unsteadily by the table in the colonel's big tent, the light from the single lantern shining full upon his coarse and bloated features as he looked scowlingly about him, first at one, then another of the four officers who were grouped in silence around his commander. Finally he spoke:

"I *did* say it, an' I can prove it."

"By whom, sir? You can have no personal knowledge of the matter."

"Well, I don't care to get any friend of mine into trouble, and I don't mean to betray him—the man that told me, I mean."

"Captain Mullane," said his colonel, coolly, "I have had more than one ugly matter to handle in this regiment during the few weeks I have commanded it.

Your reputation as a mischief-maker was known to me before I accepted the command. You and such as you forced, through your political influence in your state, the resignation of my predecessor, but it cannot touch me. Take your choice, sir. Give me in presence of these gentlemen the full authority you have for the scandal you have set afloat at the expense of Lieutenant Kearny, or go to your tent in close arrest under charges of conduct unbecoming an officer."

For a moment there was silence except for the stertorous breathing of the bulky captain. He glared scowlingly around for a moment, looked furtively into his colonel's impassive face, then thickly muttered,

"It's a letter."

"Produce it, sir."

Again he looked helplessly around, as though seeking some avenue of escape, again glanced at the unrelenting form seated there in front of him, and finally began fumbling in an inner pocket of the waistcoat he wore beneath his uncouth fatigue "blouse." From a bundle of dog-eared, thumb-soiled papers he selected an ill-favored sheet, scrawled within and without in faded ink. The colonel reached forth his hand and took it.

"Most of that letter's private and personal, colonel," said Mullane, anxiously. "Here's all there is about the lieutenant — here on the second page," and he pointed with pudgy, shaky finger.

The colonel slowly read over the indicated lines, a

look of deep disgust settling on his fine young face.
Then he glanced at the signature.

"What disreputable character is this correspondent
of yours, Captain Mullane? Who may 'P. Tierney'
be?"

"He's a scout, sir, and in government employ, with
the best of char*a*cters from General Fremont."

"And where is he now?"

"I don't know, sir."

"You may retire, Captain Mullane. I presume it is
necessary to assure you that the only part of this letter that I shall show or read is that on the second page
—which you say is *all* there is referring to Lieutenant
Kearny. But I shall keep it for the next half hour
until that portion has been copied and read to these
gentlemen, and—one moment, sir—let me say in presence of the colonel and these officers of the —— New
Jersey that I consider this story, told by a question-
able and intangible character, as utterly failing to
warrant your aspersions. That will do, sir."

And when Mullane was fairly out of earshot, the
young colonel once more conned the ill-written page,
then read it aloud:

"'You fellers needn't knuckle under to them Jersey
shanghais'"—("I do not reproduce the bad spelling,"
said the colonel, interrupting himself)—"'they've been
blowing about being so high-toned. *I* can take 'em
down a peg, and here's a tip for you. That young
feller Kearny is no more dead than I am, and no more
prisoner than you. He's got that to tell perhaps when
he gets tired of the girl, but while his comrades are

scouting and fighting, he's hiding in his sweetheart's arms up near the Gap. Next time you have a column out that way run in suddenly on old Judge Armistead's place at Hopeville, and if you don't find him skulking there I'm a liar.'"

VII.

SEATED on the broad wooden steps of the old homestead, her chin resting in the palm of one soft white
hand, her clear violet eyes gazing thoughtfully out
over the wide expanse of field, forest, winding stream,
and tiny farms, all enclosed within the boundary of
those distant heights, Lucy Armistead was lost in
maiden reverie. Again the sun was sinking behind
the wooded crests that rose in rear of the orchard.
Again the shadows were long and dark across the deserted fields below. Again the white walls of Centreville gleamed on the edge of the uplands twenty miles
away; but all was silence, and all, apparently, was
peace. Around her the droning flight of beetle, the
soft chirp of wearied bird in the branches overhead,
the flutter and subdued cackle of the hens already
roosting on the slats of the old trellis-work under the
piazza, all told of the speedy coming of night. It was
growing chill, too, and her thin white dress was far
too light a garment for the evening air along those
shaded slopes—and yet she seemed to be oblivious of
everything about her. Even when Hannah stepped
out upon the piazza and addressed a question in low
tone of voice it failed to attract her attention. The
girl stood silently a moment, looking down at her

pretty mistress ; then spoke her name—the old home pet-name—"Miss Lulie !" and still she gave no sign. Hannah's eyes twinkled with a knowing look ; her white teeth gleamed as she turned away, entered the house, reappeared in a moment with a shawl in her hands, laid it gently over the shoulders of the white figure seated there so motionless, and carefully tucked it under the resting arm in front. Then without a word she was turning noiselessly away, when Miss Armistead seemed to rouse herself to sudden question.

"Is he awake ?" she asked.

Hannah shook her head.

"He's been awake mos' of the day, an' las' night. And he asked me over and over where you were, an' if you wasn't never comin' any mo'." There was a tone of decided reproach in Hannah's voice. "He ain't as well as he was. He was gettin' well fas', so long's you went to see him ; but 'tain't so now, Miss Lulie," she continued, finding that her first remark fell short of the intended effect.

Miss Armistead turned sharply away.

"Did the judge say what time he'd get home, Miss Lulie ?" asked Hannah, after brief silence. "'Cause he wants to see him," she added, somewhat indefinitely.

"I hope to see him every moment. I've been watching for two hours."

In view of the fact that Miss Armistead's sweet eyes had been fixed on the far-away heights of Centreville, and that her father was expected to return by way of the mountain road at her back, there was something in this statement that seemed irrelevant to her handmaiden, but the latter wisely refrained from comment. There was another matter, though.

"Miss Lulie," she said, "he ain't fit to ride nohow, but he wants to go 'way."

"How do you know?" asked Miss Armistead, after a silence of several seconds.

"He *said* so. He done tole Nelse to find him *any* kind of a horse or mule, an' he pay him well when he get back to Wash'n'ton. But he *couldn't* get back, Miss Lulie, an' you know it. Dey ain't a day 'r a night the cavalry ain't all around yer, an' dey get him *sure*, an' he'd die in Libby less 'n no time, Miss Lulie."

Miss Armistead's fair head bent lower. She seemed to shiver slightly, and drew the shawl more closely about her. She would not speak, however, and after a moment's hesitation Hannah plunged down three or four steps and fairly threw herself at the feet of her mistress.

"Miss Lulie!" she broke forth, impulsively, with a sob in her voice. "Miss Lulie! The judge won't tell; he ain't a-gwine give him up now, is he?"

"*Hannah!*" exclaimed Miss Armistead, with horror and indignation mingled in her tone. "What can have possessed you? You forget!"

"Oh, I know what Mars' Henry wrote," wailed the girl; "I know he done tell you thet nobody mus' find out he's yer, but since you quit gwine to see him an' he begin talk 'bout gwine away—"

But Miss Armistead would not let her finish.

"Silence, Hannah! Whatever we have done at Henry's solemn injunction, we have in no wise harmed our country's cause. This gentleman was powerless enough when they brought him to us, and probably can never again fight against Virginia, or any one. So long as he cannot fight against us there is no need for my father to surrender him to the authorities or to speak of his being here, and he will never do it."

"But, Miss Lulie, s'pose dey find out. What makes 'em come speerin' round yer so much, anyhow? Cap'en Falconer's been to see you three times, an' it seems like he 'spect something. An' twice I hear 'em rustlin' in the bushes yonder, list'nin', after dark. I see him talkin' with two men down the road day befo' yisdy, Miss Lulie, and I thought—"

"How can they know, Hannah? No one but Nelse and you knows anything of it outside of the house. Captain Falconer is here to talk with father about his brother who was captured over at Manassas. He is anxious, and it comforts him to see father and talk with him."

"Miss Lulie, he don' come yer fur no such talk. He an' the other Cap'en Falconer don' never agree, an' anybody in Warrenton 'll tell you so. Judge Armistead knows it too. What he come yer fur is t' see you, Miss Lulie, and he's been yer every chance. Why ain' he with the rest of the gen'l'men up with the army? He jes sticks right round yer all the time."

"Captain Falconer and his squadron are charged with important duties, Hannah. They are posted at Thoro'fare Gap to see that the enemy do not get through there unless they come with heavy force. It is his duty to be alert and active. Every week, he says, the enemy appear in greater numbers, and it looks as though they were planning to ride over into the Shenandoah. He comes to consult father, too, for he has great faith in his judgment."

"Look yonder, Miss Lulie," interrupted Hannah, pointing through the darkening foliage. "It's the judge coming now. I'll run and call ole Nelse."

But before the servant could reach him, Judge Armistead rode in through the open gateway, dismounted stiffly at the steps, and threw the reins over the pommel. Very pale, weary, and anxious he looked as he took his daughter in his arms and kissed her tenderly. She searched his face with wistful eyes, striving to read his tidings as she led him slowly up to the piazza.

"I came back through the camp of Captain Falconer's men, dear," he said. "I wanted to ask that one of them should come up for the horse to-morrow. I —I cannot spare Nelse to take him back, and yet I could not have gotten over to Salem without him. It was very kind of Falconer to lend him to me. Has he been here to-day?" and the tired eyes gazed with deep anxiety into hers.

"No, father; no one. Could you hear anything of Henry? Did you—succeed?"

"No, child, no," and he shook his head sadly, wearily. "I can learn nothing. I can collect still less. Even if we *had* money, it would be difficult to buy stores now. They are almost as scarce at Gordonsville and Culpeper as they are at Warrenton. Everything is needed for the army. One thing I heard, and I'm afraid it's true, Lucy."

"What, father?"

"They say the Federals are being heavily reinforced over there at Chantilly—everywhere, in fact, from Leesburg down beyond Centreville, and that any day now they will come out, seize the gaps, cross over, and cut our line of supplies in the Shenandoah—reoccupy this whole country, in fact. Then it will be too late."

"Too late for what, father?"

"To get away from here and go to Richmond. Lucy, Lucy! Harry never dreamed what hardship and danger he was imposing upon you in sending that poor fellow to us. I had planned to start for Richmond the moment we heard of the possibility of an advance. Has he seemed better to-day?"

"I—I have not seen him, father, but Hannah says he is sleeping now."

The old gentleman took her face in his tremulous hands ; her cheeks flushed and burned as he raised it to the waning light. He asked no question, said no word, only looked in her moistened eyes, sadly, wistfully, anxiously.

"Little daughter," at last he spoke, " so long as he is here, helpless and bedridden, I must stay by him. I will not dishonor Harry's draft. I cannot go now and leave him to such care as Nelse could give him. If— if his friends come this way and find him, and carry him off whether we will or not, then are we absolved from responsibility. But, on the contrary, should our secret leak out in any way, and our people insist on searching the house, he is *gone*, and Harry's word will have been broken. If—if he were only able to ride!"

"But he is not, father. Hannah says he has been awake all day, feverish, and seeming worse. He could not ride, I'm sure; and then, even if he could go, every road and pathway is held by our cavalry as far as the heights across the valley. They all say so, and he could not escape. He would be taken, his identity revealed. Oh, father; no, no!"

And she clung to him, hiding her face on his arm, while old Nelse came hobbling around from the barn, and quietly led the horse away.

"Then listen, daughter," he eagerly spoke. "I have seen Doctor Loring to-day. He will leave Salem for Richmond to-morrow night. Aunt Nina is eager for your coming, and the doctor's daughter goes with him. He will gladly take charge of you and see you safely to the capital and Aunt Nina's roof. I will stay and take care of our guest until he is safe, then leave the old place to care for itself."

But she looked suddenly up into his face and placed her fingers upon his lips. "I will not stir without you, father. I will share whatever fate awaits you here, but not one step do I take until you too can go. Listen!"

"What did you hear?" he asked, after a moment of silence.

"I thought I heard hoofs on the rocky road through the pass—the Hopeville road."

6

Again they listened intently, but all was still.

"If it were any of Falconer's men, or any of our cavalry, they would hardly be likely to come through that way when all the main roads are open, and whom else have we to expect?" But even as he spoke the old gentleman gazed anxiously into the gloaming.

"I am going into the orchard to look. Wait here for me," she said, and, light as a bird, she fluttered down the steps and around the southern end of the house.

For a moment or so he waited patiently. The mountain road was only a hundred yards away, and there was still light enough to see any objects that might be moving. If his daughter were not mistaken, and shod hoofs were actually on the road, 'twas full time for something to come in sight. No hoof-beats were audible to him, however, and he was just turning to enter the hall when Lucy came running back. He saw her white-robed, slender form as it suddenly reappeared; he had hardly time to wonder at her haste when she flew up the steps—wild-eyed, pallid, panting—thrust a little scrap of paper into his hand, then clung to his arm, trembling from head to foot.

"Read it," she said ; "I know what it is."

"Who gave it you?" he asked.

"A man—a stranger—coming through the orchard. He said only these words, 'Danger for you and your visitor. Look out for the cavalry to-night,' handed me this, and was back in the road in an instant. Hear him now!—riding back towards Hopeville."

Hannah was lighting a candle in the hall. By its

dim rays the old man unfolded the little scrap and
read :

> "'You are believed to have a Federal officer secreted under your
> roof. Within twelve hours search will be made.
>
> "'VERB. SAT SAP.'"

"In God's name, whose work is this? What manner of man gave this to you?" he asked.

"A tall, gaunt man in ordinary civilian dress—a
man I never saw before."

"But I'se seen him, Miss Lulie, fo' er five times,"
eagerly exclaimed Hannah; "he was yer the first
mawnin' the—the lieutenant rode in," and she raised
her eyes and glanced quickly to the head of the stairs.
"'N' he's bin yer nosin' round twice. He done tole
me he was on special work, an' he hid in the barn cellar when Cap'en Falconer rode up."

"Why didn't you tell me of it?" asked the judge,
angrily.

Hannah's nervous hands plucked at her apron and
her face worked piteously. She faltered and could
not speak. At last she murmured,

"He said the Rangers kill him if they catch him.
He was a Lincoln man."

"Some spy, some skulking, rascally spy, no doubt!"
exclaimed the old man. "My God! What *can* not
rightfully be said of me? I have betrayed my own
people! I have been false to my state! But it's
over now. If they come to-night they can have him.
I have no way now to act—one way or other."

Softly a door at the head of the stairs had opened.
Noiselessly a tall, slender, soldierly form in the undress

uniform of a Union cavalry officer had limped to the railing, and now stood dimly revealed in the rays of the solitary candle below.

As the old man ceased, and dropped dejectedly into a chair, Lucy threw herself upon her knees and clasped his wrinkled hand.

"Father! Father! You forget your promise to Harry! You forget—"

But she stopped in sudden confusion, a crimson blush surging to her very temples as she sprang again to her feet. Half-way down the stairs the tall feeble soldier had stopped, clinging to the balustrade.

"Judge Armistead," he said, in a voice weak as a wearied child's. "I have been waiting only for darkness and your coming that I might say farewell. Never can I thank you—and Miss Armistead—enough. I'm well able to ride now, and go I must this very night. God grant no harm may ever come to you and yours for your kindness to Frank Kearny!"

Before either could recover from the surprise occasioned by this gaunt apparition in cavalry dress there came the shuffle of rapid feet through the dining-room, and old Nelse, his eyes bulging, his gray, kinky crop of wool seeming fairly bristling with fear and excitement, rushed into their midst.

"Fo' Gawd's sake, mars'r, hurry! De Rangers is comin' up de road. I's got de horse, suh."

Another moment—he hardly knows how he got there—Lieutenant Kearny is in saddle, clinging feebly to mane and pommel as old Nelse leads the troop horse through the darkness of the orchard and up a

winding pathway behind the house.   He is only certain of one thing.   It was Miss Armistead who whispered.

" Guide him to the hut at the old lookout, Nelse, and
stay there till I send."

VIII.

A QUESTION that occurred to Judge Armistead some five minutes later was as to Nelse's source of information about the movements of the cavalry—"the Rangers." No sooner had the old negro disappeared in the gloom of the orchard, leading the horse by the bridle-rein, than Miss Armistead and Hannah flew upstairs to the room recently occupied by the invalid, and were busily engaged in removing every trace of its recent occupation. Expecting to hear the tramp of horses' feet, the old man went proudly forth upon the broad piazza, intending to confront his accusers with all the dignity and decision of his race. He had felt almost ready to surrender his unbidden guest a few moments before, but the idea of a searching party being sent to his house instantly roused the antagonism of his nature and placed him on the defensive. For years he had lived in Virginia, and had been, when in his prime, a leading lawyer, and at all times a man honored and respected. Hospitable, openhearted, open-handed, he found in his declining years that he had laid by but few pennies for the rainy day that was so sure to come; and the education of his children, and the liberal allowances accorded them, were only made possible by mortgaging his pretty home in Warrenton. The mortgage was foreclosed after the presidential election of 1860, and not until after he had declined offers of help of every and any kind from most of the moneyed men of the community. Henry was rising in his profession in Richmond, they said, and in course of time the debt could be paid. It was not easy for the old man to say no to such kind and earnest offers, but he was proud as any of the Pharaohs, and it was his one boast that his word had ever been as good as his bond. He had still the old farm homestead up at Hopeville Gap, that had been the scene of the romance of his life, the home of the girl he wooed and won, the woman who, as his loved and honored wife, had made sunshine perennial at his hearthstone. It was hard to leave the old seat at his library window that looked out over the peaceful churchyard where she lay sleeping the last, long, dreamless sleep ; but there was soon reason why Warrenton would not have been a pleasant abiding place even could he have held his home. When the springtime came Judge Armistead was thankful he had said no to the men who would have opened their purse-strings in his behalf, for he disappointed them one and all. After fierce debates and overheated oratory the ordinance of secession went through with a yell, Virginia cast her lot with her Southern sisters, and to the very last moment, with all the earnestness and eloquence of which he was master, the old lawyer opposed it, and lost caste in a community where for a lifetime no man had so much as looked askance at him. Once taken, however, the step was irrevocable on

the part of his state, and, true to the doctrine in which
he had been reared, the Virginian threw himself heart
and soul into her service. Henry had already buckled
on the sword, and the judge not only stinted himself
that he might provide liberally for the young soldier's
needs, but sold a valuable law library that he might
contribute as liberally to the equipment of the troop
in which his boy was promptly elected cornet before
they were sworn into the service of the commonwealth.
Nevertheless there were not a few people who, in their
enthusiastic devotion to the cause of the Confederacy,
could not forgive it in an Armistead that he should
have opposed—and strenuously opposed—Virginia's
severance of the tie that bound her to the Union; and
Lucy, his sweet-faced, gentle daughter, who was heart
and soul a secessionist without having any really well-
defined idea of what its consequences might be—Lucy
was on several occasions treated by former friends
and associates with conspicuous coolness or equally
dangerous warmth, simply because of the stand he
had taken. Being a young woman of no little spirit,
despite her very cordial and winning manners, Miss
Armistead had resented these impertinences with immediate and telling effect. From that time forth she
"would have none of them," and there was civil war
within civil war that spring-tide of '61 in the lovely
old homes of Fauquier County. Perhaps it was just
as well that they moved up to Hopeville about the
time the news of Sumter came, and all the South
was crying through its journalists and orators, "*Jacta
est alea!* the day of our deliverance is come!" Lucy

Armistead, in common with nine tenths of the pretty girls of Virginia, had little doubt that it would be a matter of but a few months for the brothers and lovers in the glistening, gold-braided gray uniforms to march through Washington upon the populous cities of the North, and wring from a prostrate government the promise of future submission to the will of that imperious and warlike sisterhood, the new-born Confederacy. That McDowell and his army should dare advance into the heart of this sacred soil was temerity of the worst order. That he should be overwhelmed with panic, disaster, and ruin the moment he ventured into this broad and beautiful valley was simply inevitable, and he ought to have known it. Lucy never for an instant imagined anything else as a possible result. She had not done wondering at the abandonment of Manassas the following spring, when Jackson suddenly reappeared from the Peninsula and popped through the Gap into the very fields whereon the year before his envying comrade pointed him out, serene amid the storm of battle, "standing like a stone wall."

And now what did it mean that here under their roof there lurked in hiding nearly an entire month a soldier of the hated North, an open and avowed enemy of their beloved Virginia? By all the laws of war he ought, despite his wounds and his helplessness, to have been turned over to the care of the Confederate cavalry, whose squadrons swept by the house the very day succeeding his sudden and most unwelcome appearance, but the letter borne to the gray - haired father was one he could not disregard : it made even

the Yankee officer a sacred charge in their hands, to
be secreted, nursed back to health and strength, and
then, if not actually assisted to his regiment, at least
suffered to go in peace. There was something pathetic, too, about the condition of their unbidden guest
when, all unconscious of the test to which their
boasted Virginia hospitality was being put, he was
landed in delirium at their door. Bruised and cruelly lacerated when crushed under his wildly struggling
horse, shot through the side and through the sabre
arm, stunned by being hurled upon his head, and now
burning with fever and moaning in his fitful dreaming, helpless and dependent as a little child, and friendless as Jeanne la Pucelle before her accusers at Rouen,
he was lifted from the straw in that rude farm-wagon
and borne in the arms of the negroes to the room set
in readiness for his coming—yet not for such as he.
No words can tell the father's consternation when he
read Henry's brief but most urgent appeal, and learned
that the senseless, almost dying man before him was
an officer of the Union army and his son's once intimate and chosen friend at college. There was something he did not know even then, but that Lucy divined the instant her clear eyes glanced over that
strange letter. It did not serve to make her one whit
more kind to the stricken soldier. Anywhere else,
under any other circumstances, she could have turned
from him with bitterness and aversion. She kept her
brother's letter to reread from time to time, she said,
that it might keep her steadfast in the effort to do his
will, and whether because of it or other considerations

which she would have been the last to admit, she had most nobly acquitted herself of the task.

With Hannah's aid and that of their old cook, and the occasional services of Nelse, with her father's by no means trivial skill and experience in the cure of illness, with the youth and vigorous constitution of her patient to respond to their united efforts, Miss Armistead was soon able to assure herself that Henry's friend was on the high-road to recovery. Consciousness returned in a few days, the fever disappeared, the wounds healed rapidly; but no sooner did he realize where he was than Lieutenant Kearny began fretting himself into a fever again. He knew that in giving aid and comfort to him they would inevitably bring down punishment upon themselves, and he implored the judge to send word to the nearest Confederate post, and let them come and take him. The judge replied that it was impossible because of his promise. "My son's word is mine, sir," was his answer. Then he had to be away a day or two in search of supplies in the villages across the range, and in those days Lucy found it necessary to sit by her impatient patient for hours, reading to him, or kindly and firmly setting aside all his arguments as to the course he urged upon them. He could not understand what promise Captain Armistead had given; he could not understand why he should have promised anything at all. War is war, and both had taken up the sword with eyes wide open to its possible fortunes, good or ill. He urged that he might be permitted to see the letter, and was refused. The reason was not therein given, she said. He asked her if she knew the reason, and she rose and left his bedside and affected to rearrange the curtains at the window that she might hide from his searching eyes the blush that suffused her sweet but averted face.

As the days wore on and her manner was ever kind and grave, he chafed inwardly, and contended against the fact that it was nothing but kind and grave: a studied kindness—the professional, almost perfunctory kindness of the hospital nurse who day after day ministers to the wants of patients who must be coaxed and humored back to health. She seemed fairly inspired in the certainty with which she learned to anticipate his every need. She forgot nothing, neglected no item that could add to his comfort or promote his recovery, but with it all and through it all there was patent to him a strange, intangible, but positive *something* that told him she wished him to distinctly understand it was all for Henry's sake.

He was young, brave, gallant, fair to see, and as health slowly returned to him his good looks, despite his pallor, seemed to come with it. She was younger still, sweet, gentle, graceful, and fairer woman never yet had he set eyes upon—so those longing eyes began to tell him. Wounds, weakness, suffering, suspense, danger, and anxiety one after another became forgotten in her presence—merged and overwhelmed in a sweeter suspense, an anxiety far more potent, a wound that never yet in any man has ceased its torment save at the touch of one desired hand, and never will. Under the sloping rafters of that old Virginia farmhouse, in the peace and tranquillity of that white room, fragrant with the perfume of the flowers with which she daily decked it, and fresh with balmy air and sunshine, she moved about his bedside, or sat reading in soft, low tones, while Hannah's needles clicked through their worsted in the corner, and Hannah's watchful eyes saw what her young mistress would never have permitted her to hint, that, with all his heart and strength and soul, Lucy Armistead was loved by this young knight, this enemy of all her kith and kin, and thus that he was doubly her prisoner.

There came the day, as such days must come, when, partially at least, she too saw it. Then followed the estrangement, the neglect of him, that called forth Hannah's almost tearful plea. Impulsively, as she was rearranging his pillow, he had seized her hand in both his, all trembling as they were, and was covering it with burning kisses, when she whisked it from his grasp, and in speechless indignation almost rushed from the room, utterly spurning his plea for mercy, for forgiveness—utterly refusing to listen.

And this was still the situation the day the judge came back from Salem; and then, despite her wrath, it was she who sent him to a place of refuge which poor bewildered old Nelse would never have thought of. His one idea had been to convey as quickly as possible to his master the startling tidings brought him but the moment before by a panting colored boy, who had come full tilt across the fields to warn his brother "contraband" of the coming storm. The veriest chuckle-heads among those plantation hands seemed to have been gifted in those days of their dawning freedom with a marvellous quickness of perception and a fidelity in keeping the secrets of the "Lincoln soldiers" that beings of higher grade in the social scale might have envied in vain. The negroes who brought Kearny to the homestead in the gloaming of that autumn evening, the few servants about the farm, all must have known it was no Confederate soldier so mysteriously received and guarded; but it was not one of their number, the judge could swear, by whom he was betrayed.

Who, then, was it?

Standing on his piazza, Judge Armistead had time to decide his course of action before the troop of horsemen came clattering into sight. Two officers at the head of the little column rode into the yard and straight to the steps. One was Falconer, looking pale and grave; the other a stranger. It was the latter who dismounted and came quickly and lightly up the steps, but his manner was cold and haughty when he spoke.

"Judge Armistead, I am Major Gordon, of Richmond, and I am charged, sir, with a most unwelcome duty. It has been reported there that you are harboring an officer of the Federal army under your roof or about your premises. My orders are from the secretary of war himself, and they require me to make thorough search in every nook and corner. There is one condition on which I am authorized to suspend the search."

"And what may that be, major?" asked the judge, with bland courtesy, but with kindling eyes.

"That you assure me on your word of honor, in presence of Captain Falconer, that you have no such person or persons here."

"I give it, sir, unhesitatingly."

"My dear sir, I congratulate myself with twice— thrice the joy with which I congratulate you," exclaimed the officer, with sudden change of manner, with cordial delight in his eyes, and eagerly extending his hand. "The story was scouted in Richmond, and nothing but positive orders—"

But he broke off suddenly. Something in the upraised, not extended, hand warned him. The judge had more to say.

"I will not take your hand, sir, if in so doing I leave you under any misconception of the case. I have given you my word that no such person is here. Major, you have simply come too late."

There was a moment of silence which no man present cared to be the first to break. Then a quick, soft rustling at the door of the hallway, and Falconer, glancing sharply thither, saw Lucy Armistead turn suddenly away, her face hidden in her hands.

IX.

WHEN Major Gordon returned with his small escort to the railway, he went a much mystified man. In the discussion of the instructions which he had been charged to carry out, much stress had been laid upon the integrity of the old Virginian, who had become the subject of injurious report. Despite the opposition he had manifested before the final adoption of the ordinance of secession, every one who knew him testified, or was ready to testify, to his devotion to the interests of the Confederate government when the war-clouds rose above the horizon. No one at the Richmond War-office could trace to its source the rumor of his defection, but it came in such a shape that it could not well be disregarded—a letter from the wife of an officer prominent in the command of General Longstreet. She wrote from Warrenton to her brother, whose duties kept him for the time at Richmond, while her husband was still with his division over in the Shenandoah. She had known and honored the old judge all her life. It was "more in sorrow than in anger" that she told her brief story, and the officer sent to investigate the matter was charged to conduct no search and permit no intrusion if the old man gave his word as an Armistead that no such persons as represented were concealed anywhere on his property. This, as has been seen, was promptly given, for the judge well knew that by the time the troops arrived old Nelse was half-way up the heights behind the farm and beyond his little bailiwick.

Major Gordon had felt it his duty to inquire who the concealed officer was, how long he had been harbored under their roof, by what means he had been spirited away, and how he came to find his way thither in the first place. Mindful of the trouble in which he would involve his son were he to tell the story, Judge Armistead replied that the only information he felt it possible for him to give was this : that some negroes whom he did not know brought a man wounded, bruised, and almost dying to his door. After bearing him to a room beneath his roof, the discovery was made that he was a Federal officer. "I would not have turned a dog from my door in such a plight," he said. "We nursed him until he was able to get up and ride away ;" and that was absolutely all that he would say upon the subject.

Warned by Major Gordon that now he had subjected himself to the just suspicions, if not the punishment, of the government at Richmond, the judge simply bowed in silent dignity ; and then, when the major would have pressed him further, he slowly and impressively raised his hand and interrupted him.

"Pardon me, sir, for interposing. Your time is doubtless precious, and will be only wasted in further questioning. To such penalty as the authorities may decree, I can only submit. Meanwhile I am still mas-

7

ter here, and must not neglect my duties as host.   Permit me to offer you and Captain Falconer such refreshment as is in our power to give."

But Major Gordon conceived it his duty to decline the tendered hospitality, and to inform the old man that his imprudence had made it necessary to place him under surveillance until the wishes of the secretary could be learned. Captain Falconer was directed to remain with most of his men to throw a guard about the place that night, and assuring the captain that he would request that another officer be sent in the morning to relieve him and his detachment of so unwelcome a duty, the staff-officer set forth upon his return.

That night and for two days that followed the Armisteads were under guard. Falconer posted four sentries about the house, whose instructions were to permit no one to pass in or out until he himself had examined the person and ascertained his or her purpose : Judge Armistead was to be confined beneath his own roof.

When the morrow came there rode into sight soon after dawn the promised relief. It consisted of a lieutenant and twenty men of the cavalry command stationed with his own squadron at Thoro'fare Gap, and the lieutenant handed Falconer a letter, which proved to be from Major Gordon. In it was full authority for the captain to turn over his duties to the officer who bore the missive, since he, the writer, could not ignore the extremely delicate and painful nature of the situation in which Captain Falconer was so unavoidably placed. It was distressing to think that so old a friend of the Armisteads should have had to act for even a single night as their jailer, but it was one of the singular fortunes of such a war. "A stranger thing than this occurred to an ancestor of mine in the old days of York and Lancaster in the War of the Roses," wrote the major, "and stranger things than this might happen any day."

Then he went on to say—and this the captain read with close attention—that he wished it were possible for Falconer to remain at Hopeville at least for forty-eight hours, until the report of the case could be acted on at Richmond. The lieutenant was somewhat young and inexperienced, whereas Falconer knew the country and might be able to learn something definite of the mysterious Yankee whom Armistead had so unaccountably harbored. But it was, perhaps, too much to ask.

Falconer gave ten minutes' thought to this letter, and wrote a reply which reflected credit upon his reputation as an officer and a gentleman. Debarred, he said, by the fortunes of war from accompanying his comrades of Stuart's glorious corps in their enviable march to Maryland, he had striven to faithfully and energetically perform the duties assigned to him at the Gap. Nothing had given him such pain and surprise as the admission made by Judge Armistead, and no duty could well be more distressing to him than that of commanding the guard which his ·lifelong friends could not but consider in the light of jailers. But it was not for him to seek relief from any service

the state might require at his hands. Acting under
the request, so delicately and courteously conveyed in
his superior's letter, Captain Falconer's sense of a
soldier's duty prompted him to say that however repugnant to his feelings, he would remain at his post,
at least until further instructions, and he had the hon-
or to subscribe himself, very respectfully, etc.

It would be two days before this letter could catch
Major Gordon, two more before reply could reach
him, and meantime, thought Falconer, much might be
accomplished here at Hopeville.

Except that fleeting glimpse of her as she darted
back into the dimly lighted hall on hearing her father's
astounding words the night before, not once had he
been able to see Miss Armistead. He had begged for
an interview with her, and it was denied him on the
plea that she was too much distressed to see and talk
with any one, and had retired to her room for the
night. The judge gravely and courteously assured
him that not for a moment did they misunderstand
his position or his sentiments. His embarrassment
and his voluble expressions of regret and sympathy
the old man replied to by earnestly requesting him
to think no more of the matter. A soldier's duty was
a thing too sacred to be made the topic of a discussion. "We will confine ourselves to the house, and
give the sentries no trouble whatever," said the judge,
"and you must consider yourself entirely at home."
Hannah was ordered to prepare a room, and the cook
to rebuild her kitchen fire and serve supper for the
captain ; but Falconer protested. He *could* not tres-

pass on their hospitality so long as this hateful duty was imposed upon him. He would sleep on the piazza, or, at very best, the sofa in the hall, and spend the hours, so he wrote in a little note he gave to Hannah for her mistress, praying Heaven to bring rest and comfort and blessing to her, and prompt relief from an intolerable burden to him."

But as he had not been able to see her, Falconer, of his own volition, decided to retain the "intolerable burden" until she granted him the desired interview.

All that day she kept her room, however, and Judge Armistead, when not with his daughter, shut himself in the scantily furnished "study" which was reserved for his particular and personal use. Lucy alone ever ventured in there except at his express command or invitation.

Meantime Captain Falconer had not been idle. He had pretty thoroughly examined all the sheds, barns, and hiding-places about the premises, persistently questioned the cook and Hannah, and it was not long before he discovered that old Nelse was missing. He also knew that the horse he had lent the judge had not been returned to camp up to the time the lieutenant and his platoon left there that morning. Hannah, from an upper window, watched him as he prowled about the barn and sheds in search of the missing quadruped, and readily divined his thoughts. She flew down to the kitchen, where "Aunt Bell" was at work, and breathlessly warned her to keep out of the captain's way; he would be sure to ask her where Nelse had gone and what had been done with the horse. Meantime the girl's wits were actively at work to devise a story that would account for the absence of both, and one that no one in the house would gainsay. She took good care, too, that Miss Lucy should be fully and minutely informed of the captain's movements, and favored, furthermore, with her own interpretation of everything he did or said. This was perhaps unfortunate for the captain, as in every case her comments were heavily charged with cynicism.

It must have been nearly sundown, and all day long the inmates of the homestead had been speculating with varied emotions as to the fate of the fugitives of the previous night. Nearly two miles up the ridge was an eminence from which the country could be seen for leagues in every direction, and down among the rocks below, sheltered by thick foliage, was a little hut which had long been deserted. A bridle-path, rough, winding, and tangled with brier and underbrush, led thither up the mountain-side, and this was the refuge to which Nelse had conducted his precious charge. Never dreaming her father would boldly and frankly proclaim that he had "given aid and comfort to the enemy," Miss Armistead had hoped that some time this day she could send food and blankets to the invalid there hidden, and have tidings of his welfare. The sudden catastrophe of their being declared under guard, and so shut off from all possibility of communication with "her prisoner," as the judge once called him, well-nigh overwhelmed her with apprehension. She sprang from the couch on which she had been lying, and hurried to her window with beating heart, therefore, when, just as the sun went down in the west, she heard the stern, sharp challenge of a sentry, and a call for the corporal of the guard. She heard the rattle of Falconer's sword as he ran down the steps, and in an instant Hannah was peering over her shoulder.

There, bowing, smiling, scraping the ground with his foot, and making every imaginable manifestation of respect to the military authorities, stood old Nelse, cornered in an attempt to run the blockade through the dense shrubbery of the garden.

"Where've you been, sir?" sternly demanded Captain Falconer. "Where were you last night?"

The two faces at the upper window—one so fair and delicate, the other brown and eager—were almost ashen in the dread suspense of the moment; but almost instantly a gleam of joy shot over one, a flash of delight, not unmingled with incredulity, gleamed in the other, and both women, Caucasian and Ethiop, were shameless enough to applaud and approve a barefaced lie.

"My lawd!" gasped Hannah, "dat fool niggah got mo' sense 'n *I* ever thought!" for Nelse's black face was luminous with truth and injured innocence as he answered:

"Ober to my boy's, suh—ober on de odder side. I done tuk him a sack o' meal, suh, 'n' den dis mawnin' I fotched de hawse back to camp 'n' gave him to de gyard, suh, 'n' den I done walked all de way home, 'n' I's pow'ful tired, suh."

Old Nelse had raised his voice so that every word

was distinctly audible. *There* was a story for Hannah
and the cook to swear to! Falconer cross-questioned
in low tone. Nelse responded with loud and hearty
reiteration of his statement, and then humbly inquired
if he couldn't go into the kitchen—he hadn't had a
"moufful" all day—and the captain let him go.

In a moment Lucy Armistead and her hand-maiden
had seized the old negro, and were dragging information from him piecemeal. The fugitives had reached
the refuge in safety. Kearny had suffered a good
deal, both during the rough ride and the night that
followed, but declared he was doing well. Nelse had
left with him every scrap of the food Hannah had
hastily thrust in the saddle-bags, for when morning
came the lieutenant told him to take the horse to Falconer's camp, in order that the use he had been put
to might not be suspected, coached him on the story
he was to tell, and sent his heart's load of thanks and
blessings to "Miss Lucy an' all of 'em," as the dark
harbinger of good tidings put it.

When Judge Armistead noiselessly opened his
daughter's door a few minutes later, no answer having been given to his knock, he found her on the sofa,
sobbing as though her heart would break.

X.

THE second day of Captain Falconer's much-regretted tour of guard-duty had come, and for a man so profuse in expression of disgust at having been compelled to assume so repugnant a charge, it must be confessed that his sense of duty was commendable in the highest degree. Even while volubly damning the Fates that led to his being left behind when Stuart's cavalry were winning new laurels for themselves up in Maryland, the captain kept a vigilant eye on his sentries and on all the occupants of the house who appeared outside their rooms. He indulged Judge Armistead with another long dissertation this morning on the extraordinary freaks of fortune that had held him in the background on more than one stirring campaign, and he showed him the draft of a letter he had written begging to be relieved at once of his detail in command of the outpost at Hopeville Gap, whose principal task it was to hold as prisoners in their own house a man of such exalted and patriotic character as Judge Armistead, and a woman of such rare loveliness of mind and person as his noble and devoted daughter. As the fair copy of this eloquent appeal was not found among the archives of the War Department at Richmond some years later, it is possible that the original draft was all

that was ever written, and that its purpose was to influence no superiors in military circles, but rather to
create an impression in the minds of those who were
virtually his prisoners. Falconer hoped that the judge
would tell it all to Lucy, and that its effect would be
to bring her out from her room ready to greet him
with tender and sympathetic smiles. But although
the old gentleman begged him to come in and take
breakfast with him, he in the same breath remarked
that Lucy would have to be excused, she was feeling
far from well ; and noonday came and not a word did
he have with her.

One thing had occurred during the night that caused
him not a little speculation and anxiety. Old Nelse
had been cautioned to sleep in the house, and when
Falconer went the rounds at nine in the evening he
saw the veteran hostler's gray woolly pate bending
over a dim light at the kitchen table. "Aunt Bell,"
the cook, was making some little dish with which she
hoped, she said, to tempt Miss Lucy to eat. It occurred
to Falconer as he glanced in at the open door, and met
her smiling and good-natured greeting, that there was
a rousing big fire in the stove, and rather. a lavish out-
lay of various provender on the table. He was suspicious of everything he saw and heard, but feared to
jeopard his own hopes and prospects by interference
of any kind with the internal affairs of the household.
After all, it might only be the customary exhibit of
negro prodigality and improvidence. It was early in
the war, and the lessons of economy and the scores of
domestic makeshifts that were learned throughout the

Sunny South by the spring of '65 had not yet begun
to vex the spirits of "Aunt Bell" and her few satel-
lites. Warning the servants on no account to attempt
to cross the sentry-posts that night, as his men would
be sure to mistake them for spies or prowling Yankees,
and shoot, Falconer resumed his rounds among the
guards, and gave strict injunctions to the four men
posted about the house to permit no one to go in or
out ; then he visited his little picket-stations out on
the roads, and came back to the piazza and his soldier
slumber pretty well satisfied.

And yet the first thing he saw in the morning, just
after daybreak, was old Nelse, hobbling in through
the orchard with a basket on his arm. The basket was
half full of eggs and apples, and Nelse's old face was
"chuck-full," as he would have expressed it, of mingled innocence and concern as he listened to the captain's stern interrogations. Bless his heart, said Nelse,
he hadn't "done nuffin," just been out to get some
eggs. How did he get out? Why, "jes walked"
out. Oh, yes. He done cross the sentry's post, but
the gentleman was busy, and he "didn't like to disturb him."

This made Falconer boil with wrath. Nelse said he
walked out at dawn 'cause he wanted to find where
the hens were hiding their eggs ; it was raining, and
the sentry was trying to fix a bit of rubber blanket in
the low branches of an old pear-tree as he went out.
The sentry declared he hadn't had his eyes off the
kitchen doors and windows, and that Nelse couldn't
have crossed the post when he said he did. The cap-

tain was at his wits' end to solve the problem. Down
in the bottom of his suspicious soul he believed that
Nelse had been out most of the night—had gone somewhere with provisions, and that in all probability the
Yankee officer was hidden away in the near neighborhood. If he could *only* catch him! He determined,
after long thought, to give Nelse another chance; to
warn his men to be more alert than before, but to feign
the contrary. He planned to *let* Nelse out, but to follow him with one or two of his best troopers. It might
be done that very night, and meantime, could he not
see her and determine for himself whether she had
been interested in the care and concealment of the
mysterious Yankee?—whether, indeed, she were not
interested in the Yankee himself?

But several hours before darkness settled down upon
the range Captain Falconer found himself and his command relieved from their much-anathematized duty,
and in a manner not at all expected, at least as a result of his "application" exhibited that morning to
Judge Armistead. The news of Lee's ill success and
his retreat from Sharpsburg to the Shenandoah had
put a damper on the high spirits of many a Virginian
household, and the Armisteads at Hopeville were as
deeply disappointed as any. In sympathy with the
situation, a drizzling rain had been falling since very
early in the morning, and a mist hung over the valley
before their eyes, veiling the distant roads and fords.
The judge with his spyglass, now of little use, and
the captain with a map of Virginia on his knee, were
seated on the piazza discussing the probable outcome

of the present campaign. Moist and soaking, the fields rolled away down the slopes before them ; wet and dripping, the little patches of woodland looked black and gloomy through the mists. The road from Hopeville straight across country to Sudley Springs showed like a dun-red furrow here and there between the fields until shrouded by the low-hanging clouds, and nowhere along this cheerless landscape, outside the hedge within which the detachment was encamped, was a living object in sight. Nevertheless old Hector, the Newfoundland, lifted his head at times, pricked up his ears, and gazed attentively eastward. About two o'clock he sprang up from the mat near his master's chair, waddled down the steps, and trotted briskly out to the road in front. Almost at the same moment Hannah came fluttering down from the second story, hesitated a moment at sight of Falconer, then, never interrupting the talk of the two gentlemen, she sought to carry away the spyglass without attracting her master's attention ; but the captain checked her. "Don't take it away, Hannah ; we may want to use it," he said.

"Miss Lucy asked for it just a minute," stammered the girl. "She wants to see something."

Falconer sprang up and keenly scrutinized the misty line of road stretching away across the lowlands. Something in the girl's eager face made him suspicious of coming danger. Something in his manner as he suddenly took the glass and adjusted it attracted the immediate attention of the judge. There was an unmistakable quiver and tremulousness about the captain's hand ; there was a paler shade about his cheeks.

It made him think, all in an instant, of little hints that had been let drop from time to time, of certain impressions he had received — vague, shadowy, and intangible as—as those mist-veiled objects flitting like ghosts along the edge of the forest yonder, yet as positively pictured in his brain.   It reminded him of a reluctant expression once drawn from the lips of his son, a man who never condemned without good and sufficient reason.   "There is wide difference between the soldierly qualities of the two Falconers.   Wayne, the elder, is born to rise to high command, or fall in the attempt."   But this was not Wayne.   He had gone down before the fire of the Western brigade on the night of Gainesville, and was now languishing in a Northern prison.   This was Scott, the younger, and what he saw through that glass was not a pleasant sight. Those pallid, ghostly, dripping figures were dragoons in long overcoats or rubber ponchos, and coming this way—the advance guard, beyond question, of heavier forces in their rear.

"To horse, men !   To horse !" he shouted.   "Sound, there, bugler, and be quick about it !"   Then down the steps he ran and around to the rear of the house, where his own horse and orderly were sheltered at the barn.

Quick, from under the piazza, from the shelter of the little fruit-trees, from a dozen nooks and corners, the gray-jacketed Rangers leaped into view; belts, carbine slings, spurs, gauntlets, were hurriedly donned, bridles and saddles were whipped from the low limbs of the shade-trees, or dragged from under the bushes, and, all bustle, excitement, energy, and spirit, the little detachment rushed for its horses, and presently man after man came trotting out to the roadway in front, and the ranks were rapidly formed by their young sergeant. All athrill with martial enthusiasm by this time, the judge was standing on the piazza shouting encouragement and applause. Lucy, breathless with kindred emotion, had hastened down and was clinging to his side. The captain came riding around from the barn, and at sight of her straightened gallantly up in his saddle and gave her a soldier's salute with his gauntlet; then, as though sudden impulse possessed him, reined about and rode to the foot of the steps. "It is an advance in force, I doubt not, Miss Lucy, and there are fifty times our number in our front, but the Warrenton Rangers will glory in showing you their mettle. Some one has betrayed to them the presence of my little outpost here, and they hope to cut us off. We'll cut our way through."

"Well, but, captain, suggested the judge, "there don't seem to be many of them as yet. You can easily slip back here through the Gap, and get around to your comrades in that way. Why do you think there are so many?"

"They would not venture this far except in strong force. No doubt, if we could only see, the whole country in front of Thoro'fare is filled with them. If it is so, then we may have to fall back through Hopeville; but my Rangers never yet went back except before overwhelming odds. Ready?" he asked, as the lieutenant rode up with soldierly salute.

"All ready, captain."

"Very well. You take your platoon from the right and trot out and check those fellows till we see what they're made of."

All eagerness and spirit, the young soldier obeyed. He was a Virginia boy, brave as they make them, and it was his first chance ; his cheek flushed, his eye kindled as he glanced up one moment at Miss Armistead's glowing face. Her beauty seemed to inspire him with double rage for battle. Never heeding or listening to the captain's promise to "support him," he struck spurs to his charger, wheeled short about, and clattered out to the impatient troop. Another moment he and the platoon had disappeared among the trees down the road to the right.

The rain seemed holding up. The clouds to the west were breaking, and presently, as Falconer bowed low over the pommel and rode out to his men, the watchers on the piazza saw that the sunbeams were bursting here and there in brilliant little shafts of gold through the drifting veil. One of these broad shafts of glistening color fell full on that dun - red furrow crossing the valley eastward, and then the shadowy, spectral horsemen a mile away stood forth in bold relief. Ay ! there were the pale blue capes of the cavalry overcoats. There in their midst fluttered the little guidon—the stars and stripes in miniature. In front of them, well out across the fields, rode wary troopers peering into the bridle-paths and wood roads, watchful against surprise. Behind them, several hundred yards, covering the road until it disappeared among the distant woods, marched a compact column of cavalry. No man could say how many more there were. Those in sight were enough to swallow alive, the soldiers said, the little detachment sent down to challenge and check them.

Too late now! Young Virginia has received his orders, disappeared, and though Falconer has time to send a sergeant at the gallop to recall the youngster, and though he himself promptly moves his troop by the right flank, he gets no farther than the crossing of the Hopeville road. The Armisteads believe he has gone to the support of his subaltern as he promised, but it seems not.

All of a sudden, down at the front they see commotion among those leading and widely dispersed troopers. Then that they are opening fire ; then whirling about and scurrying for protection. Then the next thing that comes into view is a dark line, a little party of horsemen following a single leader, and, all unsupported, all undaunted by the odds against them, down the road they go in headlong charge. Twenty Virginians dashing recklessly into the teeth of an advancing regiment. There is one moment of wild yells, of sputtering hoofs, of stirring trumpet calls ; the horsemen are all intermingled in a surging mass in the muddy road, and then the whole Federal column seems to take the trot and sweep resistlessly forward. Four or five dingy gray jackets and plumed felt hats come riding lamely back, pursued by a score of sabres or popping revolvers, and the young Virginian has carried out, according to the best of his inexperienced ideas on the subject, the captain's orders to " check

8

those fellows "—but he may look in vain for the promised supports. Falconer has seen enough of the fight to warrant him in a rapid trot through Hopeville Pass, and the household at the homestead has no longer a jailer.

A riderless horse comes galloping up the road and into the gate. No one knows to whom he belongs, but old Nelse is on hand and speedily leads him around to the barn.

XI.

For nearly two hours that afternoon there was clamor and scurry down the range. Several squadrons of Union cavalry, at rapid trot, swept through the mountain road below the homestead, their trumpets echoing their liveliest peals among the rocky heights, but the main body seemed to concentrate on Thoro'fare, where vehement defence was made, and where charge after charge was necessary before the Gap was carried. The sun had come out warm and clear, and, unable to restrain his desire to see all that could be seen, and anxious to learn the fate of the little platoon of Virginians who had so daringly challenged the advancing host, the judge took his cane and trudged sturdily forth, announcing his intention of going down to the field below the heights, where some burial parties could be seen at work. It was almost sunset when the sound of distant firing and cheers and trumpet calls at last died away in the south ; the clouds lifted from the valley, and the roofs and walls of far-away villages and hamlets gleamed in the radiance of the declining orb, or blushed in the glow of the reddening skies. Lucy Armistead leaned against the old white balustrade, looking out once more upon the gorgeous panorama of the broad valley, lovelier than ever after its long immersion in the rain-clouds. All seemed still and peaceful again except the sight of those pygmy parties digging shallow little trenches down there in the fields. Nearly two hours had her father been gone, and she was beginning to feel strangely nervous and ill at ease. She had sent for Nelse, but Nelse had disappeared ; so had the horse ; and something told her that he had gone to their late guest and patient—that if possible he would bring him back. All day long her heart had been filled with wretched anxiety. Nelse had, indeed, succeeded during the night in running the blockade and carrying food and blankets to the fugitive, but he brought back word that he seemed "porely," and had evidently suffered severely. For nearly a month he had been her helpless and dependent charge. To her nursing and care and ceaseless attention he owed perhaps his life itself—he had not hesitated to say so ; he had done more—he had striven to assure her that everything life might bring to him—fortune, fame, honor—all the depth and devotion of his love he would lay at her feet ; but she had almost rudely checked—she would not listen to him.

And now his friends and comrades were here in force, and soon must come to claim their own. No longer was he hers to do with as she chose. Henry's once intimate and confidential friend, he had been intrusted to her care when life and liberty were the forfeit of her lack of vigilance. Whatever had been the cause of the estrangement that had arisen between them in their college days, the brother had assured her that the feud was ignored when they met at Richmond, and now, at

the possible cost of his commission in the service, he
had snatched the wounded soldier from the jaws of
captivity and hidden him under the refuge of his
father's roof.   There, well her woman's heart assured
her, Henry's friend became her lover ; he who sought
the defeat and downfall of her people would have won
her for his wife.   Tremblingly, in one brief interview
before he was spirited away in the blackness of the
night, he had begged her pardon for the kisses he
rained upon her hand, but told her it was love that
drove him mad—and she would hear no more.

Twilight came ; then hoof-beats and voices down
the road ; the jingle of scabbards and a trumpet call.
Another little column of Union cavalry turned into
the winding Pass and went clattering up the Gap.
Silence again, and then a halting, feeble footfall in
the darkening hallway behind her.   Her little hands
clasped tightly round the railing ; her heart seemed
to stand still one instant, then to beat tumultuously.
She knew it must be Kearny — returned to her once
more.

Slowly, painfully he reached the threshold, and stood
there leaning against the doorway, irresolute, gazing
at her with all his heart in his eyes.   At first she could
not—at last she *had* to—turn and greet him, for his
silence frightened her.   One glance at his face and she
almost sprang to his side.

"Oh, how you must have suffered !   Sit here," she
said, rapidly drawing towards him the judge's easy-
chair.   "No.   Sit down !" she insisted, as he held
back and tried to speak.   With her own hand she half

guided, half supported him until, obeying her, he sank exhausted into the seat. Then she hastened to her father's study, and presently reappeared with a goblet in her hand. "Drink," she said, and held it to his lips until he had drained the last drop.

"Is that my stirrup-cup?" at last he questioned, smiling faintly.

"Your friends are here, or all around here, as you doubtless know, but you are in no condition to travel. Father will insist that you remain until you are."

"My regiment is among those fellows somewhere; and even were they not here I could no longer stay. Even were I able to send word at once to those who are doubtless mourning me at home, I would not spend another night under this roof, even though in going I offended so courteous a gentleman as your father. You alone have power to bid me go or stay, and you have shown me all too plainly that my presence here is most distressing to you."

She was standing there before him, a light mantle wrapped about her shoulders. She was looking far away. She could not trust herself to gaze down into the pleading eyes uplifted to her face. His faltering accents, the piteous weakness of his voice, were almost more than she could bear.

"I do not want you to go until you are well," at last she murmured.

"Ah! That is where it hurts," he broke forth, impulsively. "*That* is woman's compassion—pity—for mere physical suffering. *You* would have me stay until strength returns to muscle and limb. I would have you bid me stay forever, or at least until you would go with me to the world's end. I — I have learned here to love you with every fibre of my being, to live only in the touch of your sweet hand, the smile of your exquisite face. No! no! I *will* speak, Lucy. You shall not turn from me now. Oh, for God's sake do not go, or you will break my heart," he pleaded as she would have rushed past him into the house. He seized her dress with one feeble, clutching hand, and drew its folds towards him until both could clasp it. "Nay. I'm going this night. 'Tis no disgrace, dishonor, to *any* woman, North or South, to be loved as I love you, and with me 'tis life or death. I tell you my whole heart; my very soul is filled with one infinite longing, one passionate love for you who have nursed me back to life. Oh, my darling! my beautiful! was it only to toss it aside in contempt that you aroused it all? Lucy! Lucy! Can nothing plead for me? Can nothing bring me the *right* to stay? Speak to me. I'm not the man to shrink from Fate. I *will* know why it is you spurn and turn from me. Do you hate all Northern men so bitterly that I must be only alien, enemy, and stranger from this time forth? Tell me." And now he had seized her hand, but this she would not brook, and wrenched it almost violently away.

"I never gave you grounds for such a feeling towards me," she faltered. "I strove to make you see — to make you understand it was all impossible."

"But why—why? I know all this. Heaven knows it is needless to remind me of the way you avoided and shrank from me from the first moment I was mad enough to betray myself! That does not satisfy— that does not explain. My race is as proud and as prominent as your own. Your brother held no friend- ship equal to mine; we were closest friends—devoted friends until a silly, boyish quarrel parted us for a time. I *am* a Northerner, and true to my flag and the Union. You are Virginian, and hold us as enemies. But this war cannot last forever. We are one people. Time and again did not our forefathers fight in civil feud, sometimes on opposite, sometimes on the same side, only to be the stronger and better friends till now? Will not this quarrel end as all such dissensions have ever ended? We were together when the Red and White Roses battled for the crown. We fought each other hard when the Stuarts strove against the House of Hanover. You were Roundheads when we were Cavaliers; you were with Washington when many of mine still wore the scarlet of King George, though our name had hated the house from which he sprung. Civil war has come upon us again. We battle for the Union, you for its disruption; but no nation will let such strife go on forever. Lucy! Lucy! I cannot stay, and day by day fall deeper and deeper in the toils of a hopeless love. God knows if I go this night, my heart bides here. Think, think, sweet one; have you no word of hope for me—not one?"

Still she stood there, her bosom heaving now, her head averted, drooping; her eyes — though he saw them not — brimming with tears. His pleading would have moved a stony heart if it lay but in a woman's breast, and hers was young and pure and tender, and longing to love and to be loved. She strove to speak, but words would not come just then. There rose up before her the memory of that last talk with Henry; of something he once had half confided before that time, and so long as her brother's words could live in her heart, no other answer would she give the man whose very life seemed hanging on her words.

She started suddenly from his side. There was a rustle in the shrubbery close at hand; a smothered exclamation as though a man had stumbled; then muffled footfalls, then silence.

"Some one was there—listening!" she exclaimed, startled and trembling. "I'm sure I saw a figure go skulking off towards the orchard—through there," she pointed.

Kearny had risen painfully, and now once again stood close at her side.

"No one who can do you harm," he said. "As for me, I am past harming if you will not answer me. Lucy, you are no vain coquette, toying with a man's strong love to feed a woman's vanity. Day by day I have had no thought, no study but you, and I would stake my soul on your truth."

"It is because—because you've had no other study that you think as you do," she quickly spoke, the woman in her seizing at the chance. "When once again you are among your own, 'twill not be so."

"Among my own!" he echoed, indignantly. "Among my own! You are no true woman if you do not well realize this day that on all this earth there lives but one I crave to call my own. You shall not trifle with me, Lucy. I must have my answer now, though it send me from you in desolation. You do not love me —that I know ; but is there reason, good reason, why I should never win you ? *Look* at me ! Oh, my darling, though I read my death-warrant in your eyes, I *will* see them once more," and with his trembling hands he turned and lifted her sweet, pale face until it was close to his—so haggard, so roughly bearded now, yet so eloquent and glorified with the strength and fervor of a man's love.

"Now tell me. Is there reason ?"

"Do you not know it—yourself ?" she answered at last, and her tear-dimmed eyes gazed full into his.

He started as though stung.

"Oh, my God ! I was told—I was sure— Lucy ! do you mean there is another ?"

She trembled now from head to foot. His shaking hands dropped helplessly. He waited, breathless, for her answer, and at last it came :

"You know—you *ought* to know—there is another." And she turned and fled.

He leaned against the balcony for support. All his strength, such as it was, had left him now. All his manhood, pride, vehemence, will, and passion seemed crushed and broken. He bowed his head upon his arm, trying to think, trying to understand, while all seemed reeling about him. What was it Hannah had told him ? Certainly there were men who sought her hand; certainly she had admirers, but not one for whom she cared a straw. He had not sought to pry into her se-

crets, but after she withdrew herself from his society,
Hannah had chattered ceaselessly, and he could not
but listen.   And yet—after all—after all, with her own
lips she had told him he ought to know—it was his
right to know—there was another who stood between
him and the hope of his life.   What were wounds,
suffering, delirium, death—to this?

Then there came a moment or two in which he heard
nothing—saw nothing.   He was very weak, and the
privation and exposure of the last forty-eight hours
had done their work only to be supplemented by a
blow like this.   Did he fall?   He could not tell.   He
was dazed, confused, wandering.   Was it all a dream?
Here he lay once more in the big arm-chair, a soft hand
bathing his forehead; that same sweet, exquisite face
with a world of anxiety and tenderness in the violet
eyes gazing into his as he wearily opened his own;
old Nelse standing by his side, pouring forth voluble
expression of sympathy.   *Was* it possible that for one
instant before consciousness fully returned he felt the
pressure of warm, soft lips upon his forehead?   It was
all so vague, so dreamy.   Looking up, he saw once
more the face he loved.   But 'twas all true.   She must
have meant what she said.   There was the very look
in her eyes, the very expression that hovered about her
mouth.

"Go back now, Nelse," he heard her say, "and find
your master.   It is time he had returned."

Then came trampling hoofs, clattering sabres, jingling spurs.   Half a score of horsemen rode into the enclosure.   Three dismounted and rapidly ascended the

steps, two in the uniform of officers of the Union cavalry halted short as though stunned at sight of the recumbent figure before them and the slight, girlish form at its side ; the third, in civilian dress, kept a little in the background.   It was this last one who was first to speak.

"Gentlemen, are you satisfied ?   Did I tell the truth ?"

"*Kearny !*" exclaimed the foremost officer.   "My God !   *Is* this you ?"   Then he turned.   "There is no alternative, major ?"

"None, sir.   Carry out your orders."

"Lieutenant Kearny, you will prepare to return with us at once—a prisoner in close arrest."

XII.

"THE winter of our discontent" had come upon the Army of the Potomac. The bloody sacrifices, the heroic efforts of the regimental officers and the rank and file had all been neutralized by the timid and vacillating leadership of those to whom the highest commands had been intrusted. Lee was back along the Rapidan, skilful and strong as ever. McClellan was relieved; several old favorites of the Peninsula campaign no longer rode at the head of their corps or divisions, though still wearing their general's stars in Washington, or on distant and less prominent fields. Others, like Phil Kearny and Stevens, had fought their last fight and gone to their soldier rest. A new leader transferred the scene of conflict to the heights of Fredericksburg, and the loyal and patient army tramped obediently thither only to find the crests along the southern banks of the stream bristling with the bayonets and batteries of Lee. The administration complained of McClellan that he could not be induced to attack unless his force was overwhelmingly superior and victory was certain. It seemed to demand that its generals should be made to fight, and the new commander proceeded to satisfy the nation that the Army of the Potomac would shrink at nothing by "butting its head against a stone wall," and assaulting Lee in an impregnable position.

More mourning at home; more gaps and vacancies at the front; more courts and investigations and "committees on the conduct of the war" at Washington followed as a matter of course. Another removal, another experiment, another commander, another splendidly planned passage of the fords and swoop upon the Confederate left, another senseless delay. Then, on the other hand, another daring, brilliant, defiant march from front to flank, another superb assault, and the luckless Army of the Potomac is doubled up by a single corps led by that indomitable Jackson. A winter of discontent and gloom, indeed, to all the Union army in Virginia—to all the loyal North ; and a winter of sore trial and bitter suffering for one young cavalryman in particular—Mr. Frank Kearny, of New Jersey.

No words can well describe the wrath and indignation with which he learned that a charge of desertion had actually been laid at his door. With the exception of the major and adjutant, he saw none of his comrades on the night of his "recapture" at the Gap. He was conveyed in an ambulance to Centreville, and thence to Washington, where for weeks he lay desperately ill. Influential relatives were speedily on hand to see that justice was done him. A devoted mother, a devoted cousin — Miss Paulding, of New York—hastened to his bedside, and his bodily sufferings were soothed as only women can soothe and comfort; but there are mental tortures that even the infi-

nite pity of mother-love can never reach, and, when
not delirious, Frank Kearny was a victim to a dejection too profound for comfort of any kind. The exposure, the bitter disappointment, the final shock and
outrage to his soldier honor of those last two days at
Hopeville, had brought on a relapse that laid him at
the very door of death. His regiment had pushed
on through Thoro'fare Gap on the night he was revealed at the Armisteads' to the eyes of the designated
officers, precisely as the scout Tierney, when confront-
ed, had predicted and promised. The adjutant quickly saw that his comrade must have been severely
wounded, and would have attributed his apparent desertion to that cause, but the major was a man who
had little faith in human nature. He only saw the
pretty girl at Kearny's side, and, to his mind, Captain
Mullane's scandalous report was substantiated in all
its bearings. While the —— New Jersey trotted on
up to Front Royal that next day, the talk at every
rest was of Kearny's astonishing escapade. The major had rejoined, and "had the floor ;" and Kearny,
being absent and unrepresented, could expect nothing
else than the "*toujours tort*" of tradition. Charges
and specifications were duly formulated by the major,
who cited as witnesses the regimental adjutant, now
temporarily absent conducting the accused and raving
officer to the lines of Washington, Captain Mullane,
the major himself, the general of division who on the
night of August 28th had ordered or authorized Mr.
Kearny to rejoin his regiment, the other division commander who had given him despatches to carry to

Buford, and finally the civilian Tierney, who was in the secret service of the War Department.

There was no one in the cavalry brigade to fight his battle for him; none but Confederate soldiers could tell how he strove to cut his way through their patrol and carry out his orders; none but they to bear witness that his horse was killed and he himself dragged from underneath, senseless, crushed, and bleeding; none but they to tell how he had been conveyed to a farm on the upper road, his wounds dressed, and his identity discovered by Captain Armistead. Even they could not tell and did not know that, after they rejoined their squadron on the following day, the young captain had gone back to the farmhouse where the wounded "Yank" still lay unconscious, and there wrote the note to his father at Hopewell, and having bundled the senseless prisoner into a straw-covered wagon which, with two negroes, he had hired for the purpose, he sent him to that father's home under the guidance of a sergeant of his own troop on whose fidelity he could depend to the very death. There was no one to tell how long the Union officer lay there unconscious; how he strove to communicate with his comrades when consciousness returned; how he had escaped from his would-be captors when Major Gordon came up from Richmond. It all went against him in the cavalry brigade, and the charges were duly forwarded to Washington. There, however better counsels prevailed. The surgeons were prompt to testify that with such wounds and injuries as he had evidently received there must have been some mistake. When consciousness returned the accused officer was able to tell his story, and though he knew it was Henry Armistead who rescued him from Libby and sent him to a refuge where he could be sure of care and comfort—*this* feature he was bound in honor to conceal. It would have leaked out in short order, become known to the many Southern sympathizers at the capital, and been speedily transmitted to the Confederate army, to the probable severe censure, if not disgrace, of his devoted friend. Not even to his mother did he knowingly mention this incident, but there was one who sat by his side when fever raged in his veins and wild, wild incoherencies were on his tongue. One who listened with quivering lips and tightly clasping hands to the constant moaning mention of that name —Lucy—and whose eyes filled and whose whispered prayers called down blessings at the frequent allusion to Henry — Henry Armistead — Henry's sacrifice for *his* sake. Long before Frank Kearny was able to sit up, propped by pillows and nursed by loving hands, Kate Paulding knew that his heart was irrevocably lost to some Virginia girl, and divined that it was Henry Armistead who bore him from his original captors to a place of safety. Oh, what a host of recollections was summoned up by that name! Oh, what a revelation of shattered hope and bitter loss there came to her in the still watches of the night, in the repeated mention of that other name—Lucy! When Frank Kearny returned to convalescence and was able to totter feebly about the rooms and gradually to face the situation, his was not the only heart that bore a

9

weight of silent, ceaseless, gnawing pain; but none, to look at her, would dream for an instant that the other throbbed in Katherine Paulding's breast.

Perhaps it was best for Kearny that he should have such a burden of wrath and indignation against his accusers, such a burning desire to hasten forth and confront them. Both at the War Department and Trenton, however, his case was by this time fairly represented and fully understood. Letters from officials high in rank assured him that the charges were scouted and had been returned to the brigade and regiment with the full report of the surgeons and his own statement. From the governor he received the offer of promotion to higher rank in a new regiment just being raised. He thanked everybody for the kindness extended, but what he longed for was a chance to get back to the regiment. He would never leave the —— New Jersey, he said, until he had faced down every and any detractor in it, and—but this he never mentioned to any one in authority—there was one fellow in the cavalry brigade with whom he had a score to settle. For that he must be patient and hoard his strength.

Not until the guns began to boom at Fredericksburg was he able to rejoin the regiment. He had left it youthful, buoyant, joyous, popular; a splendid specimen of the young cavalry officer — tall, handsome, erect, with glistening eyes and glowing cheeks. He returned aged as though by several years; stern, taciturn, gaunt, haggard, and bearded, with eyes that no longer glistened—they simply burned. He received the greetings of his fellows with quiet and reserved demeanor; he was contemptuously cold to several; he could evidently forgive none of them that there was no one of their number to promptly write him at the very outset that he, at least, could never believe such charge as that alleged against him. The major he "cut" dead. It was not the lot of the regiment to be heavily engaged at Fredericksburg, but one or two vacancies occurred among the field-officers and some promotions. Frank Kearny somewhat coldly thanked the officers who gathered at his tent when it was known that he had been commissioned captain within the week that followed the great and disastrous battle. He spent much time in confidential talk with the colonel and with two of his chosen friends, the adjutant and Captain Dayton. He had had complete explanations from the former and a reconciliation with him. As for the latter, he had been on detached duty at the time the story gained ground in the brigade that Kearny was "in hiding," and when it finally reached his ears no words seemed adequate to express his contempt for the originators. In some way it was whispered about the camps that Frank Kearny "didn't care a row of pins for the captaincy." It was known that the governor had offered to commission him as junior major of the new regiment, and that he had declined "until he had settled some matters in the cavalry brigade," and there was a decidedly uneasy, not to say an apprehensive, feeling as to just when and in what manner that "settlement" would take place.

Every day Kearny seemed gaining in health. His haggard face began to resume its wonted lines, and yet 'twas greatly changed. 'Twas the beard did that, said some of the commentators; but the observant men knew well that there was something behind the crisp and curling mantle of brown hair. His eyes still burned; his lips were set and stern; all the old gladness and jollity were gone; the ringing laugh was never heard. He shunned company; spent most of his time as they lay in camp drilling his men and looking after his horses; he was eager and ready for scouts and picket duty; he was in the saddle and the open air hours at a time, and was giving much attention to sabre exercise with the best fencer in the regiment, and to practice with the revolver. To the camp of an adjoining regiment, brigaded with his own, Kearny would not go at all; and it was not long before the stories of his daily occupations were made the subject of comment there.

"Look out for yourself, Mullane," said one of the field-officers. "It's you he's training for. You'd far better quit poker and whiskey now, and get in fighting trim."

And Captain Mullane laughed loudly, but his laughter was not glad. One night he asked the major if he thought a leave of absence could be obtained, "His wife lay very ill at home;" and the major told him he would do what he could for him with the colonel now commanding the brigade.

Up to this time not one word had Kearny exchanged with his brother officers as to the people with whom he had been lodged and by whom he had been nursed and tended. Though night and day Lucy Armistead was in his thoughts, he shrank from any mention of her name or allusion to her people. Inquiries had, of course, been made by comrades interested in his strange adventure, but in presence of his colonel he said to one of them: "I cannot be sufficiently grateful to this family, and the best way I can show it is to keep their secret. It would subject them to utter ostracism if their friends ever learned they had harbored a Yankee. It is my purpose to say nothing about them— until the war is over."

There had been great curiosity about the young lady. The major had learned the name of the family, but there was no one from whom they could learn particulars. After pointing out the house and the lieutenant, Tierney the scout had left them, and had avoided the Jersey regiment from that day to this. But the adjutant described her as lovely, and confided to Dayton that she seemed utterly overcome with shock and grief when Kearny was led away. It set Dayton to thinking.

One cold winter's night when the moon shone down on snow-sprinkled huts and glistening white canvas along the Rappahannock, the adjutant was sitting at the headquarters tent looking over the mail when Kearny strode quickly in.

"Is it true," he asked, "that a leave has been granted to Captain Mullane?"

"I believe it is," answered the adjutant, uneasily. He did not like the indications of storm.

"Then I want you to come with me to their camp. Dayton goes too. No; I'm not armed. You need not fear anything so serious. I want you to present me to Captain Mullane. I have a question to ask him, and you must witness his reply."

Wondering at the strangeness of the request and the oddity of the proceeding, the adjutant went. The three men strode silently across the moonlit field until they reached the sentry-lines of the adjoining regiment, Kearny slashing at his boots from time to time with the light rawhide he carried. He asked no questions and vouchsafed no information as to his purpose. The regiments were in winter-quarters, and many of the officers were living in substantial little huts. It was to a structure of this character that the three visitors were escorted by a corporal of the guard just as the trumpets along the broad, treeless plain were sounding the evening tattoo.

Sounds of revelry—somewhat bacchanalian—issued from within. An officer came forth apparently on the way to the roll-call of his company. He stopped short at Kearny's hail, and replied hesitatingly to the question, "Is Captain Mullane here?" It was evident that he scented mischief.

"May I trouble you to ask him to step outside a moment?" said Kearny, civilly.

"Who shall I say wants him?" asked the lieutenant, suspiciously, yet with a certain air of defiance. There was no love lost between the two commands, and he knew the Jerseyman at sight. "His wife is ill, and he starts for Acquia Creek in a few moments."

"Say that Captain Kearny desires a word with him."

A roar of laughter and the clinking of glasses told of the climax of some camp-story as the door was re-opened. Then came a hush; then a muttered and excited discussion. It lasted a moment, and then a coarse voice exclaimed:

"There's only three of 'em, bedad! Go on out, Mullane; I'm wid ye. Come on, fellers."

Presently out they came, half a dozen burly, half-intoxicated men, and grouped themselves compactly at the doorway.

"Which is Captain Mullane?" asked Kearny, quietly. "I have never been presented."

"I'm your man," was the answer, as a strongly-built fellow of the ward-politician type stepped a little forward, yet not too far.

"Captain Mullane, in my enforced absence from my regiment last September, you, it is claimed, started the slander that led to my arrest. I have never yet heard, or asked, the exact language. I have always meant to hear it from your own lips. Will you repeat it now?"

The "rough" looked uneasily about him. Very possibly he would have much preferred to lie out of it, but the devil of drink was uppermost in his comrades. They were many and the Jerseymen few, and there came a growl of encouragement from behind him.

"Tell him to his face, Mullane. Devil a lie was there in it!"

Thus adjured, and with sneering emphasis, the captain spoke:

"What I said was that you were a man of sense. Fighting wasn't to your taste as much as hiding away a few weeks in your sweetheart's arms."

Kearny recoiled as though struck by a heavy blow. The light switch he had meant to use dropped to the earth beneath his feet. One instant only of silence. Then came a spring like that of a tiger, and with the low, fierce cry, "You *hound!*" he flew at the brawny throat before him, and Mullane was hurled backward into the mud, Kearny going down with him.

True to their tactics, learned in many a bar-room brawl or election row, Mullane's comrades jumped to the rescue of their champion, raining kicks and blows upon his assailant. Dayton and the adjutant vainly strove to reach the struggling and prostrate pair. It would have gone hard with Kearny among those brutal boot-heels, but by this time scores of other officers, not of the Mullane faction, with the colonel himself, came flocking to the scene. Roll-call was forgotten. The "roughs" were pulled away and banished to their several quarters, and, bruised and breathless, Kearny was lifted to his feet. His antagonist more slowly regained his, and in stifled rage responded to the stern question asked him by his commander as to the meaning of such a disgraceful brawl.

"'Twas him that struck me, sir," he said, indicating Kearny, who, panting heavily and leaning on Dayton's arm, was striving to regain breath.

"How say you, Captain Kearny?" asked the colonel, sternly still, for the breach of all discipline was a sore offence to his rigidly soldierly views.

"I ask your pardon, colonel," was at last the slow answer. "Never until to-night, from that man's own lips, did I learn of the hideous insult he had put upon me. I should have known that it was one that could never be wiped out here. I will answer any just demand—make any proper *amende* to you. But, as God is my judge"—and he pointed in quivering, menacing wrath at Mullane—"that man shall answer to me."

XIII.

THE fracas in the cavalry brigade was a matter that could not well be hushed up. Men had little else to do for several weeks of wintry weather than entertain themselves as best suited their various temperaments and characters. The matter was discussed in all the adjoining camps, and the drift of public opinion may best be inferred from the brief but emphatic comment made by nine tenths of the men who knew Mullane— "I wish he had killed him." Outside of the squad of six or seven boon-companions he had not a friend in the brigade. The great mass of gentlemen of whom the officers of the various regiments were composed had never associated with him. His allies were of the class made famous in the days of "Big Six" in New York and the "Northern Liberties" of the Quaker City. A reputation as a political "boss" and a ward bully at home was supplemented by a career of drinking, brawling, and poker-playing at the front. In no battle had his voice been heard. Somehow or other he had managed to keep out of the way of hostile blade or bullet, and now he was gone, and no man regretted, though many envied, his going. Who would not have given much to enjoy a fortnight with the loved ones at home before the opening of the spring

campaign? Leaves of absence to officers and furloughs to enlisted men were only to be granted for
urgent cause, and there were not lacking those who
said they believed the letter Mullane filed with his
application was a bold forgery. He had a wife, there
was no question, and 'twas said by one of his cronies
that she was more than a match for him with her fists.
There was also a Dr. McNamara, whose attentions to
her, said the same authority, were not always strictly
professional; and though he didn't doubt that Mac
could be induced to write a certificate that a man's
wife was dying in order to get him a furlough, he
thought it improbable that he *would* be in this instance. He would draw the line at Mullane. Other
unsavory things were said by his own cronies, now
that he had gone with his winnings and left them out
of pocket. Then there came soldiers of his squadron
to the colonel's tent to complain that they had given
their captain money to keep for them, and in some
cases had lent it at his request, and he had gone without a word to them on the subject. Take it all in all,
there was no sympathy for Captain Mullane and little
blame for Captain Kearny. Most men, to be sure,
said that he should not have soiled his hands by touching such a blackguard, but no men, no man, in all the
cavalry brigade until that night dreamed what a depth
and breadth of insult had been conveyed to Kearny
by those words. Then Dayton's eyes were further
opened, and the adjutant, recalling the loveliness of
the girl whom he saw for that brief moment up by
Hopewell Gap, began to realize that it was the in-

sult to her, not to him, that drove Kearny mad with rage.

As for Captain Kearny himself, he would talk with no one. He begged a week's leave to go to Washington. Then the brigade commander sent for him.

"Kearny," said he, "give me your word that you will not follow or further molest that fellow Mullane, and I will go to General Hooker myself with your paper, and beg for a fortnight for you. No man deserves it more, and it will do you good. You are brooding too much over a trouble every one else has long since buried."

"Who has cause to remember it, sir, as I have?"

"I admit it, but let that drop. Give me your word you are not going after Mullane—will not touch him, and I can get your leave."

And it was remembered all through the brigade during the gloomy, dripping month that followed that Kearny shook his head and would make no promise.

He wrote three letters that night, and they were on the way to Washington before another sunset. Life in the old regiment had become unbearable, he said. He had accomplished the object of his return; every accusation and accuser had been faced down, but it was not in his nature to easily forget or forgive the men who so readily had given credence to his defamation. "I love and I hate with equal strength," he wrote in one letter. "There can be no half-way measure with me."

In one week's time, just as the roads were deepest in mud, and soft with the coming spring, just before the brigade began to find that stable duty could be done without the cumbrous overcoat, so long as the afternoon was sunshiny, there came an order from the War Department which authorized the immediate muster-out of Captain Frank Kearny, —— New Jersey Cavalry, "to accept promotion," and it was known that he had been commissioned by the governor as major in a new regiment just taking the field.

The officers promptly came to their comrade's tent to offer their congratulations, and then, as they strolled away in groups of three or four, the question was discussed as to how they could best give him what they termed "an appropriate send-off." In his utter change of mood and supposed change of character Kearny had not been in the least companionable since his return. No man knew the bitter sorrow at his heart; no one knew how night after night, before he sought his pillow, his eyes turned longingly to the stars in the northern heavens, and sometimes for lonely hours he sat in silence watching them, wondering if they looked down on her and the old homestead at Hopewell. Day by day the love of her burned and glowed in his vehement heart. Never for a moment could he force himself to forget her—the exquisite face, the soft, slender white hands, the graceful, womanly form, and all her dainty, soothing ways. Sometimes, like a sharp pang, the agony of that parting came back to him—the memory of her solemn words, "There is another," and he would start to his feet and stride up and down in restless misery. Who—who was the man who had won her? Who on all this earth could love and cherish and reverence her as he would ever do ? No wonder he had no more the ready laugh for his comrades' jests or joyous words for their daily greetings. Duty, stern duty alone had nerved him to his work. He had striven to forget *her*, and think only of his loyalty to the flag; but at all times—in every thought by day, in every dream by night—the face he idolized was mirrored in his brain, and life itself was wrapped in love of her.

And so it resulted that when Dayton came to tell him of the project of a regimental jubilee in honor of his promotion, and a parting "spread" to which the officers of the brigade were to be bidden, Kearny almost brusquely bade him put a stop to the whole thing. He hurried around camp, saying brief farewells. He explained that he must hasten at once to Trenton, as there were many things that had to be attended to at home before he could take the field again; he thanked them for the honor they had contemplated paying him, but said it would be impossible to wait until the designated day. Every one noted his feverish eagerness to be gone, and Dayton, who rode with him to the Potomac, and saw him safely aboard the crowded steamer that was to bear him to Washington, was annoyed when he returned to camp that night by hearing a young lieutenant remark to the captain of his troop, "I'll bet a hat he means to run Mullane to ground before the fellow's leave is up."

Standing amid the throng of laborers and quartermasters' employees at the dock at Acquia, and keenly scrutinizing every officer and man who passed the guard-line, was a tall, gaunt man in civilian dress. His slouch hat was pulled down over his eyes; his face was hidden by a heavy, bushy beard; he was evidently well known to the officer in charge of the provost-guard, for they were talking in low tones together more than once. He was also well known on the steamer, for twice he passed aboard without showing pass of any kind to the sergeant at the gang-plank. He was coming ashore from some sudden dive into the darkness of the steamer's lower deck just as Kearny and Dayton stepped upon the sloping stage. He stopped short at sight of the former, whirled about, and hastened forward out of sight. Kearny gazed after him in odd interest. There was something strangely familiar in the figure; but the face—the beard—he could not recall at all.

"Who is that man in civilian dress who just went forward?" he asked the purser of the steamer, who was at the gangway.

"That? He's a quartermaster's clerk who has charge of the stores that are run down by us. Name is Freeman. Keen hand at poker, I'm told, but the steward tells me Captain Mullane got away with most of his pile the night they went up together. Guess you don't want to play with him, though. Did you ever see him before?"

"I don't know," said Kearny, briefly. "Come, Dayton, let us go on deck."

Captain Dayton recalled the fact, a few days later, that Kearny had again inquired as to the name and antecedents of the tall, bearded stranger. "I have seen that fellow somewhere when he didn't wear that beard, but I cannot think where. I don't like him, somehow," he had said. And Dayton further noted that when the steamer pushed off and went churning her way up the Potomac the tall, bearded clerk went with her.

Captain Mullane's fortnight's leave had well-nigh expired when, on the following night, the cavalry brigade was startled by news that caused many men to gaze anxiously into one another's faces, and with eyes that questioned. The burly Irishman was found shot through the heart the very morning that Major Kearny reached Washington. The body was lying in a stateroom close to that which the major had occupied, and it was remembered by the guard on duty at the dock that the captain was there to meet the steamer on her arrival, and went aboard almost before she was made fast. No one had heard, in the noise of blowing off steam and the tramp and uproar on the hurricane deck, the sound of a scuffle and a single shot fired so close that the dead man's coat was singed with flame and his body blackened with the powder.

XIV.

The major of Mullane's regiment was sent to Washington to take charge of the deceased officer's effects and to make such investigation as to the cause and manner of his death as might be permissible by the police. He was an honest and a dutiful soldier, a man who stood high in the confidence of his colonel and of his brother officers; nevertheless, there was no little growling among the "Mullane crowd," as that particular element among the commissioned force was known, because that particular field-officer had been selected, and not one of their own number. Captain Moriarty was easily induced to go to the colonel as chairman and spokesman of this spontaneous grievance committee, and to say to him that the "frinds" of Captain Mullane considered that they had been ignored in the selection of Major Dalrymple, and, further, that in his hands it was not to be expected that justice would be done: he was, and always had been, hostile to Captain Mullane. The colonel allowed the red-faced troop commander to proceed with his harangue until his ideas gave out and he had to pause for a moment. Then, without a word, the commander held forth an opened copy of the "Revised Regulations," and pointed to the paragraph which prescribed that

10

the major of the regiment should take charge of and become responsible for the effects of deceased officers. Moriarty stumbled over this a moment, and then, after scratching his head in some perplexity, he hit on another line of assault.

"But we have three majors, sir, and only wan of 'em was frindly to Captain Mullane. Couldn't Major O'Neil be sent? 'Twould be a source of satisfaction to the frinds and family of the 'desayst.'"

"There are reasons why Major O'Neil cannot be detailed, sir; and Major Dalrymple, as commander of Captain Mullane's battalion, is the only proper one to send. That will do on that subject."

"Very well, colonel. Good-day, sir. I've simply to say in conclusion, sir, that it's the belief of all Mullane's frinds that he was foully murdered without a chance for his life, and that the man who did it was Major Kearny, sir. Good-day to you, colonel." And Moriarty went back to his friends to report the ill success of his appeal, and to spread abroad the theory that their late companion had met his death at the hands of the New Jersey major.

Remembering all that had taken place, and conjuring up, as men and Christians will, all manner of things that were of no import at the time of their occurrence, but that became of serious moment now, it must be admitted that there were strong grounds for believing that no one would be more quickly pounced upon as the slayer of Mullane than he who swore that, as God was his judge, the Irish captain should answer to him for the foul insult put upon his honor. Men

were very grave and reserved in the camp of the ——
New Jersey, and rather gloomy and vengeful in that
of their neighbors. The story went up from brigade
to division headquarters. There was no Bayard now
to stand the friend of the absent soldier. The gallant
cavalry leader, whose face had borne for years the
scars of savage warfare on the plains, had met his
soldier death at Fredericksburg, and another veteran
dragoon had recently stepped into the vacant place—
" a new king who knew not Joseph"—and when Dalrymple went on the next up trip of the steamer to
Washington he bore with him official letters that had
much to say of the late fracas between Kearny and
the murdered captain, and that told in no mild terms
of the former's furious threats.

It was four days before the officers of the Jersey
regiment were able to get the full text of Dalrymple's
report. The moment it was received by his colonel a
copy was made and handed to Captain Dayton, who
read it aloud to the assembled comrades. Not a word
was spoken even when he finished. Dayton folded
the paper and looked around at the circle of grave and
anxious faces. There were one or two in which he
read hopeful signs, but only one or two. Over in the
other regiment the reading of Dalrymple's letter had
produced but one impression : that Kearny was the
man. Here among the Jerseymen there was silence.

Summed up in its entirety, the case against Kearny
looked black as night. Coupled with his threats, his
wrath, his refusal to give a promise not to follow the
man if granted leave, the following uncanny array of

facts had been evolved, partially by Dalrymple, partially by the police, partially by telegraphic correspondence between Washington and Trenton:

Mullane's fortnight of leave of absence would have expired the second day after Kearny's departure, and he would be compelled to return on the down trip of the steamer leaving Washington the evening following Kearny's arrival at the capital. For four days after the captain's departure Kearny had been striving to obtain leave of absence himself, only to refuse it when offered him on condition that he would neither follow nor molest Mullane. Then he wrote urgent letters, and sent telegrams to the adjutant-general of New Jersey and to influential friends in Trenton, saying that he would gladly accept the majority that had been tendered him if there were now a vacancy. The governor was visited in his behalf without delay; and that very evening telegrams were sent him announcing his new commission, and saying that the War Department had been urged to order him to report at once to the governor of his state for duty in connection with the equipment and instruction of his battalion. It was known in camp that two telegrams came for Kearny four days before the arrival of his orders— these were probably the telegrams referred to—yet not a word had he breathed to any one, even to Dayton, of his coming promotion. Not a word did any of his comrades hear of it until the orders themselves were published; yet he must have anticipated their coming, for he was "packed" and ready to start almost without loss of a day. All men remembered his feverish impatience, his restlessness, his nervous irritability, when urged to "hold over" that they might give him a farewell dinner.

Then it transpired that no sooner had he received telegraphic notification of his promotion and impending orders than he addressed a letter to the adjutant-general of his state saying that urgent personal matters required his attention for a few days, and begging that he might be authorized to delay one week in reporting for duty with his battalion. To this, affirmative answer was sent by telegraph; other despatches had come to him both in camp and at the landing at Acquia, as Dayton could not but remember. The purser of the steamer recalled the fact that the major paced restlessly up and down on deck until after midnight. Other officers were aboard going to Washington on sick leave, "furlough," or duty—as many as three or four dozen—and they were having a jovial time together much of the night, but Major Kearny held himself aloof from all. "He seemed moody and preoccupied." Before "turning in" he had given orders that his trunk should be sent to Willard's and his other baggage to the Baltimore and Ohio depot. The baggage had been shipped, as "tagged," to Trenton. The trunk, duly marked with his name, had been at Willard's several days, uncalled-for.

Major Kearny had disappeared; no man knew whither.

The steamer had reached her Washington dock just after daybreak, said the guard. Several officers were there awaiting the coming of friends, and the deceased

was particularly remembered as having driven down
in a carriage with two or three men, all of whom were
noisy and intoxicated. Mullane himself was more
than half drunk and in very surly mood. He had
some words with the officer of the guard, whose duty
it was to examine the papers of all persons in uniform
either going or coming, and lurched aboard the boat
almost before she was made fast, elbowing his way
among the crowd of officers in the gangway, and being
remarked by several for his unmistakably drunken
appearance. "A gen'l'm'n waitin' f'r 'im," was the
explanation he gave to the steward at the cabin stair-
way, and that was the last seen or heard of him until
nearly half an hour later, when, in making the rounds
of the staterooms just vacated, the stewardess was
horrified to find in one of them, two doors from that
occupied by Major Kearny, the dead body of the cavalry captain. Judging from the appearance of the
clothes, it had evidently been dragged in there ; a life-
preserver had been thrust under the ghastly head ; a
little water had been dashed over the face as though
the slayer had hoped, possibly, to revive his victim,
and the pitcher was there by the side of the body ;
then the legs had been doubled up and thrust aside
so that the stateroom door could be closed and the
ugly sight temporarily hidden; then the murderer had
slipped away.

Mullane's watch, his papers, his loose bills, perhaps
ten dollars in all, were found in his pockets. Buckled
around his waist was a broad money-belt, to which
was attached a revolver holster ; his coat and waist-

coat were opened, and the belt displayed; its com-
partment for "greenbacks" was empty, and the flap
was open. This looked like robbery, since it was
known that he generally carried large sums with him.
His revolver, loaded and capped in every chamber,
was still in the holster. This put an end to the theory
of suicide. It was murder, evidently, for the victim
had not been allowed to draw in his own defence.

For their part, the police had learned enough to
blast such reputation for good as might remain to the
captain over and above his repute for ill. He had
gone home, but only for a day. His wife had not
been ill, nor had Dr. McNamara certified that she was
at the point of death, and craving to see her husband.
The police were of opinion that his arrival, all unan-
nounced, was a matter of wild consternation to the
putative partner of his joys and sorrows, but he had
turned up too drunk to know the difference. He had
spent several days in gambling and drink in Philadelphia; had reached Washington with two strangers
the evening before his untimely taking off, and it was
probable that the night was spent in gambling and
drink until these very fellows drove him to the boat
at dawn. Who they were the detectives had not yet
discovered; neither had they found the hack-driver.
Their theory was that the men were some of the
swarms of professional sharps and gamblers who hung
about Baltimore and Washington all through the war;
that they had fleeced and then gladly driven him to
the boat to get rid of him, and that he had *not* been
murdered for money. Now they were searching for

Major Kearny, who had not been seen or heard of since the moment of the steamer's arrival. Indeed, no one saw him among the group of officers eager to disembark the moment the dock was reached, and every one aboard the boat believed that he must, therefore, have been in the cabin or his own stateroom when Mullane lurched up the winding, brass-bound stairs to meet his tragic fate.

But no one saw him leave the steamer afterwards, and this was singular. True, he could have stepped off the guards, or let himself down from the upper deck to the dock; he might readily, too, have passed the sentry at the pier; for, after the rush of arrivals, and the presumable passage out of all officers and men coming up from the front, it would be an easy matter. Civilians were coming and going, quartermasters' employees passing to and fro, and all manner of distractions occurring to favor any one who wished to slip out unnoticed. Indeed, the officer of the guard could not say that Major Kearny was not among the thirty or forty officers who disembarked at early morning. He only " did not remember seeing such a name," whereas there were now one or two who began to believe that he passed out of the gate with them. They knew him by sight, and he was pointed out on the boat as " the fellow who bearded the Irish lion in his den."

Kearny's stateroom was empty. He had a satchel, a heavy overcoat, and a small leather valise when he came aboard, and these had been duly taken by the porter to his room. The valise was heavy, said the porter, and big enough to contain a complete suit of civilian dress if he had seen fit to change his clothes and go ashore in "mufti;" but with so much to carry he could not have been very "spry" in his movements, and he could not have hidden his big overcoat and long dragoon boots in that valise. Yet they were gone. Not a trace of him was left behind.

All this, though in terser form, Captain Dayton had read aloud to the gathering in the colonel's tent, and, as has been said, the report was received in utter silence. Dayton's voice was husky and tremulous when he finished, and he waited some little time. Then, raising his head and looking calmly around the circle, he spoke in tones from which the tremor had suddenly disappeared :

"Well, gentlemen, since no one has a word to say, I see that I shall have to keep the floor. In the absence of any expression of opinion from you, it may not be inappropriate for me, who have known him from boyhood, to say what *I* think. If for one moment hitherto—knowing Frank Kearny's high temper and his bitter rage against this man—knowing, too, rather more than most of you about the circumstances attending his previous absence—I had a vague but hateful doubt of his innocence, it is set at rest at once and forever by this very report. He never could have done it."

It was a strange, solemn scene, that score of soldierly men gathered there in gloomy silence to deliberate on the report which cast so dark a cloud upon a comrade's name. It was evident that there were sev-

eral on whom its effect was very different from that
declared by Dayton. It was apparent that none were
quite ready to grasp the cause of his great relief. At
last came the question,

"Will you give your reasons, Dayton?"

"Reasons? Why, man alive! think for yourself.
Mullane's pistol was in its holster, every chamber
loaded; he never had a chance for his life! Frank
Kearny might have fought him had they met, but he
is the last man to brand as an assassin, and you ought
to know it."

Dayton's loyalty to his friend, and serene confidence that he was entirely innocent and would reappear in a day or so, ready and willing to account
for every moment of his absence, had no little weight
in the camp of the brigade; but despite it all there
was widespread feeling that Mullane's sudden and
violent death was the outcome of the fray that had
been for the fortnight past the talk of every cavalry
mess along the plateau.

XV.

Just about this time there was the mischief to pay in front of Washington. While the Army of the Potomac was worrying through the winter as best it could, and huddling about the camp-fires down in front of Fredericksburg, a force of goodly size occupied the defences of the national capital. With its right resting within the parapets of Forts Ethan Allen and Marcy on the heights south of the Chain Bridge, the defending line swept through a score of powerful works until it reached the Potomac again below Alexandria. Every road was picketed, every lane patrolled, and the villages of Fairfax, Falls Church, and Vienna were occupied at most times by outposts both of cavalry and infantry. And yet, despite the strength of the defenders and the vigilance of their videttes, "the front" at that particular point was a place of unusual exposure for wearers of the blue. Mosby, an active and remarkably enterprising young leader, was at the head of a body of "irregular horse," sometimes called partisans south of the Potomac, and invariably known as guerillas north of it. In numbers these night-riders were variously estimated anywhere from one to fifty thousand. The Union pickets along that front inclined to the latter number as the more probable, and

no one who was not engaged in the delicate and hazard-
ous duty of warding off Colonel Mosby's incessant
assaults that winter and spring ought to take exception to this palpable exaggeration. If Mosby did not
count fifty thousand men in his command, and would
have been hard pushed to make it fifteen hundred at
his very best, he might as well have done so, for no
fifty thousand men in that section of Virginia ever
kept the lines of Washington in a state of livelier suspense and anxiety than did this band of hard-riding
"bushwhackers." They were nearly all youngsters,
born and bred in the old commonwealth. Nearly every man of their number knew every lane and bridle-
path from the Hazel River below Warrenton to the
broad Potomac itself, and what they did not know
they soon learned. They had relatives or friends in
every house from the Blue Ridge to Alexandria, if
not beyond. There was not a man of them who had
not a sweetheart somewhere within that range—and
not a few that had not more than one. It was not
surprising that Colonel Mosby soon enlarged the field
of his operations and took in the Shenandoah Valley
(and some Yankee paymasters—funds and all) ; but
in the early spring of 1863 he was skipping here, there,
and everywhere in the immediate front of Washington. Nobody could put a finger on him, but he put
a finger on every man who ventured forth ; and just
about the time Frank Kearny left the camp of the
cavalry brigade behind Falmouth, all the lines were
ringing with Mosby's latest exploit. He had swooped
down and carried off a "swell" brigadier-general of

the Union army from the outskirts of Fairfax, and it
was rumored that the very pretty girl at whose invitation the general had called that evening was Mosby's confederate.

For six months, ever since the transfer of the army
from Warrenton to Fredericksburg and the conse-
quent abandonment of the railway as the line of supplies, Mosby had covered the country from the Bull
Run Mountains to the Union fortifications, and no
one could divine what might be going on behind him.
Now, irritated by the boldness of this last raid, there
seemed to be a disposition on the part of the government to send out a cavalry column to capture or drive
away these lively tormentors. A story had reached our
friends of the brigade that they were to be the lucky
ones to make the attempt, and they were glad enough
to go. Very few believed there would be any chance
of capturing such a Will-o'-the-wisp as Mosby ; but
there would be scouting, fighting, something to break
the monotony of camp life, and no man in all the brigade was so eager to go as Kearny. For six months
he had been able to hear nothing of the household at
Hopeville, and day by day the longing to know something of the girl he loved had grown to the verge of
a mania. It was with bitter disappointment that he
found that the rumor of their being sent thither in
search of Mosby either had no foundation or that the
project was abandoned. It was now reported that
another command—some new cavalry regiments—had
been ordered out from Washington, but within the
Union lines there was far less confidence in the suc-

cess of the expedition than there would have been
had the object been declared a hunt for a needle in a
haystack.

Beyond the lines and all over the lovely tract of
country in the counties of Loudoun, Fairfax, Prince
William, and Fauquier east of the Bull Run range it
was a season of jubilee for all good Virginians whose
hearts were with the cause of the Confederacy ; all
households seemed wild with enthusiasm over Mosby's
exploits, and between his officers, his troopers, and the
populace of housekeeping women, children, and aged
men there was apparently but one instance of coldness
and distrust.   There were sadness and suffering at
Hopeville, where good old Judge Armistead was slowly breaking down, crushed with the weight of suspicion and calumny that had been heaped upon him
since the rescue of Lieutenant Kearny.

In less than three weeks it seemed as though every
man, woman, and child in all that section of Virginia
had been taught to point at Armistead the finger of
scorn.   He was a traitor to his people, a protector and
abettor of the enemies and invaders of his state.   He
had harbored, until he could return to his friends, the
man of all others the Virginians—the young men, at
least—most longed to have and hold : Lieutenant
Kearny; he who had driven off to captivity in Northern dungeons such chivalric fellows as Pegram, Eustis, and Falconer.   True, all three of them were by
this time exchanged, and had rejoined their comrades,
by no means looking the worse for their few months'
sojourn in the inhospitable neighborhood of Washing-

ton where old friends were allowed to visit them with as many dainties and comforts and consolations as though they had been wife-murderers condemned to hang. All the same, there was a degree of rhetorical pomp about the phrase "languishing in Northern dungeons" which made it popular for the time being, and served to keep up the sentiment against Judge Armistead. It is a community that sticks at nothing in love or hate. Life itself was too small to give to the cause, or for the leaders they loved ; and, on the other hand, no obloquy was too harsh for the man once honored of them all but now a recreant to their trust. It was universally told in farm and village circles, and it went to Richmond, Staunton, and Lynchburg, that when Armistead gave his word to Major Gordon that Lieutenant Kearny was nowhere on his premises, the Yankee was at that moment in hiding up-stairs ; there were not lacking women to say, in Lucy Armistead's own room.

For months he had been treated as a Pariah, and poor Lucy had the bitter grief to suffer alone of seeing her father breaking down under the burden of accusation and aversion thus heaped upon him. Several times had Dr. Loring been summoned from across the range, and twice since Lee returned to the Rapidan had Henry managed to reach them for a brief visit. In the army no such talk went the rounds as that which passed current among the non-combatants and the women. No rumor of dishonor attaching to his beloved father's name had ever reached the son. Bitterly he grieved at the suspicion and censure he

had brought upon his people in having compelled them
to undertake the care of Kearny, but he well knew
that the trust was sacred with them when once his
word was given. Not once had his father shown him
sign of the direful effect of all that month of secret
nursing. When the son was there, the father hid his
sorrows and made the boy welcome. Neither would
Lucy betray the true state of the case, and Henry had
on both occasions ridden back to his duties comforted
with the belief that the coldness would soon blow
over, and that by his own valor and devotion he could
soon outweigh and cause to be forgotten the apparent
defection at home. That he himself had urged his
father to harbor and protect Kearny was not known
to more than five persons ; this the father had insisted on.

One man, apparently, saw nothing in popular indignation which should compel him to discontinue his
visits to Hopeville or his attentions to Miss Armistead, and that man was Captain Scott Falconer, who
with his squadron of "Rangers" was now attached
to Mosby's command. No week had passed during
the winter without its visit from him, and sometimes
he was at the old house two or three days. The unhappy invalid, now a prisoner in his study, looked
upon these frequent appearances as his only chance
of communication with the army in whose success all
his hopes were still centred, and he welcomed them,
even though he had not fancied Falconer in the past,
and hardly trusted him now. He knew that Lucy was
the magnet that drew him thither, and he, at any other

time and under any other circumstances, would have
found it possible to intimate that such frequent calls
were not desirable. Now he could not. He knew
well that Falconer had lost caste in the neighborhood,
and Falconer, with apparent reluctance, gave him to
understand it was solely because he would persist in
association with a tabooed man. The captain made
no mention of the fact that he was generally execrated
for his conduct the day of Bayard's sweeping advance,
when that gallant boy lieutenant was killed, and still
less was the captain apt to mention the fact that
Mosby had given him the cold shoulder on many an
occasion.

It was a sunshiny day in mid-March, and the snow
was gone and the roads were thawing, and it was evident that spring would soon appear, and the spring
campaign be sure to open. For a week, despite the
softening weather, the judge seemed more downcast
than ever—more hopeless and lonely. Lucy's heart
was heavy as lead as she moved about the house,
striving to prepare from the scanty means at hand
some tempting dish for the listless invalid, striving to
sing as she went about her ceaseless avocations that
he might believe her happy and buoyant, and never
suspect how many and many a day the tears rained
down her wan cheeks even as her voice was uplifted
in some old ditty he loved. Their means were well-
nigh exhausted; the prospect of starvation was not
alluring; provisions were scarcer and scarcer every
day, and when they could no longer buy there was no
one from whom they could ask aid, even if her pride

11

had not revolted at the idea.   Henry sent everything
in his power, but captain's pay in Confederate money
was not a fortune in the spring of '63, and became a
pittance on which a Chinaman could barely live within
the year.   Shut up in his room, the judge knew not
how, one by one, the cocks and hens had been con-
verted into broth or chicken *fricassée* for his benefit
until all were gone.   That he was still nourished by
the flesh of the domestic fowl was due to Nelse, and
a predatory ability and concomitant manufacture of
statements for which may Heaven give the old darky
absolution.   Nelse stoutly swore he found the chick-
ens " up the hill," where they had established a colony
supposably beyond reach of marauders.

Lucy Armistead's heart must have been sorely torn
with care and anxiety by this time, for when Falconer
appeared she almost welcomed him.

" You see how father is failing, Captain Falconer,
and Dr. Loring has not been near us for a fortnight.
I feel as though Henry must be sent for, and can I
ask you to get this letter to him ?"

" You can ask anything of me, Miss Armistead.
You well know that my house in Warrenton is vacant;
you know it is at your service and his.   *Can* you not
induce him to move thither—can I not induce you ?"

She rebuked him gently, almost wearily.   Her uplifted hand looked fragile and white, and her face was
well-nigh as pale, though a faint color rose at his
words.   " We have long since agreed that it was impossible, captain," she said.   " Do not—do not speak
of it.   He would not go; I—could not."

"You could move him thither this very night, Lucy, and to-morrow have him in comfort and safety, and Henry only another day away. Here everything is against him, and any moment we may be driven out beyond the Blue Ridge. We know a big column of cavalry is now in front of Washington preparing to move upon us. Once they regain possession your last chance is gone. Our scouts and pickets were attacked at Fairfax and Chantilly this very morning, and I know that Mosby expects an advance in force to-night. It was this that brought me here. Can I never reach your heart?"

He would have continued, but she checked his words.

"Look! is not that one of your sergeants riding in?"

The captain turned. It was just twilight, and growing darker every moment. The man who entered the gate threw his horse's reins over a post, and, saluting Captain Falconer from the foot of the steps, held forth a letter.

"Bring it here!" said the captain. "Where are you from?"

"From Aldie, sir. A column of Yankee cavalry went through the Gap at daybreak and is over in the valley behind you now. Another is pushing out from Centreville. The 'Rangers' are ordered to cover the pike and fall back on Warrenton—so the lieutenant told me when I got in with despatches. He told me to take a fresh horse and ride up to you."

Falconer opened his letter slowly.

"What troops have we out towards the front now?"

"None, sir, north of the Warrenton pike at Grove-

ton.   As soon as it was known that the Yankees pushed
through Aldie, everything was ordered down to confront the other column ; but they're too heavy for us,
and our whole force is falling back to Gainesville now
—and won't stop there."

"By Jove ! Then there's nothing between us and
Sudley Springs yonder ?"

"None of our people, captain."

"Miss Armistead, I must see the judge one moment,
and then hasten away to join my men. This is just
what I have dreaded. Sergeant, mount your horse
and lead mine out on the road. I will join you in a
moment."

Five minutes later he came hurriedly forth. It was
nearly dark, and Hannah placed a dim light on a table
in the hall.   Old Nelse came staggering through with
his arms filled with firewood, and nearly collided with
the captain.   Anxious to send her message to Henry,
yet unwilling to have the servants suspect her appre-
hensiveness, Miss Armistead motioned to Falconer to
go on.

"I will accompany you to the gate," she said, as
they descended the steps.   "Tell me, does your letter
say whether this is a large force—one that will hold
the neighborhood for any length of time ?"

"I fear so.   It looks so."

"Then put Henry on his guard.   I had written to
him to come at all hazards before the end of the month.
Now I can no longer communicate with him.   Warn
him not to make any attempt until the way is clear.
Adieu—and thank you for your kindness."

She turned, trying not to see his outstretched hand; then, relenting, placed hers one instant in his, and regretted it, for he quickly bent and kissed it fervently, then sprang into saddle and spurred rapidly away.

The next instant a tall figure burst through the hedge close by her side, and stood silently before her. One quick glance was enough. Despite the felt hat pulled low over his brow; despite the full beard and the shrouding cloak in which he was enveloped, she knew him instantly—her lover, her rescued one, her patient of the year agone—and despite herself a low, glad cry leaped from her lips; her heart gave a great bound as she impulsively threw herself towards him; then she stopped short and covered her face with her hands.

" Yes, it is I," were the words that greeted her. " I could not bear it any longer. I had to see you again or go mad. It is best so, I suppose. Tell me—that was Captain Falconer, was it not?"

She looked up startled. She hardly knew his voice; it was so changed—so stern, so sad.

XVI.

FOR the second time there was trouble for Kearny's
friends at court, and the Jersey delegation, between
the War Department and the police, were having rather
a solemn experience. Five days had elapsed ; the web
of circumstantial evidence had been woven still more
closely about the name of the missing officer, and no
one could be found who had the faintest clew to his
whereabouts. On the sixth day after Mullane's death
there came a new actor on the scene in the person of
Captain Dayton, and Dayton had been making some
investigations at Acquia, and on the way up the river.
He had a theory of his own regarding the matter—so
he told his colonel—and had succeeded in getting a
few days' " leave " to consult certain officials at the
capital.

Meantime there had been coming from the front all
manner of tales of great doings on the part of the
two cavalry columns pushed out in hopes of capturing
Mosby. They had not caught him—that would have
been too much to expect — but they had chased the
Confederates well back beyond the mountain-passes ;
had had some sharp fighting, and claimed to have made
some important captures. The prisoners were being
sent in under guard as the despatches were penned.

All these were newspaper reports, however, and made mainly to sell. In the long period of inaction while the two armies were hibernating in Virginia there had been little or nothing to chronicle, and the correspondents of the press as a consequence had been nearly at their wits' ends. Now they were rushing despatches through, filled with graphic details of brilliant cavalry dashes and spirited combats in front of Vienna and Fairfax, and lauding to the skies the prowess and valor of certain new regiments that up to this moment had seen no service whatever, and yet were by no means averse to appearing as the heroes of the occasion. The arrival of the newspapers in the camps at Belle Plain and along the Rappahannock provoked no little derision among the veterans there assembled, since old war-dogs are always sceptical as to the unaided success of the puppies. Nevertheless there was some credence attached to the stories as read around the fires of the —— New Jersey, for one of the officers prominently mentioned as commanding one column had served as their senior major in '61, and was now full colonel of a new regiment. Under Graham's leadership anything might be possible, and everybody waited for Graham's official report. One thing was certain, our cavalry, for the time being at least, held the gaps through the Bull Run Mountains, and Mosby had gone elsewhere.

The first report that came from Colonel Graham was one that gave rise to some consternation at the War Department; and as Graham was a New Jersey man, it happened that some of Kearny's friends, in their inquiries at the adjutant-general's office, were favored with its contents. Dayton was not among them, and he only heard of it later. It seems that the colonel had set forth with every hope and expectation of capturing the partisan leader himself, and punishing severely his command. He knew the very house in which the renowned raider was to spend the night; he had accurate maps, and full and reliable information as to the position and numbers of the various outposts as well as of the main body. He had given no sign of a move that night, but, after the usual trumpet calls for tattoo and taps, had saddled at ten o'clock, and at midnight had surrounded the indicated building only to find that his bird had flown, and with him all his troops. Their flight had been hurried, but as the advance was rapid they could not have slipped away except by the receipt of timely warning; and this warning, he wrote, could have been given them by a certain man in civilian dress—a tall, bearded fellow whom he well remembered as having been a scout or secret-service employee in the Bull Run campaign of the previous year, and who even then was looked upon with some suspicion. His knowledge of the country seemed so perfect, and his acquaintance with every household, so far as their names and numbers were concerned, so accurate, that it was considered rather remarkable that one who claimed to have been long a resident among these people should now be serving their enemies. Furthermore, it was remembered of him that he rode to and fro, by day or night, all over the country, and was never molested. It was hardly possible that the Virginians had not an inkling of his connection with the government service, and it was extraordinary that, knowing the nature of the duties he was supposed to be performing, they did not string him up by the neck to the nearest tree. For several months, wrote Graham, he had lost sight of the man, but remembered him the instant he was brought into his presence the night of the advance—remembered him despite marked changes in his appearance, for a heavy, bushy beard now covered the sallow face and "lantern jaws" of the previous year. It seems that he had been halted by the outermost sentries, and held until the head of column came up, and he was disposed to be very indignant at such treatment. His papers were beyond question. There they were, all neatly filed in a big, flat pocket-book—his orders, his passes, certain letters of instruction, and even a sort of circular "to-whom-it-may-concern" commission, which enjoined all officers to give the bearer ("whose signature will be found to correspond with that exhibited hereon") every facility in their power, and permit him to pass to and fro without delay.

Despite these papers, Graham's mind was not set at rest. The man had been held by the outposts because he was seen galloping through a little winding lane among the trees beside the pike, instead of holding to the road itself. He was nervous, excited, eager to push ahead, and it was his manner that made the guards suspicious. After carefully reading his papers by the light of a little camp lantern, Graham required him to affix his signature to the page, and though somewhat hasty and tremulous, there could be no doubt that the "William L. Tierney" in the exhibit of the War Department and that thus hurriedly scrawled at the outskirts of Fairfax were written by the same hand. The colonel bade him mount and accompany the headquarters party, explaining that "as they were going the same way they might as well ride together," and Tierney seemed to want to protest, but apparently thinking better of it, "fell in" behind the staff and trotted along with them. The night was very dark, and in not more than ten minutes he had disappeared. It was probable that he took advantage of the intricacies of a cut through a piece of woods to slip away, strike spurs to his horse, and put a mile or more between himself and the column before his absence was noted. At all events, he had not been seen from that time to this, and Graham believed that he was playing a double game.

But the chief of the secret service could not harbor such a thought for a moment. When Graham's letter was shown him he proceeded to say that there always had been a jealousy between the cavalry and his scouts. The officers and men could not but envy the "roving commissions" granted the latter, and it was true that the scouts were prone to put on airs at times and give offence. "But Tierney's an invaluable man," he said; "he was raised in Prince William County, and knows every family in it; he was a wild fellow, and ran away from home and enlisted in the army, and has served two years in the cavalry. I got him discharged in the fall of '61 purposely to put him on this duty, but after

second Bull Run he told me the people were beginning to know him, and it might be well if he made
himself scarce for a while ; so I had him transferred
to duty hereabouts, and on the Eastern Shore a while,
then put him on the quartermaster's boat to look after
certain matters the Secretary of War desired to have
watched ; even the officers of the boat thought him a
clerk detailed to keep track of the stores, and he has
been most efficient—just the man for the place, the
Secretary says—and it would astonish some officers of
the Army of the Potomac to see how much he knows
about them and their opinions. Oh, it isn't nice duty, I
admit ; but some one had to do it—the Secretary can
satisfy you as to that—and I put Tierney at it," exclaimed the chief, in conclusion. Questioned by the adjutant-general as to the authority given him to leave the
steamer and go into Virginia again, the chief replied
that Tierney had a sweetheart down near Manassas
Junction, and he presumed that, hearing of the forward move of the cavalry, he had seized that opportunity to run out and visit her. There was no time
for formal application for permission, and it never had
been customary. The secret-service men had to be
trusted, or they were of no use. Tierney would turn
up in a day or two, and come in full of valuable information, and completely vindicate himself.

But there were some among the few officers present
at this conference who did not share the confidence of
the chief, and it was found that some subordinates in
the department had long been suspicious that all was
not square with Tierney. *They* said he was a gambler

and an associate of gamblers, and that he had some
intimacies among a low class of men in the army that
were impairing his usefulness.   There was a time in
'62 when he was drinking hard, and possibly the gentlemen from New Jersey might be interested in knowing that it was Tierney's babbling that gave rise to
the first stories at the expense of Lieutenant Kearny
the year before.   He had been drinking and playing
cards with Mullane, and it was he who was reluctantly
compelled to admit that he was Mullane's authority,"
and it was he who guided the major and the adjutant
on their memorable visit to Hopeville.

It was a pity Dayton could not have been there to
hear this story.   Then came tidings from the other
column—that which had passed through Aldie Gap
and swooped down upon the roads in rear of Thoro'-
fare in hopes of cutting Mosby's retreat should he
escape the clutches of Graham's command.   They had
had but poor luck despite the flourish of trumpets with
which the papers had hailed their "storming of the
pass" and capture of important prisoners and documents.   The pass in question was watched by a small
troop of Virginians, perhaps forty in all, but they
made things lively for the head of that blue column,
and it was only at the cost of much smoke, noise, and
expenditure of carbine ammunition that the little band
was induced to fall back, leaving their dead and wounded among the rocks by the roadside where they fell.
Then the pass was stormed in great shape, and the
new regiment went "charging" through in column of
fours, cheering lustily and brandishing their sabres,

and finally reining up and unsaddling on the other side, while the colonel made his enthusiastic followers a congratulatory speech, and then sat him down to write his despatches to the War Department, not forgetting one or two highly picturesque descriptions for the benefit of the local papers of the counties from which they hailed. Meantime, of course, the Virginians were riding rapidly down the westward valley, giving warning of the coming of the "Yanks;" and when the despatches were finished and the column one more *en route*, pretty much everything and everybody worth capture was spirited out of the way. When the command reached the road that night, late, it was only to learn that they were much too late. Mosby had given them the slip.

Of course the colonel could account for it. The country was overrun, he wrote, with spies and scouts in civilian dress. These men were mounted on fleet horses, and despite the rapidity with which he advanced they carried in every direction the tidings of his coming. There was reason to believe, he said, that several of these men thus disguised were officers of the Confederate army visiting their homes and families on brief furloughs, or possibly sent thither for the purpose of watching the movements of the cavalry. He urgently recommended that strict orders be issued that all men found within the lines of the advancing force be arrested and tried by drumhead court-martial as spies. The colonel was a man of much political influence at home, and his opinions and recommendations—good, bad, or absurd—could be treated only with deference.

The War Department issued no new orders, but the colonel was authorized by a letter, sent within a few days, to make an example, if necessary, of Confederate spies, but he was warned to exercise caution in the matter, and be sure that the persons taken in civilian dress or other disguise were *bonâ fide* officers of the Confederate service, and within our lines for treasonable or unlawful purpose.

When this letter reached the colonel he was commanding a force of some two thousand cavalry holding the gaps of the Bull Run Mountains and scouring the adjacent country. He was for the time being his own master, and virtually in charge of a district in the enemy's country. For Colonel Graham, his superior in both rank and experience, disappointed at the failure of his expedition, and attributing much of his lack of success to the junior's delays, had gladly left him at Thoro'fare, while he with nearly three thousand sabres at his heels went clattering off to Front Royal in pursuit of Mosby.

An ardent patriot was the soldier left behind. Treason was to him a thing to be made odious, and no man, woman, or child whose sympathies were with the Southern troops could be anything less than a traitor, and a menace to the security of the state. Nothing short of summary execution was, in his private opinion, the proper method of convincing such people of the error of their ways. It boded ill for the already sore afflicted household at Hopeville Gap that they should find themselves all of a sudden placed under the surveillance of a soldier whose soul was burning with zeal to uphold the supremacy of the law, but who preferred to crush the rebellion by extreme measures at the fireside rather than to face it in the field.

And now, while Graham was beyond communication except by courier, there came to Washington a genuine surprise in the shape of a paragraph in his second report—a brief summary sent from White Plains—of the result of his dash at the gaps after the escape of Mosby. There had, indeed, been some spirited cavalry fighting in his column, and an entire battalion of Virginia troopers had been cut off, surrounded, and captured near Groveton. Captain Dayton, who was still in Washington, was hurriedly summoned, together with two Jersey legislators, to the office of the adjutant-general.

"Listen to this," said that perplexed functionary, " and tell me, if you can, what it means :

"'I deem it my duty to add,' writes Colonel Graham, after detailing his capture of the —— Virginia Cavalry between Groveton and Haymarket, 'that this success was mainly due to the presence of my former regimental comrade, now Major Frank Kearny, of the —— New Jersey, who, having a brief leave of absence, joined me as a volunteer at Centreville, and his accurate and intricate knowledge of the roads enabled him to plan and carry out the surrounding of the rebel force. It was he who guided the turning column to their rear; and the officers unite in praise of the brilliant and daring manner in which he led the charge that broke their line.' Now, gentlemen, who can explain this freak of Major Kearny's ; and who can tell where to find him?"

There was a moment of wondering silence, then Captain Dayton spoke :

"I believe I can, sir."

XVII.

THE night of Frank Kearny's sudden reappearance
at Hopeville was one that Lucy Armistead has never
yet forgotten. Probably she never will. For a few
moments after asking the abrupt question about the
officer who had just ridden away, he stood in silence,
gazing into the darkness, as though longing to see the
man once more. He was breathing heavily, as though
wearied by recent exertion, and the sigh with which
he turned aside spoke of utter dejection. Anxiously
she scanned his face, but his eyes seemed to avoid
hers. Then, as though nerved to sudden action, he
quickly stepped to the gateway, and stood one moment listening. Then he abruptly spoke:

"I left my horse at the foot of the pathway leading
down through the wood. May I ask you to send
Nelse for him? And now I have business of importance with the judge. Can I see him?"

"He will be rejoiced to see you—but—you look so
worn, so ill? Have you not overtaxed your strength?
Is there not grave hazard in coming hither?"

"I came because I could not live and not look
upon your face again. Even though I know now
that it is as you said—there was another—I had to
come. Now I have seen. I must go. Five minutes'

12

talk with your father will be enough—and then—it
is good-bye."

He half turned towards the house, then back to
where she stood silent, wondering, and here he bent
as though for one last look into her eyes. The sight
of her sweet, pale face, so wan, so pathetic, and yet so
lovely, was more than he could bear. He had left her
when weak, broken down with wounds, illness, and
sorrow. He returned to her stalwart, bearded, a model
of soldierly grace and strength ; yet his voice was full
of a weight of trouble that wore heavily upon him.
His eyes gazed one instant into hers, then, as though
utterly overcome by the force and vehemence of his
love, he suddenly clasped her in his strong arms, and,
straining her slender form to his breast, his lips rained
kiss after kiss upon the rippling hair and smooth white
forehead. "Oh, God ! how I loved you !" was his one
smothered cry ; and then, almost rudely, he cast her
from him, turned sharply away, and hastened to the
house.

For a few moments she stayed there, leaning against
the gate-post, breathless, startled, and unnerved. Not
until she could regain her self-control did she attempt
to enter the hall. Then, sending Hannah for Nelse
with orders to bring Mr. Kearny's horse from the
lower field, she shut herself in her room. She could
hear the voices of the two men before she closed the
door : her father's, so weak and broken, apparently in
vehement protest ; her lover's, deep, strong, earnest,
yet with such weariness and sorrow in it. Then suddenly the door closed heavily ; spurred boot-heels

clinked through the hall and descended the steps,
where there was brief pause and a word with Nelse.
Then hoof-beats in the yard below, down the neglected drive, out to the road beyond, and he was gone
—gone without another word to her. She sat there
in her cold, dark room, shivering. Then Nelse's voice
was heard calling her name, and she knew her father
had need of her. Down the stairs she found the old
darky with his eyes fairly starting from his head, holding out to her half a dozen Treasury notes—money
such as he had never seen, yet well imagined the value
of—that had been thrust into his hands as the major
rode away; and in the study she found her father,
seated before his open fireplace, trembling, agitated,
and vainly striving to read a letter by the flickering
light, while in the torn envelope on the table by his
side she could see a packet of similar Treasury notes,
left, evidently, by the same lavish hand.

"Read it for me, daughter; I cannot," he said,
feebly. "He has been most kind, most thoughtful,
but of course he could not be made to understand that
it is all out of the question—out of the question. We
can accept no man's bounty, much less one of that
uniform."

Obediently she took the sheet, and, sitting at his
feet, where the firelight fell upon the page, she read
these lines :

"I write because it may be impossible to see you—
impossible to explain. No words can tell you the depth
of my gratitude for the tender care and the infinite
kindness shown me under your roof. I dare not con-

jecture what it may have cost or may yet cost you among your own people. In kind, it will be beyond my power to repay you, nor do I know that in any way such repayment can adequately be made; but, my kind and generous host, it is necessary for my own peace of mind that in some way I attempt to show my appreciation. Forgive this intrusion into your personal affairs. I could not but know that the very necessaries of life are hard to be obtained even where money was in abundance, and I am tortured by a fear that your means have been grievously straitened by the unhappy strife between the sections. This money burns my hand. I implore you to take it, use it, consider it a loan if you will not otherwise accept it. I ask it for your own sake, for Henry's sake, nay, more, for the sake of her whose name I cannot breathe without a blessing, whose—whose—' "

She hesitated, her head drooped lower, a wave of color surged up over the lovely face, and, hiding it from his eyes, she held forth the letter with shaking hand.

"I—I cannot read it further. There is only a little more."

He took it slowly, waiting until he could brush the moisture from his eyes. Presently she rose from her stooping posture, lighted a candle and placed it by his side, then quickly sped from the room. Slowly he found the place where she had ceased.

" —whose welfare and happiness must ever, henceforth, outweigh any earthly consideration except the duty I owe to my country. Sir, though she has taught me its utter hopelessness, I love your daughter, and shall love her to my life's end."

An hour later, when she stole noiselessly into the room, the old gentleman was sitting there in the flickering light, almost as she had left him. He had extinguished the candle, for candles were already as precious and scarce as the coarse currency that formed the one circulating medium in the country towns. Kearny's letter was still in his hand, and on the table by his side was the package of Treasury notes, unbroken. She bent and kissed his forehead and the gray curling locks above, but said no word.

"Daughter," he presently spoke, "you will find some large envelopes in the lower drawer of my desk. Give me one, dear."

Silently she obeyed him. Then he took the "greenbacks," still in unbroken package and more than half hidden in what remained of the torn wrapper; carefully stowed the entire packet away in the heavy, lawyer-like envelope she gave him; then asked for light, his heavy seal and the wax from their nook in the old-fashioned desk. Sealing the packet with practised yet tremulous hand, he then carefully "docketed" the thick paper with the date and the major's name, then looked up into her eyes.

"He meant well, dear. It was natural that he should seek some way to be of service to us, but we cannot touch his money—we Armisteads. Hide it somewhere where it will be safe until it can be returned to him by trusty hands. He will not come again, daughter; he will not come again."

That night, when Hannah knocked twice at the door of her young mistress and could get no answer, she softly entered and found her, not asleep, but lying on the little white bed, sobbing as though her heart would break.

Stirring trumpet - calls roused the echoes of the heights at early dawn, and when the little household peered from the windows they found the fields at the foot of the slope all alive with horsemen in light blue overcoats. For two days there remained in camp there a force of perhaps three squadrons; while others, apparently of the same regiment, were posted high up in the Gap or patrolled the roads to north and south. The commanding officer, with others, twice called at the homestead and asked to see the judge, and as he was too feeble and ill to be disturbed, they inquired on their second visit for "the lady of the house," whom Hannah vainly sought to excuse. Miss Armistead would gladly have avoided an interview, but the lieutenant-colonel commanding sent up his card, and courteously requested that she would see him, as he had orders to communicate to some responsible member of the family. Determined to shield her father from every possible annoyance, she descended the stairs and found her visitors standing in the hall. It was late in the afternoon, and the light was dim.

"Will you step into the sitting-room?" she said. "The servant should have shown you there. We have no parlor."

"The servant did so, madam," said the elder of the two officers, "but explained that she had no light, and we did not wish to intrude more than was absolutely necessary. I called earlier in the day, but was unsuccessful; now I had no choice but to persist. Pardon me, may I ask who it is whom I have the honor of addressing?"

The lieutenant-colonel was a stately gentleman of over fifty years, and he spoke with a slightly foreign accent. It was evident that he wished to behave with all the consideration and courtesy possible, and Miss Armistead failed to experience the feeling of repugnance which, a year or two before, she was sure would manifest itself at the appearance of a "Yankee." She answered coldly, as became a daughter of Virginia, yet she liked the old soldier's manner.

"I am Miss Armistead," she answered. "My father is in feeble health, and I seek to spare him any care or worry. Did I understand you to say that you had orders to carry out, and that they concerned us in any way?"

"I deeply regret that such is the case, Miss Armistead"—and both officers were evidently trying to see as much of the fair face before them as the dim light permitted. "Orders which are imperative in their tone have reached me this day from the officer commanding all the Union forces now serving in this neighborhood. He has information, he says, that several officers of the Southern army, whose homes are in Fauquier and Prince William counties, are now somewhere about here. One has already been found, and among those believed to be hiding near at hand is Captain Henry Armistead, of Stuart's cavalry—your brother, I fear.

It is most distressing to me to have to communicate this to one so young, so fair, so apparently unprotected," went on the gallant old dragoon, "but I am ordered to make strict search and to maintain a vigilant guard over the premises."

Lucy's heart sank within her. She knew how it would affect her father—it was her one thought now. She dreaded to think of the risk Henry would run if, despite the verbal caution she had charged Falconer to give him, he obeyed the summons in the letter she had earlier written. Resistance, protestation, she knew, would be useless. Frankness and courtesy might disarm even the enemy when he came in such courtly shape as that before her.

"I thank you for the consideration you show us, sir," was therefore her reply. "My brother is not here, if my word will suffice and save my father's privacy from disturbance; but there shall be no hinderance to making your search as thorough as you deem necessary. When will you begin?"

"That, at least, I reserve to myself, Miss Armistead. My orders did not say *immediate* search, and—it shall be at your convenience. My sentries, of course, were early posted so that none could pass in or out; and if you will kindly say how soon we may begin—I fear it must be this evening—I will myself be present, and you can rest assured that no intrusion will afterwards be allowed. Who are you, sir?" he said, sharply, and turned in evident indignation upon a distinguished-looking officer who had suddenly appeared at the doorway. "I gave orders that no officer or man was to enter here without my authority.   I do not know your face.   What is your regiment?"

"The —— New Jersey, colonel," responded the officer, saluting, "which will account for my not knowing that you had given such orders.   I am Captain Dayton, sir, and have just arrived from Washington. These papers will explain the object of my journey, but, as it is too dark for you to read them, let me say briefly that I am sent to find Major Kearny, who is believed to have accompanied your command, and whom I hoped to hear of here at Judge Armistead's."

Lucy started at the mention of the name, and stepped forward where she could more distinctly see the newcomer.

"Mr.—Major Kearny was here two nights ago, for not more than ten minutes," she answered, in low tone.

"And he went back to Washington or Alexandria the next morning, captain," said the field-officer.   "I saw him start."

In deep and evident disappointment the stranger paused a moment.   "Then my errand is fruitless," he said, as he slowly turned away.   "My escort is tired with a long day's ride, colonel, and, with your permission, we will bivouac beside your command."

"By all means, sir, by all means.   I will accompany you now.   Miss Armistead, a thousand regrets for my unavoidable intrusion.   I will leave my adjutant to receive your answer," and, bowing low, the courteous old soldier took his leave.

An hour later, in silence and with every exertion of gentleness and consideration, the searching party—an officer with half a dozen men—ransacked every room in the house from garret to cellar, with two exceptions. The colonel forbade their entering Miss Armistead's or that of her father, by whose side she had taken her place. Underneath the window other soldiers—two officers, apparently—were talking in low but excited tones. What she heard nearly froze the blood in her veins.

"I tell you it is true. He was found dead as a door-nail, shot through the heart, and there's no doubt that Kearny was the murderer. That's what they want him for."

XVIII.

Anxious days were those that followed. A wet, cold, driving storm set in, deluging the lowlands, turning the mountain brooks into foaming torrents and the country roads into quagmires. Most depressing was the effect upon the broken-down old man who cowered drooping and despondent over the lonely hearthstone. Lucy would not leave, yet could not cheer him; he seemed fallen into an abyss of hopelessness and woe from which nothing could rouse him, and yet there were moments when he became almost vehement in obstinacy. She had sought to induce him to remain in bed the third morning of the storm, but though he had passed a restless night he was oddly bent on being up and dressed. Nothing would convince him that Henry was not coming that very day; coming with friends at his side and gallant gray riders at his back to sweep the range of their oppressors and drive the hated invaders to the Potomac. Twice on the previous day she had thought him wandering, and her sore heart nearly ceased its beating at the mere suggestion of his failing now when it was beyond human possibility for Henry to reach him. Twice or thrice during the night he was even wilder in his words, but the silent, tearful watcher by his pillow tried to teach herself that 'twas only dreaming, that the morrow would bring relief. Once, late that afternoon, the strain became more than she could bear, and seeing the old cavalry officer on horseback at the gate, and remembering that he begged her to believe they warred not on women and the helpless ones at home, and had urged her to call upon him if he could be of the faintest service, she asked the sergeant in charge of the guard now pacing silently around them to say to the colonel that she begged to speak with him. He came, the gray-haired, ruddy-faced old hero, and, dismounting at the steps, saluted her as he would have done homage to a queen. The sight of the grief and anxiety in her face, and the pallor, due to suffering and ceaseless vigils, went straight to his heart.

"Dear young lady," he said, "I beg you tell me how I can serve you. Think! yonder across the Potomac—only as far from it on that side as we are on this—is my home, and there, almost as lonely as you, lives my daughter. I ask to serve you in your distress as I know any gentleman in the gray you love would treat my child under like conditions. Who knows how soon your battle-flags will be on our fields! Twice already has your Stuart ridden within rifle range of her windows. Miss Armistead, war is bitter enough. Do not make it worse by refusing the little service we are permitted to give!"

In her loneliness and desolation, who can blame her that the tears gushed from her eyes? It was a minute or two before she could control herself sufficiently to speak. Two or three of the guard looked curiously on from the shelter of their ponchos as the old soldier led her to a chair and bent sympathetically over her.

"You are more than kind," she answered at last. "My anxiety is all on my father's account. He seems failing so rapidly, and our physician, Dr. Loring, has not been near us for days. The roads are in dreadful condition, I know, but we have no one who *can* go. Would it be possible to send one of your men over to him and beg him to come either to-night or the first thing to-morrow?"

The old dragoon's face was clouded with sorrow in a moment.

"If he could be brought to you by any act of mine I would send a guard for him this moment. Miss Armistead, I fear I have sad news for you. I would go for him myself, but it would be useless. For some reason, I know not what, Dr. Loring was arrested by my superior officer, the colonel commanding this district in the absence of Colonel Graham, and two days ago was sent to Washington. We have an excellent physician with us—the surgeon of my regiment. He will be up from Thoro'fare before dark; I pray you let me send him to your father."

"Oh, how cruel, how wrong it seems! Pardon me, Colonel Westerlo, I ought not to speak of it when you have been so kind; but Dr. Loring was almost the sole dependence of scores of families, left now without a protector; husbands, brothers, fathers, sons, *all* in the army, and the women and children left alone. What possible cause could be assigned?"

The colonel shrugged his shoulders. "I know not,"

he said; " we had not wars like this where first I drew
the sabre. There be men who say that in no other
way can the South be brought to terms. My commander keeps me here against my will. I prayed to
be sent with the column to the Shenandoah. I like
not this search of defenceless homes, this warring on
non-combatants at the rear; but I can but obey. His
captures include but one officer, I am told, and he—
but you know him, perhaps—a Captain Falconer."

" Captain Falconer !" she faltered. " When—*when*
was he taken ?" and she clasped her hand to her heart;
a deadly pallor o'erspread her face. What if he had
been captured before sending warning to Henry not
to make the attempt ! What if Henry had received
only the hurried letter in which she implored him to
come !

Westerlo was aghast at the effect of his words.
" *So ?*" he muttered to himself; " and yet I thought
not so carpet-knight a soldier could have won a heart
like this."

He bent over her all sympathy and sorrow.

" The captain was taken by our advance at Thoro'-
fare the night we reached there—the night Major
Kearny visited your father," he said. " He was alone
with but a single orderly at the time. He—he is per-
fectly safe—unhurt—he will soon be exchanged. I
beg you not to grieve."

But she had covered her face with her hands, ap-
palled at the thought of Henry's peril. *Now* no word
of warning could reach him, and acting on the prayer
contained in the last letter she had sent him, he would

spare no effort, shun no risk, to reach his father's side. Even though warned at Hedgman River or the lower fords of the Rappahannock that all Fauquier and Prince William counties were now held by the Federal cavalry, he would seek his way by night; he was sure to come.

"I bitterly regret that in my stupidity I have added so great a grief to your load of anxiety, dear young lady," said Westerlo, rising. "Let me ask forgiveness. Let me go, at least, and send our doctor to you. Oh, grieve not, grieve not, pretty one; he is really safer now than he would be here. There, there, I will go."

She sprang to her feet and sought to restrain him.

"Oh, no! It is not—it is not what you—" But she broke off short. Was not *any* supposition of his preferable to his discovering the real cause of her anxiety and distress? "You must not send the doctor," she hurriedly continued, abruptly changing the subject. "I *am* grateful, but—but father would not see him—at least not yet. Indeed I *will* call upon you if need there be."

But the old dragoon rode away, shaking his head. "I have made a mess of it. I might have known she had a lover—and he was just from here; yet, a *poule mouillée*, like that—a fellow with no fight in him for all the bravery of his attire. Ah, the sergeant was a hero—*he* got through!"

True to his word, he sent his surgeon to the house at dusk, and the doctor had a brief talk with Miss Armistead. She had begged her father to see this gentleman, but to no purpose; the old Virginian was indomitable in his pride and his resolution. So long as he had life in his veins, he said, he would refuse all aid from "Federal" sources, and she knew well that it would only irritate and worry him to plead further. The doctor was not invited to the sick-room, and, falteringly, Lucy told him why. He seemed in no wise surprised or annoyed, asked several questions, and quietly took his leave, saying that he would send some little remedies in a short time. If Judge Armistead had dreamed that the glass of sherry she so smilingly gave him with his chicken broth that night had come from the field stores of the Yankee doctor it might have choked him, but he swallowed it eagerly, and was allowed another thimbleful. At an hour before daybreak, when she stole into the room to see how he was sleeping, he looked up with sudden question about Henry, and soon after sunrise he began to dress and to call feebly for Nelse. Nothing would persuade him to remain in bed. Something, he said, kept telling him that this day would bring Henry home to him again, and he must be in readiness to welcome his boy and his friends. He smiled grimly, lifting a tremulous hand and warning them to listen in silence as the trumpets of the cavalry were heard playing some bright, spirited calls while the guard was being mounted under the dripping trees. "They'll be playing a different tune before night," he said. "They can't see twelve hours ahead, or they'd be scampering now."

And though the roads were deep in mud and the clouds hung low, the wind had died away, and towards

noon there were signs of breaking of the storm. The
rain ceased to patter on the roof, the light slowly increased, and then, early in the afternoon, there came
visitors. She heard clanking sabres and clinking spurs
upon the piazza without, and her father listened with
frowning and impatient mien. He could not bear it that
she should so frequently be called upon to receive these
haughty and triumphant invaders. Yet he longed to
question her as to Kearny. Yank or no Yank, he liked
that young fellow, and though he would not approve,
he could not wonder at his love for such a girl as his
peerless Lucy. Not once had that name passed the lips
of either father or daughter in conversation with each
other since the sealing of the packet that contained
the treasure he had left with them. Not once, however, had it left her thoughts since the moment of the
dread announcement made by that officer under her
window. She longed—even though she shrank from
asking—to know more of that extraordinary story.
It was not that she for a moment believed Kearny
could be guilty; she simply needed to hear of him.
Twice had she striven to muster courage and ask
Colonel Westerlo about him, but the words—the name
—would not come. Now it was with fresh excitement that she heard from Hannah's lips the announcement that the colonel was at the door, and begged to
see her on important matters. She went at once, and
found the old soldier, with the surgeon and his adjutant, all equipped for the march, their horses saddled
at the gate.

"We are come to say farewell," he said, with sad-
13

ness and courtesy mingled in his voice. "Orders reached me an hour ago to leave one squadron here at Hopeville and march at once to Salem with the rest. I have instructed Captain Wise, who remains in command, to visit you daily and inquire if in any way he can be of aid to you, and believe me, Miss Armistead, it is with heavy heart I go. Will not your good father see our doctor now, since it is our last opportunity?"

But Judge Armistead refused flatly. He desired his pleading daughter to express his appreciation of the proffered courtesy, but to say that he could not be under obligations. "Lucy," he whispered, tremulous and excited, "it is as I told you. It *must* be so. Henry and our boys are coming, and the warning has reached these fellows. They flee from the wrath to come."

She had to return to the kindly old soldier, and tell him, with tears in her eyes, that pleading was useless. Her father would not see the doctor, and that medical gentleman bade her be of good cheer; so long as the judge was combative and obstinate there could be no immediate danger. They would be sure to meet again, said the colonel, as he bent over her hand to say adieu. Never would he visit this section of Virginia without coming to find the old homestead, and to inquire for her welfare.

And then they were gone. She had found it impossible to ask one word about Kearny, and she could have buried her head in the pillows and wept in utter anxiety and desolation. Her father here, failing day by day, his mind clouded, his strength gone, his system practically starving for nutritious food, and his palate pining for the delicacies to which it had been accustomed; Henry, she knew not where, but something kept haunting her hour after hour, warning her that the brother she loved was in desperate peril, and plunging deeper and deeper into the toils. And then Frank Kearny. Could she ever forget him as he looked that night? Could she ever forget how he had clasped and kissed her? The change in him; the worn, haggard look about the eyes and mouth; the sternness of his soldierly face, the weariness and sorrow in his voice. All this she recalled—all this—and the fact that between him and her there was that forbidding shadow that bade her send him hopeless from her side. Motherless, friendless, she was bearing her weight of sorrow and care practically alone and comfortless.

An excited controversy in the kitchen afforded temporary relief—Aunt Bell and Hannah in lively but partially suppressed altercation. The former was urging that Miss Lulie be instantly summoned to see and rejoice in something which had been deposited by a squad of soldiers at the cellar door, whereat Nelse could be heard capering in delight. But Hannah was positive and peremptory. "Don' you do no such fool thing! You hide 'em, 'n' keep 'em, 'n' just dish 'em up 'thout sayin' one word 'bout it. *I* knows." And Hannah's wisdom prevailed. The judge was regaled for supper that evening with viands for which he had longed in secret, and for which he thanked his silent

daughter with loving eyes and loving kisses. She
would ask no question; she, for his sake, would not
reject the good things that had been thrown in their
way. She could have found it deep down in her
warm, Southern heart to have thanked and blessed
that thoughtful old Dutch-Yankee dragoon, for she
well knew it must have been his doing.

Just at dusk Captain Wise appeared to her as she
was flitting through the hall. He was a man she had
not before noticed among the officers passing to and
fro. He was not the like of Westerlo, but he meant
to be civil and courteous. He called, he said, as instructed by his commander, to inquire how Judge
Armistead had passed the day, and whether there was
anything he could be of service in. She thanked him.
It might be necessary to send old Nelse over to Hopeville village on the west side of the range if the roads
were better on the morrow. Could he be allowed the
use of a spare horse or mule? The captain looked
much disconcerted. His orders strictly forbade it.
In fact, "not to put too fine a point upon it," said this
martial Snagsby, it was his belief that Colonel Westerlo had been sent away because the district commander suspected him of giving too much aid and
comfort to the enemy, and he, Captain Wise, was
warned on peril of his commission to see to it that no
one passed to and fro along the Gap without the order of the energetic colonel commanding the cavalry
brigade now holding the neighborhood.

"It was his own adjutant who brought over the
orders," said the captain, "and he told me the reason

they had to be so strict was that the colonel felt sure there were Confederate spies lurking around us, and he was fearful that while Graham was away a brigade of Stuart's men might gallop up from the Rappahannock by way of Sulphur Springs, and capture him and his whole crowd. He says the one thing the colonel prays for is to capture some one of these disguised soldiers, and then he can make an example of him."

"What could he possibly do—what right would he have?" she asked, with wildly beating heart, Henry—Henry and his peril—occurring to her at the instant.

"He has authority, he says, to summarily hang any Confederate officer or man who may be found disguised within our lines. It will go hard with any man he catches, for he is a fanatical old fellow, and I believe he would do just what he says."

And this was the comfort that came to Lucy Armistead when that long, hard day was brought to a close.

XIX.

A NIGHT of sleeplessness and weary vigil followed. Not until hours after dark would the old judge consent to be led away and put to bed. Nelse, the sable groom of the bed-chamber, had thrice vainly importuned his master before success rewarded his efforts. Lucy sat by her father's side an hour and read to him, hoping to soothe him to sleep. At last he fell into a fitful slumber, moving nervously from time to time, and muttering or moaning when he stirred. Exhausted, yet unwilling to leave his bedside, the girl bowed her head upon the coverlet, and, still clasping the worn, withered old hand in both of hers, so white and soft and smooth by contrast, yet so thin and fragile now, she too presently dozed away. The only light in the sick-room came from the flickering blaze on the hearth, the only sound, save the old man's fitful breathing, or an occasional sigh, was Nelse's monotonous snore from his mat in the hallway, where the faithful old darkey had elected to spend the night. Once or twice, when she found it time to give him medicine or the drink that the doctor had left for his use, Lucy roused herself, and once she called Nelse and had him replenish the fire. As the night wore away the old man grew wakeful again, and fanciful in his talk and ideas. Lucy again strove by reading aloud awhile to distract his thoughts from that one strain—Henry's coming. It was torture, agony, to her to think of it now; yet it was the burden of his every sentence—he would talk of nothing else. Twice he started up, declaring he heard horses' feet on the road through the Gap, and once he made her go to the piazza and look and listen. Throwing over her shoulders a heavy shawl, she obeyed his wish, and, softly opening the great hall door, stepped forth to the head of the stairs. The clouds had gone at last, the stars were shining placidly through the chill and silence of the night. Far over to the east there were dim lights along the valley, the glow of distant camp-fires. Down in the fields where the battalion had pitched its white tents but a few days before, all was now emptiness and gloom. The fires had burned there merrily even through the three days' storm; but now not a glimmer could be seen. In the orchard south of the house a bright fire blazed in front of the white tent pitched there for the use of the guard, and she could see one or two forms wrapped in the long blue cavalry overcoat huddling about in the smoke of the moist and hissing logs. In front of her, not ten yards away, a sentry paced silently to and fro; and others, she knew, guarded the flanks and rear of the old homestead. How could Henry pass such warders undetected, even if it had been possible for him to make his way through the miles and miles of guarded roads that lay between the Rappahannock and his father's bedside? She shuddered as she thought of the peril. Even now,

might he not be a prisoner caught in the attempt?
Might he not even be cold in death, murdered in determined effort to force the Yankee lines?

Over the horizon a pallid light told of the near ap-
proach of day. She had hardly slept an hour during
the night, and was cold, weary, hungry too. Possibly
now if she could assure her father that dawn had come,
the Federal cavalry were still at their posts, and no
sign of Henry had been seen or heard, he might again
doze, and she, too, could get a little rest. Just as she
would have turned away to re-enter the house there
fell upon her ear the faint click, click of distant iron-
shod hoofs upon a rocky road—a horse coming through
the Gap and at rapid trot. Probably the officer of the
day returning from an inspection of his picket, she
said to herself, and still waited to hear more. Looking towards the fire, she saw that two or three of the
men in blue were hurriedly tumbling up, and, carbine
in hand, running through the trees to the stone wall
at the roadside, where they were lost to her view.
Presently there came sharp challenge ringing out on
the chill morning air, then the clatter of the hoofs as
the horse was suddenly reined in. She heard prompt,
cheery, confident answer, in a tone almost laughing
and rollicking. "Don't shoot, boys, I'm all right,"
or something to that effect. She heard orders to dismount, and, still talking loudly and cheerily, the stranger seemed to be leading his horse into the orchard,
while the guard clustered around him. What was
there in that voice that almost stopped the throbbing
of her heart? Henry's—Henry's beyond all possibil-

ity of doubt — Henry's — and yet laughing, joking, chatting loudly with a squad of Federal cavalry! Presently she could see them at the fire—the sergeant and one of the men closely examining a folded paper, while others held the stranger's horse. As for the stranger himself, he bent over the flames, totally indifferent to their scrutiny of his papers, and seemingly intent only on toasting his hands, and then flapping them across his broad chest as though striving to quicken the circulation in a frame numbed by a long night ride. He was garbed in a long blue cavalry coat like those worn by the troopers, and wore a soft black felt hat and high top-boots. A thick, bushy beard concealed all the lower face ; but that form, that voice—Good Heaven! was he mad to take such desperate risk? It was her brother beyond shadow of doubt.

Presently she saw the young lieutenant who seemed to be in command of the guard coming from his tent, and him the stranger greeted cordially. "Sorry to disturb you, lieutenant," he said, "but these men don't know me yet as the rest of the cavalry do, and I had to have you called to satisfy them. There are my papers, sir," and he nodded carelessly towards the sergeant. "Oh, here's another batch that will help out in case you don't remember me. I'm Will Tierney, the scout. Everybody knows me hereabouts."

Trembling with apprehension, she clung to the balustrade and looked with staring eyes. She saw the lieutenant studying one paper after another, and then, as though satisfied, engaging in quiet conversation with the new arrival. Then the weary horse was led away by one of the men, and she could see that the others were again disposing themselves for rest around the fire. Henry, her brother, was coolly shaking out a couple of blankets, as though he meant to lie down in the midst of his enemies.

It was nearly sunrise when she stole back to her father's bedside to tell him the startling news, and warn him of the imminent danger in case of suspicion or discovery. It seemed to rouse his weakened faculties and bring back new lease of life.

After brief statement of her plan, and gaining his approval, she roused old Nelse, and warning him that all his wits would now be needed, told him of "young mars'r's" presence among the guards in the orchard, and bade him go about his work and keep his eyes open for a chance to aid him. Then Hannah and Aunt Bell were called, and at an early hour these excited domestics were down in the cellar levying on the box of provisions sent there by Colonel Westerlo, and busy in the preparation of breakfast. An hour later, unhindered by the sentries and escorted to the house by the lieutenant himself, the tall young "scout" sauntered into the yard, strode up the steps, knocked at the door, and politely inquired of Hannah whether he could see the judge or Miss Lucy. While she was gone to carry his message he stood carelessly at the head of the steps, his hands in his pockets and his glib tongue telling the lieutenant how many years he had lived in Prince William County before the war. A moment later he was bidden to enter, and far back in the dim recesses of the hall threw off the bushy beard and clasped his sister in his arms.

"Father! How is he?" were the first words he could say.

She clung to him, sobbing in speechless thanksgiving that, if only for the time, he was safe, safe in her embrace. She gloried in the address, the daring, the devotion that had enabled him to thread his way through miles of foemen to come at her call, and gladden the fading eyes of the father who so loved him—who had so suffered for his sake. Yet she was all unnerved. The sorrows, the privations of the long winter, had told upon her more than she dreamed until now, and, weak as a child, she lay on his breast, crying her heart out in mingled joy, relief, and apprehension. At last she looked up in his eyes.

"He is very feeble; he will be so overjoyed to see you—but oh, Henry, did you not receive my warning? Do you not know your very life is perilled by this disguise?"

"It was too late to warn after your first letter reached me, sister mine. I hardly dared hope to find him alive after these interminable delays. I started the instant leave was granted me and before the movement of the Federals was known, but they got first to Warrenton, and it has been sharp work since. Heaven! If I could only send back word this night! If Stuart only knew what I know—how few—how scattered they are! We might rush a regiment or two up here and ride off with the whole gang. Take me to father. There I can tell you the rest."

That meeting need not be dwelt upon. For an hour the old man lay there clinging to the hand of his stalwart son, while Lucy sat by her brother's side, drinking in his every word. Both father and daughter were thrilled at the story of his perilous journey. It would have been utterly impossible for him to get through so long as he wore any item of Confederate dress or equipment. The line of the Rappahannock was closely guarded all the way to the forks of the Hedgman River. He expected to find no Federal troops west of the Orange and Alexandria Railway, but the sudden expedition to capture Mosby had filled the country with cavalry, and every town and every road from Sulphur Springs northward seemed infested with them. Near Amissville chance befriended him. He found there the scout Tierney, who, with the full knowledge of both Stuart and Mosby, was in the employ of the Federal "Secret Service." It was his business to spend most of his time with the lines of the Army of the Potomac, but to slip out and give prompt information of important moves, while feeding his employers with any such pap in the way of reports of the position and numbers (the latter purposely exaggerated) of the Confederates as he thought they would swallow. It was a dangerous game, and one he could not long expect to carry out. Both sides began to suspect him, he said, and he had had trouble within the Federal lines, and experienced great difficulty in getting out to warn Mosby. He had been seized by the Yankees despite his papers, and only by the skin of his teeth had he escaped and made his way through the wood roads in

" As for the stranger himself, he bent over the flames, totally indifferent to their scrutiny of his papers, and seemingly intent
only on toasting his hands."

the nick of time. Now, of course, the game was up, and he could no longer return. He was seeking to get farther south, and appealed to Armistead to aid him, confident that as one of Stuart's most trusted officers he would be able to satisfy the Confederate officers along the line to Gordonsville that he was not a Yankee spy, but a loyal Virginian. Henry saw a chance at once; making a temporary exchange of "mounts," and borrowing Tierney's hat, overcoat, and Federal passes and papers, and gaining from him such information as to the names of the officers, the regiments, etc., he would be apt to encounter *en route* as he needed, the young Virginian pushed boldly forth, rode unhesitatingly among the very first party of blue-coated horsemen he sighted across the stream; told their commander he was Tierney, hurrying through with important information; showed his papers; scrawled with a rough pencil a not bad imitation of the scout's signature; gave a good deal of information about the condition of things south of the river, and was allowed to ride on, mainly by night, avoiding pickets and patrols when it was possible to do so, and thus escaping delay; but being bold, communicative, and jovial whenever he *had* to meet them, he succeeded at last in making his way to Hopeville village, and then pushed through the Gap. Up to this moment he had not been recognized by either friend or foe outside the walls of his father's house. But it had taken time; there had been unavoidable detentions at more points than one; nothing but the imminent danger in which he feared his father's life to be would have prompted

the risk. Now the question was how to get back, for
he dare not stay.

Several times during the day he felt compelled to
go out and chat with the men of the guard, examine his horse, and talk of the ride before him as soon
as he was well rested. By four in the afternoon he
had decided that his best chance for success lay in a
bold trot down the pike to Warrenton. If Tierney's
defection had been discovered and reported by Colonel Graham, those passes would soon be worse than
worthless. He must utilize them while they were
yet good.

But they had done their work already. Just as he
had resumed his disguise, and was about to say farewell, Lucy was startled by the scurry of many hoofs;
the shout of men surrounding the house, and the sudden entrance of two officers in the Union blue followed
by several men.

"That's the man!" exclaimed the foremost. "Seize
him!" and almost before Henry had time to think,
two stout dragoons had thrown themselves upon him.
The *rôle* he was playing occurred to him at once, however, and while Lucy, almost fainting from terror and
distress, sank back against her father's door, he boldly
faced the officers.

"What on earth does this mean, captain? Surely
I saw you last night over near Salem. I showed you
my papers—Tierney."

"Unluckily for you, Tierney, you did, as I happened
to remember when orders came this morning to make
every effort to find and arrest you."

"On what charge, pray?"

"On the double charge of having murdered Captain Mullane at Washington on the 10th of March, and of deserting to Mosby's guerillas that same night."

XX.

RETURNING to Washington as soon as he could obtain a fresh "mount" for himself, and leaving his escort to follow by easy marches, Captain Dayton reached the capital late on the evening after his meeting with Westerlo. As they sat by the camp-fire, sheltered by a tent fly, the two officers had talked for half an hour or so before the younger bade his host goodnight, and rolled himself in his blankets for such rest as was possible to a man whose heart was filled with anxiety. Already, he found, the very troopers of his little escort were talking of the murder of Mullane, and of the strong circumstantial evidence against Kearny. The story flew from mouth to mouth in the camp of Westerlo's detachment, and one or two officers came and questioned him as to the truth of the rumor. Dayton could only say that Mullane was certainly dead, and that Kearny was a passenger on the boat about the time the tragedy occurred, and there had been previously a quarrel between them. Knowing the major, however, from early boyhood, he felt confident that he was not the murderer. But the officers knew that the object of his ride to the neighborhood was to search for Major Kearny, who had certainly accompanied the column. What possible ex-

cuse could Kearny have had for joining a command
and an expedition where he had no official position?
Did not that look queer? This question made Dayton
hot, and his answer was, therefore, decidedly cutting.
Major Kearny, he said, knew more about this section
of the country than any of the officers going out with
the column. He had a week's "delay," doubtless had
heard of the start of the command, and instantly re-
solved to follow and overtake it, and tender his services as a volunteer. Such conduct might seem in-
comprehensible to the questioner, but was most char-
acteristic in Major Kearny, and had been very hand-
somely recognized by Colonel Graham in his report.

All the same, Dayton was feverishly eager to get
back to Washington and join his friend. He more
than suspected that it was a longing to see the fair
girl at the Armistead place that prompted Kearny to
seize the opportunity to come with Graham's command, and it was evident that he had returned to
Washington as soon as the brief interview was completed. Something had told him that there was a love
affair back of all this gloomy and restless demeanor
of Kearny's. He *knew* there must be from the fury
with which he had resented Mullane's accusation; and
now he was confident that, thus far at least, Kearny
had not prospered in his suit. He had only dimly
seen the sweet face in the dark hallway, and he ventured to ask Colonel Westerlo if he had met the young
lady.

"Ah, I have—two or three times," was the reply.
"And I grieve for her. Her father is going fast, I
    14

fear; her brother is an officer of Stuart's cavalry; her lover—a handsome fellow—was captured by our advance the night we got to Thoro'fare; and she is utterly alone in the world.   And, you mark me, captain, she is a thorough-bred; she is a *lady*.   Ah, my heart aches for her."

"Who is the lover?   Did you see him?"

"See him?   Yes.   Worse luck, I 'gobbled' him; and, worst luck of all, I told *her!*   It almost turned her into stone.   I thought I had killed her.   She reeled and nearly fainted, and was deathly white.   Oh, but she is game, that little one; she is brave!"

"And who is the man?"

"His name is Falconer.   He is from Warrenton, and is a captain of cavalry.   He had been visiting her when he got the news of our coming, and he ran into our advance while trying to make his way to his people in the Gap."

Late the next night Dayton reached Willard's, after a journey that had been an all-day affair.   He had left Westerlo at the peep of dawn, and was tired out and splashed with mud when he strode into the office of the familiar old hostelry.   Dozens of men in uniform, of all grades from major-general down to second lieutenant, were grouped about the marble pavement, and many ceased their talk and looked curiously at him as he entered.

"Has Major Kearny returned?" he asked, with eagerness he could not conceal.

The clerk glanced up quickly.

"Captain Dayton?" he asked.   "Yes, and wants to

see you at once on your arrival. There are one or
two gentlemen with him now. Will you go right
up ?"

And Dayton, too anxious and impatient to feel the
weight of his weariness, was ushered at once to his
comrade's room. Two officers were sitting with him,
and a portly man in civilian dress lounged in a big
arm-chair. All arose as the travel-stained soldier entered, and Kearny sprang eagerly forward and grasped
him by the hand.

"Dear old fellow ! what a time you must have had
—and all on my account ! Where have you been ?"

"I'll tell you that presently. Tell me first that you
have cleared these muddy heads hereabouts, and put
an end to their suspicions."

"How is it, gentlemen ?" said Kearny, with a grave,
sad smile, turning to his visitors. "Let me present
my old chum, Captain Dayton. Major Ross; Captain
Foster of the staff. The senator of course you know.
From all accounts, *mon ami*, you needed no evidence
to clear me in your loyal heart, but an alibi is the
least point on which the defence rests the case. I
wasn't there."

"I'm glad to hear it, Kearny; and where did you
leave the boat ?"

"At Alexandria. I was up and dressed when we
reached there, and on the dock whom should I meet
but Stockton, of the regular cavalry. He told me that
he was going out to join Graham's command under
orders from the War Department. He knew the object of the move, but neither of us supposed that Gra-

ham would start that night. I was delayed in getting a suitable horse, and it was late that day before we reached the camp of Stockton's troop. We were together all day long, so that ended the case against me. Next morning I galloped forward and caught Graham at Centreville. Of course I was amazed at the charge against me, but it was all set at rest by Stockton. Now the question is—who did it? Have you any theory?"

Dayton hesitated a moment, then slowly answered:

"I have some vague suspicion of a man whom we saw on the boat the night you started for Washington, but who disappeared immediately after the murder. I gave his name and description to the police, but as yet have seen none of them since my return. It was that tall, lanky fellow, Kearny—the man with the big, bushy beard, whom you noticed and spoke of having seen elsewhere in different dress. You remember they told us on the boat he was a quartermaster's clerk—name of Freeman—and that Mullane had won a lot of money from him."

Kearny's eyes gleamed with eager interest. "I do indeed!" he said. "Go on!"

"Well, I cannot, further than to say that he did not come back to Acquia with the boat, and that he has not been seen aboard it since; or had not up to the day I started in pursuit of you."

"I have already explained to these gentlemen, Dayton, that while I was glad of an opportunity to be of service to Graham and his command, I had hoped to find it possible to make my way out to Hopeville Gap to personally visit the family that saved me from death or imprisonment, or both, after the Gainesville fight. But for this dash after Mosby I might have been unable to get out there at all; yet that was the object of my requesting this week's delay."

The captain of the staff, who had been seated quietly at the farther end of the sofa, now rose and came forward.

"I am going up to the Department, Major Kearny, and have only waited in hopes of seeing Captain Dayton on his return. It was a matter I did not intend to mention until later, but I want to congratulate the captain on being the first man to hit on the true solution of this case."

"You mean I am right—that it was Freeman who did it?" asked Dayton, eagerly.

"You are right, although it wasn't Freeman. To-day's discoveries at the Secret Service office establish the fact that Freeman, so called, wrote a letter to Mullane telling him he had evidence to prove that Mullane had cheated him at cards, and won all his money from him by a scoundrelly trick; so he bade him be at the landing, and come to his room on the boat prepared to restore every cent, or he would have him arrested and cashiered in disgrace. The letter, signed by a very different name, but one we know equally well, was not obtained by the police until this morning, as it lay in the hack where Mullane had dropped it. The hackman was frightened at the murder, and had kept in the dark until ferreted out, and then gave evidence that he had been employed by some 'out-of-town sports' to drive them with Mullane from a certain low saloon to the boat; thence he took them to the Baltimore depot, and could hear them quarrelling among themselves over the money out of which they had fleeced the captain during the night. They had won almost every cent he had, and he was drunk, ugly, truculent, and butt-headed at the time he went aboard. There was evidently a quarrel, a grapple, and then the death-shot. Whether intentional or not, it was fired by a man then employed as a scout and agent of the Secret Service Bureau, who immediately thereafter crossed into Virginia, got his horse and field equipments, joined that night the column under Colonel Graham, and made his escape in time to warn Mosby of their coming."

"By Heaven!" exclaimed Kearny, "it was that scoundrel Tierney. The same who betrayed me last year."

"The very man," calmly answered Captain Foster. "And there is no question that he has been a two-faced villain all through, and serving the rebellion while drawing pay from us. You never saw any one so taken aback as the chief. He has stood up for that fellow through thick and thin, and now he looks as though he wanted to go and hang himself."

"Better hang Tierney, if they can lay hands on him," suggested the senator.

"Oh, never fear as to that! provided they catch him; but he'll never be fool enough to get within our lines again. If he should, and any of Graham's brigade lay hands on him, up he'll go to the first tree."

"No wonder he slunk away and kept out of sight the evening we boarded the boat at Acquia!" said Kearny. "I always knew that it was his doing that the blackguardly story about my stay at Hopeville was first whispered abroad. We could not recognize him in his disguise, but he knew me. What orders have been given in the case, captain?"

"They go out to-night, warning all commanders of columns or detachments in Virginia to be on the look-out for the ex-scout Tierney; giving a description of the man, and copies of all his orders and papers. No instructions that I heard of at the office were given as to the disposition to be made of him. I fancy that is left to the imagination. And now, major, I know you and Captain Dayton have much to talk of—I will report your return to the adjutant-general, captain—and I'll say good-night. You leave for Trenton in the morning?"

"I hope to," answered Kearny, with the same grave, quiet smile. "I trust no new accusation or suspicion may attach to me by that time, or the governor may decide it best to declare a vacancy, and make another major."

Then the senator and Major Ross decided it time for them to go and leave the friends together; and no sooner were they alone than Dayton threw himself wearily back in the big arm-chair. Kearny stood over him, placed his hand on his shoulder, and looked down in his face.

"Did you see—her?"

"For a moment only, yes."

" Was all well with them ?"

"I fear not, Frank. I met old Colonel Westerlo there, commanding a detachment of the —— Pennsylvania Cavalry, a fine old soldier, and he is deeply interested in their welfare ; but he tells me the judge is proud as Lucifer and stubborn as a mule. He won't accept anything in the way of attention—won't see anybody; refuses even a visit from the doctor ; and he had heard from the negroes that the old gentleman was very ill and weak, and Miss Lucy nearly starving ; they had been daily expecting a visit from the family physician, and needing him, but the very day I got there Westerlo heard that that red-hot old martinet Van Duzen had ordered Dr. Loring's arrest, and had sent him under guard to Chantilly."

" On what possible charge, pray ? If anything, Dr. Loring is a Union man in his innermost heart. What will old Van do next? He is too flighty and rabid an old dragoon to leave in an independent command there. He'll be for hanging somebody yet."

"Kearny, from what Westerlo tells me, I am seriously worried about your friends there. Can you not write a letter to Van Duzen and commend them to his care and courtesy, because of their long kindness to you when you were under their roof ?"

"I'll do it this night, of course ; but as we are strangers to each other I must get the senator and some other dignitary to endorse it. Then it must go safely to Van Duzen ; such a thing would only hurt them if it should fall into Southern hands. I hope my visit resulted in the relief of their pressing needs.

It did not help me, God knows. Yes, I know your natural supposition, and—it is true. I am hard hit—hard hit. All to no purpose, too ; she told me frankly there was another."

"Yes, I heard of it; Westerlo told me. I know it has been the cause of all your misery this winter."

"What did Westerlo tell you?"

"He was well-nigh used up," answered Dayton. "Utterly unconscious of the fact that it was her lover he was speaking of, he told her of his capture, and she nearly fainted away. He said—"

"Whose capture—when?"

"That very night, by Westerlo's advance-guard—Captain Falconer. Wasn't that the man she told you of?"

"Falconer !—captured again? Yes, that's the man."

XXI.

Night, dark and cheerless, had fallen on the old homestead at Hopeville. Except in the room of the aged invalid, not a gleam of light shone from within its walls. Around the house the sentries paced as usual, and with an air of increased alertness and importance. The capture made just before dusk was one that rewarded hours of hitherto seemingly senseless vigil. There was something, after all, about this mysterious household, whose members they saw only at ten yards' distance, and whom they were enjoined to treat with scrupulous respect, but on no account to pass in or out. Either they were spies themselves or harborers of deserters and spies, so ran the camp-fire stories, but this evening's business had probably ended their career of plotting. A strong guard had ridden away into the dark gorge through the range, bearing with them, strapped and bound to his horse, the two-faced spy, murderer, and deserter to the enemy—the scout Tierney, who had trotted so confidently down the pass that very morning, and spent the day in private interview with the invisible owner of the place. Things looked black for that young Virginian, said the officers in their talk with one another. The captors brought the news that "old Van Duzen" had received from Washington the day previous a full account of the crimes with which the man was charged, a description of him, and copies of his passes and papers, and the orders were to find him if a possible thing. It was speedily transmitted to the outposts, and that very night "Tierney" himself had been heard of at one of them. An officer galloped in to Van Duzen's headquarters with this important news, and in less than an hour several strong detachments were roused from their night's rest, and sent forth at early dawn to scour the country in pursuit. One of these had easily traced the man to Hopeville village, and thence through the Gap. Now they were riding back in triumph, and with the rising of the morrow's sun "old Van" would be in possession of his coveted prisoner. It was a bet of five to one that he would hang him inside of twenty-four hours. If Graham got back from the Shenandoah in time to interpose, the man would doubtless have the benefit of a trial, but otherwise the "short shrift and sudden cord" was the least he could expect.

And yet how cool and calm he was! Captain Wise, who was present at the capture, seemed greatly troubled for the young lady, who had been shocked beyond description by the abrupt announcement of the charges against Tierney, and the somewhat violent means of his arrest. No one supposed that he was a person of any social position or consideration until that moment, but it became instantly apparent that he must have been of great consequence in the eyes of Miss Armistead, and *that* established beyond question

the belief that he must come from the same grade—
one of the old families of the grand old commonwealth. She had for an instant seemed stricken dumb
with horror; had almost fainted; then had rushed forward and seized his arm.

"Gentlemen," she cried, "it is some fearful mistake; it cannot be true!"

But it was Tierney himself, said Wise, who suddenly and proudly checked her.

"Miss Armistead!" he loudly and firmly spoke, "not
one word—unless you would make it worse for me.
You know I am not guilty of such crime, and I can
satisfy all accusers at the proper time." And with
anguish in her eyes she had fallen back to a seat, and
bowed her head in her hands, but said no more. Who
could the man be? His whole manner and intonation seemed to change when he spoke to her, and was
obeyed as one in her own station who had the right to
advise or command. This was a matter over which
Wise pondered long and deeply that night when he
was again left alone with his little command; but he
pondered to no purpose. The problem was too much
for him.

Could he have but seen the sight in the poor old
father's room that bitter evening, no doubt would
have remained. Judge Armistead, lying on the old
sofa in his study, had heard every word. His rallied
faculties had quickly grasped the whole horror of the
situation, and the imminent peril of his beloved son
flashed upon him in an instant. It was better—better
for the time being, at least—that he should appear as

the murderer, the deserter, the double-dealing scoundrel Tierney, than be known in his true character—an
officer and a gentleman of the Confederate service
caught disguised and with false papers within the
Union lines.

In the first predicament, as Tierney, he could stoutly deny the murder, the desertion, and demand trial.
They would not be apt to hang a man without proofs
of his crime, and he would probably be taken to
Washington; possibly not until then would his identity be discovered.   On the other hand, if discovered
here and now—if recognized and pointed out as Henry
Armistead while yet he stood within the control of
Colonel Van Duzen—his doom was sealed.   No proofs
could then be lacking or demanded.   And had not the
whole country-side been warned that if any were captured in disguise and found to be Confederate officers,
their lives would be the forfeit?   When he heard the
escort ride away, and listened to the stern, brief orders given to shoot the prisoner dead should he attempt to escape, the father's heart sank within him.
He cried aloud in anguish that his son could be thus
torn from his side and he be forced to stifle every
word of sympathy or love at parting, lest in so speaking he betray him to a fate worse even than the plight
in which his recklessness and devotion had plunged
him.   The old gray head, bowed with grief and ills
and bitter sorrow, was hidden in his arms when poor
Lucy staggered to the bedside and threw herself, de-
spairing, on her knees.   Ah, God!   There were sore
hearts and desolate homes far in the wintry North,

far in the balmier fields where the Gulf winds blew, but we never knew such suffering and such sorrows as did they who dwelt "between the lines."

It was in the hour of their direst need, after a night of sleepless misery, that there came to them late on the following day the gray-haired veteran Westerlo. He had obtained leave to ride over and see them, he said; and Lucy, weeping and exhausted, could almost have fallen into his arms and sobbed in mingled relief and anguish on his fatherly breast. In few words he told them what he knew and what he feared. She had led him to the bedside of the sore-stricken man, and before he spoke at all Westerlo's suspicions were confirmed. He was at headquarters when Van Duzen received his prisoner that morning. The manner, the bearing, the eyes of the tall and soldierly fellow who stood calmly erect before his questioners were not those of a traitorous wretch such as Tierney was known or believed to be. As Westerlo stood there and studied him, and then listened to the story of his arrival at the homestead and the incidents of his capture, he became possessed with a violent longing to go without delay to the stricken ones at Hopeville. Opportunity presently came; some little strings of evidence as to the alleged Tierney's wanderings were needed. Westerlo tendered his services to his superior officer, and by noon was galloping furiously away.

"I come to speak to you of this scout," he said to these prostrate foes after a few inquiries of the judge as to his health. "I ask you nothing. I seek not to pry into any secret. It might not do for me to know, but he stands accused of crimes that, if proved, would hang him, and he says they cannot be proved, and he demands that they take him to Washington and let him there establish his innocence. My superior is a most ardent hater of this unholy rebellion; he is very bitter. It becomes me not to speak of my commander, and I must not criticise. Nor could I urge him to send his prisoner to the capital to be tried by the slow process of court-martial. It is an example *here* he needs, and there was only one way I could stay him. Two different stories had been told of what he said—of the accounts he gave of himself—to the guard here and to the picket at Hopeville village. I am sent to get the truth, and I come at speed, but not so do I return. My commander will not act until I get back, and I will pray that Colonel Graham is already *en route* and will be there before me. Then he will not hang; he will be taken to Washington; it is possible I go with the escort, for Colonel Graham is my kind friend. I ask it that I may have a day or two and run up to my home and see my own little girl. Now, dear young lady, dear sir, I hear of late a strange story. They tell to me that this our brave Major Kearny was brought to your house, was nursed, tended, concealed from the troops of your own friends, restored to health, to his home, his country, his comrades, through your merciful kindness. My commander, Van Duzen—he did not know this until yesterday, and then it comes to him straight from Washington—no! not from Major Kearny—from the War-office—and he is distressed to think he had so

harshly included you in his orders. He gives me permission to see you, to see how we can serve you, and
for this I rejoice. But he can do little. Now I suppose a case: you have a son, a brother, a noble fellow,
if he is my enemy, whom in open fight I could not
shield; but war has its strange fortunes. Suppose he
should be captured; suppose he be in our hands—in
danger. Would not a great nation, a great people
like ours, rise and say, 'It was he who shielded our
soldier; it was his people who brought him back from
the shadow of death. Now we ask mercy for *him*.'
Dear young lady, if that *should* happen, if it should
be that your brother stood in danger of his life, is
there not some paper, some letter, you could trust to
me that I may show the powers at Washington and
restore him to you?"

The old gentleman lay on his pillow with averted
face, listening in speechless thanksgiving to this wily
and diplomatic dragoon. Lucy, weeping and beam-
ing by turns, blessing in her heart of hearts the generous and thoughtful soldier who had come to them
in their depth of woe, bringing hope and cheer and
consolation—Lucy, who had once believed no man in
the Federal blue could ever win a kindly thought from
her, now seized the colonel's rugged hand and clasped
it in both her own. For a few moments she sat trembling and expectant, waiting for her father to speak, but
at last she bent over the silent form and saw the reason; he too was weeping, yet striving to hide his tears.

Impulsively she turned, and with brimming eyes
looked into Westerlo's face.

"We *have* such a letter, such papers. We have here the very pages my brother Henry wrote to us the night he captured Mr. Kearny. Without them we could not have concealed him here. With them, we could not say no ; and yet—and yet—oh, Colonel Westerlo, there are words in them that will wring my brother's heart if shown or known. They tell of matters he would never speak of even to me. They give a reason for his determination to save Mr. Kearny from going to a Southern prison or taking his chances with other men. Father ! *Would* he forgive me if I let it go ? He bade me keep it until the war was over, that he might show how he redeemed his pledge."

"It can be in no safer hands than those of Colonel Westerlo, my child," answered the old judge at last. " He will guard it for us, to be used only in such case as he described; and let me say this to you, sir: there are other papers, there are letters which it may be in our power to show you that will strengthen the impression which you predict as a result of this. And again, look at our situation ; since the hour it was known that we had befriended a Federal officer, and stood between him and capture and imprisonment, every friend we ever had in all this state turned from us on the instant. We are utterly alone. Sir, we will not accept aid or comfort for ourselves. Let *this* prove my words"—and he turned to Lucy—"the package, daughter, with Major Kearny's money; bring it here. I shall ask you, colonel, to see that it is safely restored to him. We will not, I say, ask or accept

15

aid for ourselves, but should you ever hear of my boy in danger of his life or honor, you will not forget?"

"Forget? By Heaven! I could as soon forget my mother's face," answered Westerlo. "With every time I look upon your daughter's eyes I am ready to implore that you should let me take you—take you and her to my home. There you are safe, at least, as my own; there you can have tender care and nursing, and your health will return. Judge Armistead, *surely* it can be done."

"You are a noble, a knightly soldier, Colonel Westerlo. From my heart I thank you. It is too late—too late. I shall never leave Virginia; but when I am gathered to my fathers, she—my child—will be utterly alone here. If then—if then—"

"Hush! she comes. Then, now, at any time henceforth, she shall be as my own. You have my word."

And Judge Armistead's trembling hand sought and clasped the broad and sinewy palm extended to him as the two men looked in each other's eyes. Then Lucy re-entered the room, and handed to her father the sealed packet and some letters.

An hour later Colonel Westerlo had bidden them adieu and started on his return. He had exchanged a few words with Captain Wise, and given him some hints as to the propriety of diminishing his guards and augmenting his personal courtesies to the stricken household. He had made arrangements to have the assistant surgeon sent up to see the failing old man, and he had stolen into the kitchen and had a brief consultation with Aunt Bell, as a result of which some more boxes were smuggled over from the camp of the cavalry detachment. Then, bearing his precious documents, he waved his hand in adieu to Lucy, who appeared one instant on the piazza, and set forth on his return.

Two miles outside of headquarters he came upon the cavalry picket at a fork of the road. The sergeant looked up eagerly as he saluted the popular old field-officer.

"They're expecting you back, colonel, and are getting mighty impatient, from what I can learn."

"Why, what has happened?"

"Oh, nothing much, except that the man we took to be Tierney isn't him at all. It is a Reb officer we've got, running our lines as a spy in disguise. There's going to be a hanging at sunrise."

"My God!" was all Westerlo could say as he struck spurs to his horse and urged him to the gallop.

XXII.

DESPITE the vigor of his actions as temporary commander of the district, "old Van Duzen" was a sorely
perturbed official. Some one had succeeded in arous-
ing in his mind grave distrust as to the security of
his position. Mosby, it is true, had scampered away
to the Shenandoah, and was frequently heard of at
various points along that beautiful valley. Graham,
with three regiments, had given chase, and was now
separated by many a long mile from the inexperienced
soldier whose years had pointed him out as a good
man to leave behind when rapid marching was expected of the column, and whose prominence in poli-
tics gave him, supposably, some qualifications as a
manager of local affairs. It was by no means a tur-
bulent neighborhood. All the people who had elsewhere to go had long since left so dangerous a field as
that which lay subject to incessant incursions from
troopers of the opposing forces. Most of the little
towns were well-nigh depopulated. Few of the farms
had other tenants than the birds of the air; but what
made the region full of wordless terrors to the old
politician-colonel was the close proximity of the fords
and bridges of the upper Rappahannock—only a long
day's march away. Beyond them his scouts dare not

venture, and who could say what that restless rider,
Stuart, might not be doing on the southern shore?
Night and day Van Duzen's dream was of a sudden
rush past his outposts, and a furious descent upon his
scantily garrisoned camp. He had pickets and outposts covering every road for miles to the south and
east. He sent couriers every day to follow the Shenandoah column, and he besieged the War Department
with despatches urging that he be strongly reinforced. The country, he said, was full of spies. He
had every reason to expect a dash of Rebel cavalry
any hour of the day or night. He was ready to fight
to the last man, so he declared in ringing reports to
an admiring constituency at home, but he begged his
friends to urge their representatives at Washington to
insist on his being instantly and greatly strengthened.
By this time, as was well known at the War Department, Stuart was kept very busy along the lower Rappahannock watching the movements of Hooker's dragoons; but Van Duzen was one of those men who
could hardly believe that the cause of the rebellion
cherished one higher ambition than to capture and
carry off to Richmond no less a personage than himself, and he would sooner be shot, he said, than fall
into the hands of the Confederacy. Yet he enjoyed,
after a way of his own, the prominence of his position. In the absence of news from other sources the
representatives of the press had no trouble in getting
whole columns of sensation from his oracular lips.
"Special correspondents" were easily obtainable
among his henchmen, and the vehement and vigorous

efforts of the gallant Colonel Van Duzen in the suppression of the rebellion were daily thrilling thousands and thousands of readers with reviving hope, and people were already wondering how long an ungrateful administration would delay his promotion to a generalship; and Major Kearny had just marched across the Long Bridge with his new regiment when he was startled, and many a reader electrified, by the tidings that Colonel Van Duzen had captured within his lines, disguised as a Union scout and amply provided with authentic orders, credentials, etc., an officer holding confidential relations with General "Jeb" Stuart—"a distinguished scion of the F. F. V.'s"— Major Henry Armistead of the Confederate Cavalry; and that it was probable that the fate of the spy, death by hanging, would be the penalty of his rashness before the setting of another sun. He had safely penetrated the lines, said this glowing account; had obtained most important information as to our forces, their numbers and position, and was just about returning when arrested by the vigilance and unerring judgment of Colonel Van Duzen. At first he stoutly maintained that he was what his papers represented him—a scout and secret-service employee, but he was recognized at once by several "intelligent contrabands" who had known him for years, and when arrested was in the act of bidding farewell to his venerable father at his home near Hopeville Gap. The case against him was clear, and it was absolutely necessary, said the scribe, that a stern example be promptly made. Ample authority had already been given

Colonel Van Duzen in the premises, and there could be no question that so fervent a patriot and sterling a soldier would do his full duty.

And so it happened that Kearny, miles away, and Westerlo, close at hand, were spurring that night to reach the scene before the fatal order could be carried into effect. Westerlo was on the spot and in presence of the district commander as the cavalry trumpets were sounding tattoo. Kearny was clattering through the streets of a well-nigh deserted village with an all-night ride before him. Few words were needed to gain the desired permission. His new colonel was an old soldier of the *ante-bellum* days, who knew the story of his young major's rescue and preservation by that very family, who already half suspected that his heart was left behind him in the shadows of the Bull Run range, who had noted the eagerness with which he rode forth upon the well-remembered highway beyond Fort Runyon when they reached the "sacred soil" that morning; and who knew his suspicions were well grounded when at nightfall Kearny came to him, paper in hand, trembling at the lips with anxiety and emotion, to proffer his request to be allowed to push ahead without delay.

Meanwhile old Westerlo had lost no time. Briefly reporting to his superior the result of his observations during the day, he asked the honor of a private interview, and Van Duzen, hardly knowing what to make of the matter, acceded. He stood a little in awe of the educated soldier whom the fortunes of a war replete with oddest fortunes had thrown under his command.

"I hear from several sources as I return to camp," began Westerlo, the moment they were alone, "a strange story. Is it true, colonel, that our prisoner is recognized as Captain Armistead, the son of the poor old gentleman at Hopeville?"

"It is true, sir, beyond a doubt. His identity was discovered to us just after you left by a faithful colored man, and corroborated by several others. It is a most important arrest—a most important arrest. I telegraphed the news at once to Washington—at least, my adjutant assures me it went at once, and the line is fortunately up. They make no reply. It is evident they have full confidence in my ability and intention to carry out the custom of war in like cases."

"And, pardon me, you will wait no instructions?"

"I need none, sir," was the stately reply. "I know my duty—painful though it be. So flagrant a case, after all we have published as to our intentions, cannot be overlooked. Why, sir, it was sheer bravado— Southern braggadocio—that prompted that young coxcomb to dare me in this way. I have not a doubt, sir, he has seen my proclamation to the people of this district, and he and his fellow-rebels put up the scheme to make me a laughing-stock—a laughing-stock. He dared to ride clear through my lines, sir, and doubtless vaunted himself on the exploit, and now was going back, laughing in his sleeve at me, to bring Stuart and his whole force at his heels to drag us off to Libby. But I beat him at his own game, sir, and we'll see how he'll laugh to-morrow."

"You will hang him then, I judge?" said Westerlo, quietly.

"What else? What said our immortal Washington of André—'He was hanged as a spy'—did he not?"

"Words to that effect, colonel, as I remember; yet, was there not something else? 'He was tried as a spy.' Have you tried Captain Armistead?"

"*Cui bono*, Colonel Westerlo, *cui bono?* Why attempt to prove a self-evident proposition? What could be clearer than his case?"

"Colonel Van Duzen, I am too old a soldier to argue with my senior; I am too respectful to you, personally and officially, to venture a word of advice without your full consent and by your invitation. I have asked a private interview that no man might know I ventured to ask you, my commander, to consider one little point. Sir, while I have been a soldier from boyhood, humble and accustomed to obey, yours has been the proud gift to be a ruler of men, a swayer of the public mind. Yours is a name with which our state resounds—mine is known but as your loyal subordinate. I would not for one moment question your judgment in this most important matter. It is to present to you a phase of the question you cannot yet have heard that I am here—to ask it of you, not as a right, but as a favor."

Van Duzen was disarmed. The subtle tribute to his greatness was more than the statesman of the Susquehanna could withstand.

"Proceed, Colonel Westerlo," he answered, with becoming dignity, yet with softened manner. "I shall be glad of the counsel of so eminent a soldier."

"They tell me, colonel, he is to hang at sunrise. I question not that you are satisfied your authority is ample, and that the government will interpose no orders or delays. I look upon you, indeed, as having final jurisdiction in the matter, and realize that the fate of this unhappy youth is solely in your hands. It is to you, therefore, I bring these papers, confided to me as a sacred charge, and ask your consideration of one point. He is here, this young rebel, in disguise and with false papers. This brings him within the penalties of your proclamation, and yet, if I prove to you he came not as a spy, but solely to pay a last visit, as he supposed, to a dying father, will it not induce you to defer his execution until another day, that he may see once more the dear ones of his home."

"And meantime have Jeb Stuart rushing in and whisking the whole crowd of us off to Libby? Thank you, Colonel Westerlo, but delays are dangerous. I tell you, sir, this war has been conducted too long on the kid-glove principle. The nation—the people—demand of us that we now take the bull of the rebellion by the horns and crush the viper to earth." (Van Duzen's metaphors, with his toddies, became mixed in equal proportions, and Westerlo looked anxiously around him, sure of seeing somewhere the demijohn of Monongahela which was an invariable accompaniment of his senior's campaigning.) "I conceive it to be my bounden duty to make an immediate and telling example of this case, and I have so decided."

"One moment more. Bear with me, my colonel," said the old trooper. "Last year a young officer of high connections and distinguished family was shot and captured while carrying despatches. Ah! You know the story. I will not weary your patience, sir. It was the father and the sister of this gentleman now your prisoner who braved the wrath of all Virginia, who sacrificed their social standing, who lost every friend they ever had in this community, to save that suffering comrade from a fate you declare to be worse than death. You know the circumstances, but you cannot know, as I do, the sorrow and the sufferings of these noble but most unfortunate people. Sir, the revered old judge who so humanely gave Lieutenant Kearny the shelter of his name and fireside now lies at the door of death, heart-broken at the calamity that has befallen his only son. The fair, lovely daughter whose tender care nursed our Union soldier back to life and strength, whose quick woman's art found him a hiding-place when the Rebel authorities searched the premises for him, the only sister of this condemned Virginian is at her father's bedside sustained from despair and utter prostration only by his imminent need of her care. When you hang Henry Armistead, you kill one, perhaps both, of those loving souls at his home across the range. Sir, I implore you, grant us respite for one brief day. I say us, for I have learned to know and honor these people. I say us because their grief has become mine."

Van Duzen was silent. He would gladly have found a good way out of the mire in which his high-flown proclamations and portentous threats had plunged him. On the other hand, would not all the morning papers of his native state and of the waiting North be filled with details of the energetic measures taken by Colonel Van Duzen to crush the rebellion at its very core? Of his pursuit and capture of this dangerous and desperate man? Of his stern but soldierly course? Of the last night of the condemned man on earth? It would never do to weaken now. Never!

"I appreciate your feeling, Colonel Westerlo. I would gladly show these people how we value the services they rendered to a loyal son of the Union, but they cannot ask of us the life of a spy for the life of a soldier. Depend upon it, this misguided young man would be among the first to condemn their action and upbraid them for their disloyalty to their state. It would be very different had we been indebted to him for Major Kearny's life."

"You admit, do I understand, that it would induce you to suspend sentence if it were young Armistead to whom we owed Kearny's life?" tremblingly asked Westerlo, though striving to veil his deep anxiety.

"Well—ah—at an earlier stage of the proceedings it would have had great weight—great weight. Things have gone so far, however—"

"Colonel Van Duzen, forgive my haste. Forgive me that I interrupt, but listen; Henry Armistead and Frank Kearny were intimate and devoted friends in their college days. A romantic incident separated and made a coldness between them. It was the fortune of war that threw the latter, wounded, senseless,

and bleeding, into the hands of the former. It was
Armistead who tenderly cared for his captive for two
days and nights until he found means to send him to
his father's house. It was he who exacted of his people that they should conceal him, nurse him, restore
him to life and liberty, and the service of the Union
again if need be, that his promise might be kept unsullied. Here is the letter he wrote. Listen:

> "'IN THE FIELD, NEAR GAINESVILLE, *August* 30, 1862.
>
> "'FATHER,—The strangest fortune that ever fell to soldier's lot is
> mine to-night. You know the old intimacy and friendship that ex-
> isted between Frank Kearny and me at Princeton. We were like
> brothers until our senior year, when there came between us a cloud—
> a woman. I loved her—and the quarrel was my fault. In the win-
> ter of '60–'61 he came to Richmond and we met as friends, but there
> were subjects, this among them, on which we could not speak. In
> the spring that followed, after Sumter's guns, I hastened hither from
> New York, where I had gone to see *her*. She told me gently that my
> hopes were all in vain—that her heart was his—that he had already
> volunteered for the war. There is no need to tell you what this
> meant to me. Before we parted she had won from me this promise
> —God knows I gave it solemnly, and, pitying her fears and sorrow,
> with my heart in my words—that if ever he fell into my hands, and
> it lay in my power to save him, save him I would.
>
> "'Thursday night, late, I had ventured with a small detachment to
> strike the road between the Federal cavalry and the lines at Hay-
> market, hoping to pick up staff-officers or stragglers. Luck was with
> us. An officer strove to cut his way through, and in the excitement
> and darkness my men almost killed before they could capture him.
> Then, by the faint light of a camp-fire in the woods I examined my
> unconscious prize, and found myself face to face with—my promise.
>
> "'Bleeding, senseless, stunned, and bruised, he has lain here hid-
> den for two days, nursed by the negroes who bear him to you and
> tended by a surgeon whom I brought to him. I had to leave him all

day to take my part in the glorious victory we have won. The Yankees are in full retreat upon Washington. We go at dawn with Jackson to strike their flank. Honor calls me with my troop—my word of honor is given here. In your hands and in Lucy's I place my captive and my faith. As you love me, as you would preserve my honor unsullied, receive this helpless enemy of our cause beneath your roof. Conceal him from those who would take him to imprisonment in which he would languish and die. When occasion offers, restore him to his friends, and when all is over—the war or my life—send this to her, that the woman I loved may know how an Armistead kept his word—even though it was to give her to another's arms.

"'Lucy, you know her name. Do not speak it to a soul until this letter is to be sent to her. Dear ones both, God bless and guard you, and sustain me in the cause we love.

"'Yours ever,   HENRY ARMISTEAD.'"

There was a moment of silence in the room of the old Virginia house in which the colonel was making his headquarters. Then Westerlo spoke again.

"Colonel Van Duzen, would you hang as a spy a man like that—when he hasn't been spying at all?"

XXIII.

THERE were some sorely disappointed men among the "camp followers" around district headquarters during the next few days. Full and graphic details of the hanging of one of the most distinguished sons of a most distinguished Virginia family having been prepared in advance, several correspondents having spent the night in writing touching descriptions of the manner in which the Rebel spy refused all friendly offices (he had simply declined to be interviewed), and one energetic gentleman having "pre-empted" the telegraph wire at no inconsiderable expense, it was hard luck that they should be greeted with the rising of the sun with such cheerless tidings as that the condemned man had been accorded a respite. The soldiers broke ranks after *réveille* roll-call, and scattered about their fires and coffee-kettles with unfeigned alacrity and cheerfulness. They were all "ready and willing to blaze away and kill Armisteads by the dozen in fair stand-up fight, or sabre them in a cavalry charge, where every man had a show for his life," said one old troop commander; "but this here hanging a fellow in sight of his friends and neighbors is too one-sided a business for most of us, and d—n me if I wouldn't rather see the whole thing stopped."

Around the house in which Armistead had spent
the night a dozen soldiers armed with loaded carbines
paced restlessly to and fro. A dim light burned in
the room where he sat writing his last messages. At
dusk the adjutant had waited upon him, and with a
voice that shook despite his efforts to control it, announced to him that under authority of the President
of the United States, and by order of the district commander, he would be hanged as a spy at daybreak.
The idea of being executed without trial other than a
mere search and a verbal examination—on his own admission, too, that he was Henry Armistead—had not
occurred to him as possible. He turned very pale, but
stood and looked calmly in the officer's eyes.

"Do you mean that this is true? Do you mean
that I, who am in no sense a spy, am to be executed
as such without the form of a trial and in such inde-
cent haste?"

"Such are the orders, sir. I have no alternative
but to tell you so and to ask how I can serve you
meantime."

Armistead was silent a moment, then, to the surprise of his much-embarrassed visitor, replied,

"By leaving me alone to think over this for half an
hour. Then, if you will call, I will thank you."

And the adjutant bowed and withdrew, giving orders
to the sentry at the door to keep his eyes on the prisoner, and permit him to make no attempt on his life.

When the adjutant returned at the appointed time
he found the Virginian seated at a little wooden table.
He raised his head.

"I presume you will permit me to see one friend?"

"It is the intention of the colonel to send at once for your relatives at Hopeville. He has just succeeded in getting an ambulance up from Thoroughfare."

"Spare them that, and all knowledge of this—murder—until it is done. My father lies in an illness that may be fatal. My sister cannot leave him. The man I ask to see is our old family physician, Dr. Loring. He lives not far from here."

"I regret that Dr. Loring has been sent to Washington. We cannot reach him."

"Then let me have writing materials and freedom from interruption of any kind. It is all I ask of you."

And it was all he would accept. Two officers besought him to let them be of service. He returned their cards with courteous but positive refusal. Others sent steaming coffee and a hot supper. He would not touch it. The correspondents vainly pleaded for an interview, and, his patience being exhausted, Armistead begged the officer of the guard to secure him against further annoyance. He was still writing when, near midnight, the adjutant entered, followed by an elderly officer with iron-gray hair and the appearance of a man who had been for hours in the saddle over muddy roads.

"Captain Armistead, I come to you far more gladly than I did at retreat. I am ordered to say to you that Colonel Van Duzen has been pleased to grant a respite of two days in your case, and I present to you Lieutenant-Colonel Westerlo, who will explain."

They were closeted together, talking in low tones,

16

after the first few formal words, for over an hour, and parted with fervent shake of the hand. Then the old dragoon went to his tent. It was after one when his head rested at last upon his soldier pillow, but his face wore a smile of hope and content. "A good night's work, you old schemer," he muttered, addressing himself, "a very good night's work. All I need is two days, and I'll have this fine fellow out of danger of your halters, Colonel District Commander Van Duzen. Good-night to you, and blissful dreams, and may you soon be in Congress, where you want to be, or heaven, where you deserve to be, or anywhere out of the army, where you've no business to be."

The sun was high over the Bull Run range, and pouring in at the open flap of his tent, and his small darky servitor had slaved for hours removing the mud from his garments and equipments, and polishing his huge top-boots and spurs, and still he slept. Not until the trumpets pealed for guard-mounting did he start from his pillow, and found on the camp-stool by his bedside a card :

"Frank Kearny, Major —— New Jersey. The very man, by Jupiter ! Here, Guyascutus, my Ethiop ; where are you ? Where is this gentleman ?"

"Just done come," was the effect of the darky's reply. "He's gone to speak wid de officer of de gyard, cunnel."

"Seek him, and bid him breakfast with me, and see to it that breakfast is ready quick. Go !" exclaimed the veteran, as he hastily garbed himself. He was the picture of soldierly trimness and precision, when in half an hour he emerged from his tent, and hastened in search of his visitor. Kearny, on the other hand, haggard, wearied, splashed with mud from his all-night ride, looked ill by contrast.

"Something told me you would be here without delay, Major Kearny," said Westerlo, grasping his hand. "Come to my tent at once. We will have breakfast there, and be uninterrupted. Where heard you first the news of this affair?"

"At our camp a few miles this side of Alexandria, late yesterday afternoon. I left at dark, the moment I could get away."

"So? Then you have had a long, long gallop. You are worn out, but have heard the good news."

"I have; and how much is due to you and your efforts? Colonel Van Duzen told me on my arrival. I hardly dared hope. Colonel, I pray God that no inkling of his possible fate has reached the family at Hopeville."

"Bad news travels fast, but I send the surgeon over there this morning, and he will reassure them if any other story reached them. Still, they are in grievous anxiety. My God! think of that poor girl—father, brother, lover, all going or gone at one fell swoop!"

Kearny's face looked more haggard and worn than ever as he sank into the camp-chair set for him by his host. He made no answer.

"And a noble fellow is this Armistead," continued Westerlo, "a friend worth having. I like him better than the lover."

"You knew him?" asked Kearny, with averted face.

"I saw his capture; a poor fight he made of it. One looked for something better in a man who won the love of such a girl. Ah, Kearny, she is a heroine, and he—this Falconer—who *can* account for women's tastes? Yet he is handsome, winning I doubt not; but a soldier—bah!"

Breakfast seemed to have few attractions for Kearny, and Westerlo, wondering at the sombre mood and spiritless bearing of his new friend, attributed it mainly to excessive fatigue. He hospitably pressed him to eat, and finding that he had no appetite, and could do but faint justice to the steaming soldier fare so lavishly set before him, he urged him to remove his boots and mud-stained garments and sleep a few hours. But Kearny was restless, and eager to see Armistead —a favor promised him by the colonel commanding in course of the morning. He had other questions to ask. He longed to hear of Lucy, and he plied Westerlo with inquiries as to the condition in which he left the judge and her. He astonished the old dragoon by grasping and squeezing his hand when he spoke of the provisions he had forced upon their acceptance. He more than surprised him by the consternation and dismay with which he received back the package of money which up to that moment Kearny fondly hoped was keeping the wolf from the homestead door. It began to dawn on Westerlo that here was a new complication, and Kearny's next inquiry strengthened the conviction.

"Colonel Van Duzen told me of Armistead's letter. He was on honor, he said, not to reveal its contents, but that you had it. I know that originally I owed my life and safety to his letter, though they showed me far more than it ever called for of devoted attention and watchful care. What I never could understand was why he should have demanded such a sacrifice of them—the loss of all local friends if they stood discovered. Colonel, I want to see that letter. You have it, have you not?"

"I have, but it was confided to me with the condition that no one be allowed to see it except to save his life. It has served its purpose and shall be restored to her. I will send it by our doctor to-day. When will he be here, boy?" he asked.

"De doctor done gone, suh. Went las' night to de odder camp an' ain't come back."

"Good God!" cried Westerlo, starting to his feet. "Then he has gone there this morning and knows nothing of the reprieve."

In less than an hour, despite his all-night ride, mounted on a fresh horse, Frank Kearny was spurring for the Gap in the desperate hope of reaching the homestead before the fatal news. There was just time, before his steed was ready, for him and Westerlo to prepare despatches—one to go at once to Colonel Graham, another to the senator from New Jersey, and both were fervent appeals to remove Armistead from the custody of Van Duzen, and afford him fair trial. There was no moment in which to see the prisoner—Kearny was galloping northward striving to beat a rival that has downed the best horses that ever ran.

XXIV.

BAD news travels fast. Long before the major could reach the western entrance to the pass the assistant surgeon had ridden along the eastern base of the range from the camp of the cavalry outpost at Thoroughfare, and in answer to an almost imperious demand from Lucy had falteringly told her of the discovery of "Tierney's" real name and identity, and then was compelled to admit that the order had been issued for his immediate execution. He expected an outburst of womanish tears, possibly hysterics and wild lamentations, but he could have spared himself that anxiety.

"It is confirmation of my father's fears and mine," she said. Her face was bloodless, her lips quivering and almost bluish in hue, as though bitterly cold ; her glorious eyes were tearless now, but dark circles had formed about them, and their gaze was hard and stern. "Monstrous and murderous as the decree may seem to us, I presume it is useless to appeal to your commander for mercy," she presently continued. "You are sure Colonel Westerlo had returned, and had seen him?" and for an instant there was almost piteous appeal in the look she gave him, and in the tones of her voice.

"Yes, Miss Armistead, I grieve to say he was closeted with the old colonel a full hour before I came away, and we heard of no change in the order. Still, I beg you not to abandon hope."

"Hope!" and a flush of indignation rose for a moment to her wan cheek. "What have we to hope from men like him? At least, I presume, he will not refuse me one last word with my brother, or if I come too late for that, the poor privilege of bringing home and burying here all that is left to us."

"I feel sure he would not; but, forgive me, I fear it may be now too late."

"You do not mean—you cannot mean that they would have killed him already!" she exclaimed, with horror in her face. "Oh, this is monstrous! this is worse than tyranny!"

"I hope not. I pray not," answered the doctor, hastily. "But when I left it was the understanding that it was to occur soon after sunrise, and if—if you were able to ride over—"

"I will go instantly—instantly. Meantime you will stay with my father, will you not? Colonel Westerlo gave me to hope that you could remain here throughout the day."

"Depend upon me, Miss Armistead; I have duties here with Captain Wise's detachment that will detain me until the morrow, and I can spend most of the time at your father's side. First, can I be of any aid in getting your horse? My orderly is here."

"No, no! Come at once to father. Say nothing to him of my going. Conceal from him, if you can, the possibility of my brother's fate, and if he awake and discover my absence and demand the reason, then let him understand I have gone in hopes of saving him. Father was awake all night, and has only within the hour fallen asleep exhausted."

"And you have a horse?"

"None; but Colonel Westerlo left some instructions with Captain Wise, and he will surely let me have one. My habit and saddle are left; our horses were taken long ago."

And so, almost at the hour when Major Kearny set forth from camp, Lucy Armistead, mounted on a spare horse of Captain Wise's, and escorted by that gentleman himself, rode westward up the pass, and was soon across the range. Wise had been summoned from his early breakfast by a message from the guard, saying "the young lady" wished to see him at once. His half-hour's talk with Colonel Westerlo the previous day had filled his soul with sympathy and sorrow for the unhappy occupants of the homestead, and Miss Armistead's beauty had long since undermined the soldier sternness with which he had entered upon his duties. He obeyed her summons with alacrity, but was aghast at sight of her white, quivering face and trembling hands. She was exerting every effort to preserve her self-control, but the struggle was painfully apparent. In few words she told him almost coldly of her brother's death-warrant, and begged that she might have a horse to ride over into the valley and down to Van Duzen's headquarters. There might be time for one last appeal, or for a few words of farewell. Wise never hesitated a minute. Miss Armistead should have the best horse in his squadron, and he himself would escort her. Captain Wise added, below his breath, "Court-martial be blowed; I can't stand this!" Miss Armistead assured him she needed no escort; but he knew better, and when she would have declined it, he told her he was sorry to force his company upon her, but as his orders were to allow none of the inmates of the homestead to get beyond his lines, he must make those lines as elastic as possible by going with her himself. In twenty minutes she was in her riding-habit and the saddle; had printed one kiss upon her sleeping father's forehead, breathed one brief prayer to God for divine protection and guidance, and then rode past the pickets with her cavalry escort at her horse's heels, the admiration of every soldier of the guard.

They had not reached the village of Hopeville when, thundering up the rocky road, his horse all foam, there came suddenly into sight a horseman in the Union blue. Miss Armistead had been urging the pace at every practicable stretch of the winding passage through the range, and her sad eyes were gazing eagerly ahead as they turned a shoulder of the heights to their left. She reined in, however, the moment this solitary rider came in view, and if Wise had not been looking at him instead of at her, he would have noted how her pale cheek began to glow the instant the expression of her eyes changed from mingled surprise, incredulity, and hope to undoubted relief and joy. The next instant the tall horseman had

trotted up, whirled his steed to the left about, and was
at her side, bowing with cavalier grace over the pommel of his saddle, and baring his close-cropped head
as he saluted her. Wise, riding on her right, noted
the gold leaf on the cavalry strap, and made up his
mind that this could be no other than the Major
Kearny of whom he had heard so much. She had
turned away from her escort to greet the new-comer,
and her face was for the moment hidden from him ;
but the instant he heard her voice responding to the
major's salutation, the captain concluded it his duty
to fall back and give a word of instruction to the
brace of troopers who followed them. Before he could
carry out his intention, without being too abrupt, he
heard her almost breathless inquiry for Henry, and
Kearny's deep-toned answer :

"Reprieved and probably safe. Something told
me you would hear the contrary, and I came at once."

For a moment she could make no reply. She bent
forward over her horse's neck, covering her eyes with
her slender hand in its worn old riding-glove. Kearny
leaned towards her, his eyes yearning over her, his arm
half outstretched as though eager to catch and support her should she sway or reel. No word was audi-
bly spoken in the next minute, but Wise could see in
half a glance that Kearny's lips were moving, and that
he was murmuring something intended probably for
her ears alone. The three horses were ambling peace-
fully abreast, glad of the chance of a breathing-spell,
and Wise glanced over his shoulder at the troopers in
the rear and concluded that now was his time. He

reined back, but she missed the click of the hoofs on her right, rallied in an instant, and, brushing the tears from her eyes, raised her head and called him.

"You gentlemen have not met before?" she asked. "Major Kearny, let me present Captain Wise, who has been very, very kind to us to-day."

And Kearny drew back his panting steed, and extended a gauntleted hand to the captain over the croup of her horse. Wise remembered the force of that grip for weeks afterward. Again he would have retired and yielded his place to his senior officer, but again it was she who interposed. The road was wide enough for three now that they were fairly out of the Gap, and she would not hear of his going. Wise looked uneasily at the major, but could read nothing in his impassive face. Kearny plainly saw that, the first emotion and excitement over, and her anxiety as to Henry's fate measurably allayed, she was again mistress of herself and of the situation. She did not mean to be alone with him to the exclusion of any other man, and he was as proud as she.

He was worn and jaded from his all-night ride and his hours of vigil and sleeplessness. He would give her no hint of the pains and labor he had undergone in Henry's behalf and on her account. He somewhat bitterly said to himself it was a matter she would not care to know, and he never dreamed, as he rode in moody silence by her side, or spoke calmly and with simulated cheerfulness of his confidence in her brother's transfer from the hands of the fiery Van Duzen, that down in the bottom of her sorrowing and tender heart

she well knew he could not have been with the neighboring command on the previous day. Indeed, had
not Westerlo told them he was with his new regiment
en route to Washington? and that in some way he
must have heard the news, and, like the knight he was,
had hastened to the rescue and then to her side?
Even in the anguish of her anxiety and dread there
was a joy in this consciousness against which she
strove in vain. What but love for her could have
brought him here—here at her side? Gratitude and
a sense of obligation might have hurried him forward
to Henry's prison, but he would have stopped there,
his work accomplished, had he not loved her and
longed to bring her the tidings of the reprieve.

And yet no sign of this would she let him see. Was
there not still *another* between them?

Late that afternoon brother and sister were seated in
his guarded room, holding a few moments' converse
while the captain was making preparations for her return. Not without difficulty had Westerlo and Kearny
succeeded in obtaining for her the privilege of spend-
ing those intervening hours with the prisoner. "Old
Van" was already beginning to repent him of his
clemency, and to mourn what might be a lost opportunity. He had read of Southern women who furnished lovers or brothers with means of escape. What
was to prevent her giving him poison with which to
cheat the government of its punishment of the spy?
Kearny clinched the matter and put an end to the
argument by saying that he gave his word of honor
that nothing of that kind would be attempted; and

when Van Duzen looked dubious, he added brief mention of one or two senatorial names, at which the Penn-
sylvanian surrendered.   He was politician enough to
know the influence of the Kearnys and the New Jersey
delegation, and to yield gracefully in presence of such
odds.

At one hour of the day Westerlo and Kearny were
allowed to hold a consultation with the prisoner and
his sorrowing sister.   Ostensibly it was to confer with
him as to his "last wishes," for, in the absence of instructions to the contrary, Van Duzen had announced
that on the following day at sunset he must pay the
penalty of his crime against the laws of war.   In reality
it was to comfort him and her with details of the rapidly growing sentiment in the entire command against
his being regarded in any other light than that of an
ordinary prisoner of war.   Westerlo had taken pains
to tell all over camp the story of Judge Armistead's
possibly fatal illness, and the gallant effort made by
his son to see him just once more.   So, too, he had
told how they had shielded and succored Major Kearny, and the stories grew as they went from man to
man.   By noon that day "the Reb" was decidedly
more popular in that particular camp than its commanding officer, and there was talk of starting a
"round-robin" petition in behalf of the former.
Then, too, at any moment now despatches might
come from Colonel Graham or from Washington
setting Van Duzen's edict aside.   Kearny had long
since sent a mounted man over to the military telegraph station with additional despatches and with or-

ders to wait for replies, and he and Westerlo were in a feverish state of anxiety. Armistead alone was calm and composed.

At last it was time for her to go, for she felt that she must be with her father overnight. Wise, of course, had turned back one of his troopers at Hopeville to tell the doctor of the reprieve, but she well knew the dread anxiety night would bring to the failing old man. The officer of the guard and a sentry, as required by their orders, still stood at the open doorway of the prison-room, but the two field-officers withdrew that the brother and sister might have a few moments of whispered confidences. Her horse had been resaddled, and now, with those of Captain Wise and his orderly, was in readiness outside. Kearny's, too, was being led up and down in front of Westerlo's tent a short distance away. He had determined, despite his fatigue, to ride to Hopeville and spend the night at Wise's camp. It was a desire to see Judge Armistead once more, and strive to be of service to him, that would excuse this uninvited visit; but he longed inexpressibly for a few words with her. This was no time, he knew, to seek to undo her determination or to strive to discover whether her heart as well as her hand was pledged to this unknown rival. He had been strangely moved by what Westerlo let fall concerning Falconer. It was not possible that she, an Armistead, could deeply love a man whose courage was questioned, and whose name was mentioned with covert sneer. These were matters on which he could not speak to her, and yet what man who loved as he loved would abandon hope so long as there was left one tendril on which to cling?

And now 'twas full time they started, and old Westerlo had tiptoed into the dark hallway and tapped at the casing of the open door. None but he saw that parting. It was still some minutes before he could lead her away, and then, with bowed head and hidden face and faltering step, she came forth leaning on his strong arm. A group of a dozen officers stood not far away. Beyond them had gathered a number of the men; all curious, perhaps, but all silent and sympathetic. Some one of the former removed his forage cap, and in a moment every man in both groups stood uncovered. This was the Virginia girl who had saved Major Kearny's life: It was reason enough.

Westerlo lifted her into the saddle. Wise reined up on the other side. Kearny could be seen swinging astride his horse over at camp, and she was bending down saying a few words of thanks and tearful farewell to her stanch old friend, when there was a buzz of voices out towards the Thoroughfare road and the clatter of galloping hoofs. Kearny came trotting eagerly down to meet the arriving messenger, who suddenly darted into sight around a neighboring building and almost rode over the major before he could check his steed.

A joyous light flashed over the Jerseyman's face as he read the brief words of the despatch thrust into his hand, followed by a shade of disappointment. Quickly he rode to her side, and without a word handed her the paper. This was what she read—she cared nothing for the address or signature—she knew it must be true:

"Orders by telegraph direct Colonel Van Duzen to place the prisoner Armistead under your charge. You, with sufficient escort, to bring him at once to Washington."

XXV.

MARCH and April have gone. So has Van Duzen's camp at White Plains. Stirring times have those cavalrymen been having on both sides of the Bull Run range, but little of it, outside of "Old Van's" Congressional district, did the people hear. Matters of far graver moment have been occurring farther south along the Rappahannock. Chancellorsville has been turned and lost. Stonewall Jackson has made his last triumphant attack in flank, and has led his enthusiastic Virginians for the last time. May has brought sunshine and cloudless skies and soft and perfumed breezes to the once lovely valley in front of Hopeville Gap, but the roads are all dusty again with the tramping hoofs of scouting dragoons, and all is wild excitement and whispered confidences among the people who still occupy the homes and cottages of Warrenton and the villages to the north. June is here before we realize it in the whirl of hurried raid and rapid marching, and the war-clouds are sweeping up the Rappahannock, up the Hedgman River, and those tireless horsemen of Stuart lead the van and clear the way. Two strong divisions of blue jackets—our old friends of the —— New Jersey among them—cross the stream and boldly grapple the advancing columns, and at Bev-

17

erly Ford and Brandy Station the troopers of the
North and South clash in the first real cavalry battle
of the war.   But within another week the dingy gray
jackets and plumed felt hats are riding jauntily as
ever up towards Luray, and through every pass, one
after another, the Union horse dash in to the attack.
And still they stay not.   With the end of the second
week in June Lee's advance is far down the Shenandoah, and miles and miles ahead of the Army of the
Potomac on a race for the North.   Another week,
and as the Union columns pass over the well-known
fields of the old battles, and trudge on up to Edwards
Ferry, what should that bold raider Stuart do but
double on his tracks, come back down the Luray Valley, camp once again around Salem and White Plains,
and then, cutting loose from the entire army of his
commander, circle completely around the rear of
Hooker's marching columns, cutting off trains and
stragglers at will, cross the broad river between
Washington and its defenders, and then go galloping
straight away for the Susquehanna.   No wonder our
Union dragoons are kept " on the jump."   No wonder
Major Kearny finds his hands full in handling his new
battalion.   No wonder his heart turns with longing
and anxiety to the old homestead at Hopeville Gap,
and he prays for opportunity to ride over thither
and satisfy himself as to Lucy's safety.   He has not
seen her; he has not heard one word from her since the
night she left Van Duzen's camp to return to her father's bedside, while her brother remained—his prisoner.

He had faithfully carried out the instructions most reluctantly transmitted to him late that night by the irate and disappointed colonel. With an escort of a dozen troopers he had conveyed his friend and captive to the provost marshal's office at the capital. He had had one long talk with him on the way, but not an entirely satisfactory one. There was an odd constraint in Armistead's manner which Kearny could not understand or account for, and which the former did not see fit to explain. They parted in Washington without removal of the veil, and the major went back to his regiment sad at heart and more restless than ever.

One thing, however, he accomplished as a religious duty. He lost no time in acquainting the authorities with Armistead's story, and in reminding them it was to his people he owed his life. He found where Armistead was to be confined, and wrote to his mother and other relatives in New Jersey, enjoining upon them that they should do everything in their power to repay through him the obligation owed to the Armistead family. The authorities offered to release the captain on parole, and the captain refused it. All *he* asked was that they should exchange him as soon as possible, and permit him to rejoin his squadron under Stuart. Kearny rode back to Virginia, and was presently hurried out to the front and heard no more of his prisoner for many a long day ; when he did, it was to be informed in several letters that came all at once that Captain Armistead had fretted himself into a fever; that he had been and still was seriously ill; that in his helpless condition the rules had been re-

laxed, and Mrs. Kearny and others had been permitted
to have almost exclusive care of him in a comfortable
room set apart for the purpose, and that he was now
on the mend.   About the week before he rode into the
charge at Brandy Station, Major Kearny had other
letters.   Armistead had almost regained his strength
after a long convalescence; and, "I once thought,
Frank," wrote his mother, "that something more than
a school-boy-and-girl affair was going to be the result
of your long association with Kate Paulding.   Indeed,
I was almost certain she thought so too, but I am
bound to say that the present state of affairs is a puz-
zle to me.   For the first month of his incarceration
she seemed to avoid the possibility of going to see
him with me or with your sisters.   Now the days are
few that do not find her ready to go and read to him
by the hour."

It was a piece of information at which Kearny
smiled.

But early in June there came a time when once
again the fortunes of war seemed bearing him towards
Hopeville.   Despite the desperate fighting at Beverly
Ford, Stuart had pushed on northward, using the Bull
Run Mountains for his screen, and Kearny, with his
battalion, had been held guarding the trains of the advancing Army of the Potomac.   How he prayed for
release from this humdrum duty, and longed to be
with Gregg and Buford and McIntosh in the columns
that had dashed off northward, along the familiar old
range, in pursuit of the wily raider !   Twice in person
and several times in hurried letters he appealed for re-

lief, and begged to be sent on to join the other command, but it was useless. His new regiment was comparatively undrilled, uninstructed, and the men had not shown the steadiness and cohesion of the older troops in the one day of desperate hand-to-hand fighting. The general decreed that they with others in like predicament must stay and guard the trains, and Kearny perforce had to stay with them. Time and again he wished himself back, a troop or squadron leader in the old regiment, but 'twas too late. Not until towards the 20th of the beautiful month of June did he find his white-topped charges slowly crawling into view of the Bull Run range, and one day he wrung reluctant permission from his senior to take half a dozen men and ride over towards the gaps to inquire for his friends. It was late in the afternoon when he trotted through the well-remembered hamlet of Gainesville, and out on the Thoroughfare Pike. It was nearly sunset when he reached the Aldie road, and soon was plunged in the shadows of the heavily timbered range. It was twilight, and still as the grave, when he came in sight of Hopeville Gap and the dim cross-country trail to Sudley Springs. Far to the east the heights of Centreville were still bathed in rosy light, and the white walls gleamed in the last rays of the sun, invisible to him by reason of the barrier at the west. He remembered how Lucy's big Newfoundland used to trot out on the red road in front of the hedge, and challenge with deep-mouthed bark at the sound of advancing hoof-beats; but here he was in sight of the orchard and the heavy foliage of the old trees about the house. Behind him his men were chatting and laughing as they rode at ease, and still no sound of life came from the homestead. Something like a chill seemed to strike home to his heart; something like dread presentiment overcame him. Unable to bear the suspense, he spurred rapidly forward, and in another moment was at the gateway, gazing with straining eyes and choking breath upon a scene of desolation.

There was the old piazza; there the tall brick chimney, still proof against wind or weather. There were the broad steps and the dingy white urns and the little squat pilasters of the blackened balustrade, but all else was a gaping ruin. The dear old homestead was gone.

For some moments the shock well-nigh unmanned him, but the presence of his escort, chatting in low tones, and speculating as to how and when and why this destruction had occurred, restored him to himself. Riding in on the ruined drive, he dismounted ; sent a small party of his men up the pass to watch for possible raiders from the western side of the range, where Stuart was known to be in force, and then began a sad search for anything that might give a clew to the mystery. When could this have happened? How did it take place? What had become of her and her father? These were the questions that were uppermost in his mind.

The roof of the old portico was gone with the rest of the house, but the floor and the big white columns still stood. They were protected by the stone wall which formed the basement, though the columns were charred and blistered on the inner side. Within the rectangle formed by these stone basement walls was one yawning pit half filled with heaped and blackened timbers. Over in the northwest corner where was Aunt Bell's domain—the kitchen—were the remains of the big stove which she was wont to keep in such glistening coat of polish. Beyond that the trellis-work and the low fruit-trees among which the sentry paced the night old Nelse found him "so busy" he "didn't like to disturb him" and so slipped out unseen. Beyond these the now abandoned henhouse and the gaping doorways of the old barn; but nowhere was there sign of life of any kind. Busy, scratching hens, neighing steeds, lounging troopers, watchful old house-dog, Nelse with his limping gait, Aunt Bell with her cheery black face, Hannah with her alert, intelligent, eager eyes; the patient, sad-featured old father—all were gone, and with them the girl he so fondly and faithfully loved.

Late that evening, heart-sick, and weighed down with anxiety, he was pushing eastward again to restore his escort to the command. With Stuart's troopers just across the range and likely to come through at any moment, it was no place to spend the night. Alone, he would gladly have remained until some tidings could be gained, but he was responsible for the safety of his little party, and stern duty demanded his prompt return. With an entire army straining every nerve to reach the Potomac and check a dangerous invasion, it was indeed

"No time for love or sighing,"

and though it well-nigh tore his heart, he had to go.

Splashing through the shallow waters of the Catharpin, his escort aroused some sleepy watchers on the eastern bank, and sharp challenge greeted him. A patrol thrown out along the left flank of the army had halted for the double purpose of resting their horses and guarding the road to the Gap. The men were springing to horse as Kearny answered, and it was with difficulty he could persuade their commander that he and his were friends. A moment's parley, however, satisfied them as to his identity, and then the two officers dismounted for brief consultation.

"We were going to venture out early in the morning, and go as far as the Armistead place in the Gap," said the lieutenant, presently, "but some negroes in an old cabin here told us it was burned down six weeks ago."

"Where are they?" asked Kearny, with sudden interest.

"Just in the woods there at the edge of the clearing. One of them lived at the place."

A dim light was burning in among the trees. Thither strode the major, his heart thumping in his breast. In answer to his resounding knock the door was slowly opened, and a venerable kinky head peered forth.

"Nelse! old man! Don't you know me?" was the instant exclamation.

"Oh, my lawd! Mars'r Kearny!" cried the negro, in reply, and then tears and sobs choked his utterance.

The poor old fellow broke completely down, and, clinging to Kearny's outstretched hand, wept like a little child.

It was some time before he could tell his sad story. Dr. Loring had been restored to his friends and patients soon after Colonel Graham returned and relieved Van Duzen, but he came too late. Day by day the judge seemed to sink lower and lower. The cavalry were withdrawn, falling back to Fairfax again, and the Rangers reappeared. Even the sight of the Confederate gray failed to rally the broken old man, and one stormy night, just before they heard the news of Chancellorsville, he passed quietly away. They buried him in the little church-yard down at Warrenton by the side of his wife, and thither Dr. Loring had escorted Lucy and Hannah, leaving old Nelse with Aunt Bell to take care of the homestead. One night, soon after they took the judge's remains away, there came a dozen men on horseback. Some were in uniform, some were not, and they ransacked the house and drank up all the store of "apple-jack" that was left, and drove him and Aunt Bell out into the fields, and swore it was the last time that place should ever shelter a Yankee, and then they burned it to the ground. Did he know where Miss Lucy was now? No, only that she was with Dr. Loring's family either at Warrenton or perhaps Salem again. Did he know any of the men who fired the house? Only one of them—the gentleman that came to see the major with the officers once —Mars'r Tierney.

XXVI.

"No time for love or sighing," indeed! "On to the Potomac!" "On to threatened Pennsylvania!" were the watchwords. Though his sore heart clung to Virginia, duty and honor called Frank Kearny to his post in the marching column. There was only time to sit him down by the flickering light of the camp-fire, and on scraps torn from his pocket-diary to write her a hurried letter full of sympathy, sorrow, and wordless devotion. Of his love and constancy he made no mention, but no woman could fail to read their presence in every line. Thrusting in old Nelse's brown palm a roll of treasury notes, at sight of which the eyes of the recipient nearly bulged from their sockets, Kearny bade the negro reward his fellows for the shelter they had afforded Aunt Bell and himself, to keep the bulk of the money for his support and hers until the major should come again, but to fail not in setting forth with the rising sun and to bear that letter to Miss Armistead, even if he had to follow her to Richmond; and Nelse promised faithfully to obey. Then, measurably comforted, Kearny roused his sleepy escort, and, bidding good-night to the officer commanding the patrol, rode away eastward in search of his trains.

Who has forgotten the days that followed — the breathless hush of anxiety and suspense, the rueful stories of invasion and disaster, the loud alarum in the valley of the Susquehanna, the thrill of dread in Washington and Philadelphia, the excitement and almost defiant rejoicing in Baltimore, the flaming skies above Columbia and Carlisle, the plumed squadrons of Stuart's raiders whisking past the outlying pickets of the national capital, sabring their way into the thick of the Union trains, and then trotting jauntily through the very streets of York, the dusty skirmishers of grim old one-legged Ewell scaring the whole country-side into refuge at Harrisburg? All over the astonished North consternation and dismay. All through the Army of the Potomac the thrilling sense that now at last their turn had come ; that now, at least, it must be do or die.

Far in rear of the marching columns when he reached the Potomac, still chained to the hateful task of guarding trains, Major Kearny heard with eager delight that a sudden change had been effected in the organization of the cavalry. A foreign officer who had long commanded the scattered division to which he belonged had been relieved at Frederick, a new leader placed at its head ; and now, under men like Buford, Gregg, Merritt, Custer, and Farnsworth, the troopers of the Army of the Potomac, in three strong divisions, were scouring the country in front of the trudging infantry. Beyond question they would be the first to grapple with the foe, and Kearny was about the last man in the array who could rest content with the duty assigned him. No sooner was he north of the stream than he intrusted to the care of a staff-officer hurrying to the front an earnest appeal to the commander of the cavalry corps to be allowed to come forward in any capacity whatever, and in a few days the welcome order reached him, "Report for immediate duty to the general commanding the second cavalry division now marching on Hanover." With eagerness unspeakable he turned over his battalion to the senior captain, and pushed on that very night.

And so it happened that once again he greeted his comrades of the old regiment. He found them haggard, dusty, worn with ceaseless marching and sleepless nights, cruelly thinned in numbers, but "still there," and Dayton with them. There, too, grimy with dust, like their comrades, was the regiment in which Mullane had lived his brief and inglorious year; but with him had disappeared the faction of which he was the acknowledged leader and exponent. A dozen officers from its ranks spurred forward to greet and welcome the new-comer who sat in saddle in rear of the long skirmish line of dismounted Jerseymen, shaking hands with captains and lieutenants by the dozen. The whole brigade seemed to feel that it must do its best to show Major Kearny the pleasure his coming afforded every man. They all knew how he had never ceased his importunities to be sent to the front until the order was granted, and here he was just in time for Gettysburg.

Two anxious days had passed since Buford, far over on the left, had discovered the advancing infantry of

Pettigrew and Archer, and, true to his instincts, had rushed straight at the throat of his foe and striven to hold and pin him there, west of the Lutheran Seminary, until the Army of the Potomac could come up and man that priceless ridge below the quaint old Pennsylvania town. Now the morning of the 3d had come—the climax of it all. In vain had Ewell forced his columns—Jackson's old men—to the assault of the bowlder-strewn slopes of Culp's Hill. In vain had Hood's Texans hurled their charging lines on the Round Tops at the southern flank. The Union ranks had reeled and staggered under the repeated on-sets; the Union colors had been steadily beaten back from the Pike and that famous peach-orchard at the angle of Sickles's front; but all the crest of Cemetery Ridge was crowned with black-mouthed batteries and panting but determined battalions in the grimy blue; all the curving, wooded slopes at the north were watched by keen-eyed Northern riflemen; all the broad plateau to the eastward, far over as Westmin-ster, was powdered with the dust of tramping columns, and glistening with sunshine reflected from the canvas covers of countless wagons. Here, too, were parked the reserve batteries; here, too, the ammunition trains and the scores of ambulances; and all the beautiful undulating, fertile farm-land between them and the north lay open to the advance of hostile cavalry but for the covering skirmish lines of the Second Division; and of these the old —— New Jersey was farthest to the front, crouching along the rail-fence by the road-side and watching with eager eyes the fringe of wood on yonder opposite slope. "Stuart is back!" "Stuart has rejoined Lee!" These were the words that passed from mouth to mouth that gorgeous July morning. Now look out for squalls! Just at noon, when men and horses were gazing longingly at the forest shades along the ridges, and seeking shelter from the fierce rays of the July sun, there came the staff-officer galloping over from Meade's headquarters with the stirring message, "Look well to your front! Howard reports that he can see from Cemetery Hill great masses of cavalry marching out north of you. They must be forming behind those ridges now."

All the long, hot morning has been spent in comparative quiet. Custer and his "Wolverines" have scouted all the roads for a mile or more above the Hanover Pike. There are skirmishers in gray out beyond Wolf Hill, where McIntosh and his dragoons joined the extreme right of Howard's corps. There are little scouting parties of Confederate horse twinkling through the woods and farm enclosures up towards the York road. But just at one o'clock Custer with his fine brigade has started away under orders to march to the Round Tops across that intervening plateau whereon are all those dust-covered reserve batteries, ammunition wagons, and trains. He moves reluctantly, and with a shake of his curly head and a lingering glance over his shoulder at the wooded crest behind those substantial farm-buildings a mile away northward across the open fields. "You may be attacked any minute," he says to the brigade commander. "Those woods are full of 'em by this time."

And now, just as Kearny is shaking hands with his comrades, there bursts upon the startled ear the roar of the fierce cannonade that ushers in the afternoon of the 3d of July—a roar that speedily swells into the deafening thunder of the most stupendous duel of batteries ever heard on this continent. It is the two hours' prelude to Pickett's memorable and heroic assault, and for a few minutes the cavalry out on the distant flank can only look on and listen, awed by the magnificence of the sight and sound. The western edge of the plateau, three miles or more away, is presently shrouded in a cloud of sulphur smoke which, perpetually being rent and torn by flashing shells, closes promptly over the gaps and only gains in density. Then comes the call to action on the right. "Skirmishers forward!" ring the trumpets, and Dayton clasps for an instant Kearny's hand, then draws his sabre and gallops over to his advancing squadron. The brigadier has determined not to await attack, but to see for himself what is to be found along those forest-fringed heights across the level field. Whoever occupies them commands a view of the country for miles to the south and takes "in reverse" the line of battle of the Army of the Potomac and its parks of reserve batteries and supplies. What if Stuart should already be there? What if even now, screened by those woods, he is forming his charging columns and preparing to come sweeping down on these slender lines, brush them to either side, and then go careering madly on, playing havoc among those defenceless trains? Who can doubt the effect of such a dash when coupled with the grand assault now beginning from the west? Who can say where ruin and disaster will be checked should this indeed prove to be his plan?

Kearny has ridden back towards the Pike to rejoin the division commander, who comes spurring up with an anxious look o'erspreading his soldierly, bearded face. Together they rein in on a little knoll at the southeastern angle. Behind them in the highway Pennington's rifled guns are still unlimbered, for Custer's column is not yet clear of the field, and he does not move until his cavalry comrades are all on their way. In front is Chester's section, the cannoneers lying or squatting about the guns, the drivers dismounted and resting near their drooping horses. To the left, drawn up in close column of squadrons, are battalions of Union horse almost grilling under the blazing sunshine; but the eyes of all men follow the movements of that long skirmish line swinging boldly out across the farm fields towards those solid-looking buildings of the thriving Pennsylvania husbandman. "Rummel's barn" becomes the object of an interest it never knew before.

Suddenly up from the earth spring the men at the guns. A murmur of excitement flies along the mounted ranks. "Look at 'em!" "Yonder they come!" are the cries, and all in an instant, out from behind the farm buildings, out from the big, substantial barn, running into line, agile as monkeys, come scores of skirmishers in gray rushing for the low stone wall. In an instant both lines have opened fire, and the cavalry combat at the right flank has begun.

"Ha, I thought so!" exclaims the general.   "Look
at the guns!   Stuart himself, as a matter of course."
And out on the heights in the rear of the farm buildings—those coveted heights from which the whole field
can be so plainly seen—two horse batteries trot briskly
into view from the leafy shelter in which they have
been lurking, and in an instant are whirling around
into position.   Before a shot can be rammed home,
Chester and Pennington have saluted the new-comers,
and with spiteful shriek the shells go whizzing over
the heads of the intervening skirmishers, and the batteries have joined in the general uproar.   Just about
the time when the Union guns along Cemetery Ridge
are cooling down for the reception of the assault so
surely coming, far out here on the right flank their
comrades with the cavalry brigades have taken up the
chorus, and in a moment every gun is in full song.
The Rummel barn is jetting fire-flash and smoke; it
is packed with sharpshooters, before whose sheltered
aim many a gallant fellow of the Jersey regiment is
going down.   Kearny feels a sudden sense of keen
anxiety for Dayton, and longs to be allowed to dash
out to the front, but his general knows a more effective
plan.   A word to the young officer commanding the
advanced guns and the muzzles are depressed, the trails
whipped suddenly to a slight change of direction, and
in the next instant the shells are bursting under the
barn roof itself, ripping and tearing the brittle wood-
work, firing the hay-stacks, and emptying it of its human contents in the twinkling of an eye.   The whole
brigade sets up a cheer and laugh as the discomfited

18

sharpshooters come tumbling out and, bending almost double, scurry for the shelter of the low stone wall. Another and a louder cheer bursts forth when, with a blare of trumpets, Custer, "ever ready for a fight," comes galloping back at the head of his gallant Michigan brigade and ploys his excited troopers into close column of squadrons, ready for anything as their sabres flash in air. One regiment he hurriedly orders in dismounted to cover the left of his column; another to aid the thinned and bleeding rank of Jerseymen; a third, in saddle, dashes for the stone wall along the little stream at the western edge, just in time to meet there the flower of Virginia's cavalry and be borne back in the rush. There are ten minutes of wild excitement and stirring battle-cries—ten minutes of rally and countercharge, in which the Virginians in turn are outnumbered and hurled back. A brief breathing-spell for the horsemen while the gunners concentrate their fire on the batteries on the Cress ridge, and then—then comes the glorious episode of a never-to-be-forgotten day.

Just as Pickett's devoted lines are breasting the slopes for the final and desperate attempt to pierce the Union centre, Cavalier Stuart, with all his chivalry at his back—six thousand glittering sabres at his beck and call—darts in to carry out his share of the well-planned combination. Watching from his leafy covert at the summit back of Rummel's house, he hears the signal guns of the Washington Artillery far across the plateau; he notes the mass of trains and wagons down towards the south, shielded only by that thinned, and travel - worn division drawn up in front of the Hanover Pike. The time to strike has come, and, like poised falcon, his compact columns wait ready for the swoop. Behind him, in the open fields of the Stalsmith farm, are the brigades of Hampton and Fitz-Hugh Lee. No leader on earth need seek for braver men or keener riders. There they sit in saddle, eager for the word—eager for their great part in the drama of the day—and now it comes.

Kearny has just galloped back to his general's side, his eyes flashing with excitement, the sweat pouring down from his forehead, panting with his exertions in rallying the scattered troopers on the left. Another regiment of the Michigan brigade has just trotted into close column under Custer's eye. The Jerseymen and Pennsylvanians are slowly retiring, with emptied cartridge-boxes, to where their horses await them in the woods by the " Low Dutch " road at the eastern verge, leaving the " Wolverines " to oppose the gray skirmishers along the little stream and among the farm buildings at Rummel's, when, at the very northern edge of the open fields—just at a gap in the forest-covered ridge—there rides into view a pageant at sight of which a murmur of admiration bursts from the Union ranks. Sweeping out upon the gentle slope, with fluttering guidons and waving plumes overhead, with sabres at the carry glistening in the unclouded sunshine, moving with stately ease and deliberation, forming squadron front as soon as the columns clear the gap and reach the broad expanse beyond, then closing in mass as they steadily advance, side by side come

the famous troopers of Wade Hampton and Fitz-Hugh
Lee.   Here are the men who have borne the flags of
the Carolinas and Virginia to the very borders of the
Susquehanna, and made them famous on a score of
fields.   Here are the raiders who have followed Stuart in many a dash around our jaded flanks and rear.
Watch them as squadron after squadron gains its
front and distance at the trot.   Mark the steadiness
and precision of every move.   Note that slow, stately
half-wheel to their right as they descend the slope.
That means they are coming square at Chester's guns,
now just one mile away.

See the rush and scurry among the dismounted skirmishers midway up the field!   Out of the way with
you, lads!   Run for your horses, every man of you!
Never heed those peppering riflemen in the barn-yard
now.   Here come foemen worthy of your steel, and all
the Union cavalry is athrill with excitement and enthusiasm.   "Mount! mount!" are the shouted orders.
"Steady, now, men!" the caution from many a squadron leader as the very horses seem to plunge and tug
at the bits as though eager for the fray.   Look at Custer, his curls floating in the rising breeze, his eyes kindling like coals of fire, his sinewy hand gripping the
sabre-hilt, trotting up and down in front of his heart-
throbbing lines giving quick, terse words of instruction and warning.   Bang! bang! go Chester's guns,
sending their whirring compliments to the massive
gray columns still placidly advancing at the walk; and
a cheer of exultation, not unmingled with low murmurs of soldierly pity, greets the sight of the explod-

ing shells square in the midst of the beautiful division. But not one whit do they swerve or slacken. On still steadily they come, and now the field in front is cleared; and now all the guns are hurling shell and case-shot; and now the slow, stately advance becomes suddenly shimmering and tremulous to the eye; it only means that the pace has been quickened to the trot. A quarter mile at that gait, another at the gallop, and they will be here.

Now for our side! "Meet them, McIntosh! Meet them, Custer!" are the general's quick orders; "but let them get well down this way. Do not charge until they are in line with the woods; then we've got 'em on both flanks, too." Capital plan that. Lining the fence by the roadside on the east are hundreds of kneeling troopers ready to open fire as the columns come sweeping by. Over on the west side, too, along the little run, are other skirmishers all ready for the coming host. Possibly Stuart does not see this—possibly does not care. Heedless of bursting shell and hissing lead; silent, stern, inflexible, in exquisite order and perfect alignment, the Southern horse sweep grandly down the field. "Keep to your sabres, men!" is the order passed from rank to rank. Brandy Station, Aldie, and Upperville have taught them the lesson that the revolver is no weapon to cope with the blade wielded by brawny Northern arms. On they come, the ground trembling and rumbling under the quickening tread of these thousands of hoofs. Listen! "The gallop!" *Now*, Michigan! *Now*, New York and Pennsylvania! tighten your sabre-knots; take good grip;

touch boot to the centre; keep your dress; eyes straight to the front, and *forward!*

"Major Kearny, gallop round to the —— New Jersey. Mount every man you can find, and order a charge on their left flank the instant we check them here! Give 'em canister now, Mr. Chester !" These are the last orders Kearny gets from his general this day of days. Putting spurs to his horse, he darts around the rear of Chester's guns just as " the advance " is ringing from the trumpets ; clears the front of the squadrons issuing from the woods at rapid trot, and, glancing over his shoulder, sees the rush of the " Wolverines " up the field ; sees Custer, four lengths ahead, darting straight at the plunging host in gray ; hears the sudden burst of terrific yells with which the men of Stuart welcome the signal " Charge !" hears the fearful crash with which the heads of columns come together; marks the sudden silence of the cannon, useless now when friend and foe are mingled in death-grapple at the front, and with a din of savage war-cries, orders, shouts, shots, clashing sabres, and crunching hoofs ringing in his ears, he speeds on his way to the fence and the wood road, wild with eagerness to rally his old comrades and lead them in.

Back among the trees to the right, whither the led horses had been conducted out of range," there is mounting in hot haste," and thither gallops the young major, flashing his sabre in air, and calling to his old comrades to form their line. Rapidly he rides along the fence. "Mount, men, mount ! Quick, Dayton ! Quick, Hart !" he shouts. " Form your men, and get in here

on the edge of the field!" But all along that fragile
barrier are scores of troopers, kneeling or lying prone,
blazing away at the dense, dust-covered, struggling
mass of gray horsemen only three hundred yards away;
and in the thunderous din no voice is audible beyond
a rod or two. Dayton spurs up and down in the roadway until he has driven a dozen men back in search
of their steeds. Hart gallops southward to where his
squadron, mounted, is guarding the led horses in among
the trees. Half a dozen Pennsylvanians, officers and
men, come trotting up to Kearny, eager to be "counted in" if there is to be a charge; other troopers tear
down a panel or two of fence, that the forming squadrons may get in from the dusty road. Out in the
broad fallow field the uproar of the fierce combat
swells and rages, and though the long, compact columns are still pushing on, the headlong speed of the
charge is gone, the leading squadrons are swallowed
up in cheering clouds of swordsmen dressed in the
Union blue. The Southern leaders are hewing their
way, fighting like tigers and yelling command and
encouragement to their men, but those "Wolverines"
of Custer have barred the path; scores of troopers
from all over the field are bearing down on front
and flanks; Chester's guns have torn fearful rents in
their now beleaguered column; hundreds of steeds are
rolling in agony on the turf, and hundreds of riders
are bleeding and thrown. Eager troopers dash from
their places in the rearward lines and rush yelling to
join the combat at the front. Hampton's battle-flag
is waved on high and spurred through the mass of

swaying chargers to animate the Carolinians to renewed
effort; but it is all practically unavailing; the impetus of the attack is done, and now, though outnum-
bering the horsemen swarming upon them from every
side, Lee and Hampton are almost helpless. Relying
on dash, weight, and inertia to sweep everything before them, the Southern leaders have failed to provide
for just this possibility. Now their gallant men are
jammed together in one great, surging mass; only
those on the flanks or front can use sabre or pistol;
the rest are useless as so many sheep. In vain their
officers shout hoarse commands to open out, to cut
their way to right or left. From east and west every
instant fresh parties of Union horse come dashing in
with new shock and impetus, hurling men from the
saddle, adding to the clamor and confusion, utterly
blocking every attempt of the gray troopers to wheel
outward and hew a path to the relief of their struggling comrades in the foremost lines. Kearny notes
it all with mad exultation; Dayton's half - score of
men and the Pennsylvania troopers are hurriedly
ranging themselves in rank, when through the dust-
cloud they catch sight of that battle-flag of Hampton's struggling forward in the midst of the Confederate column. "There's our point!" he shouts as, with
flashing eyes, he turns to the little troop. " Come on,
men !" And, with Dayton at his side and the cheering line of horsemen at his back, down he goes in
headlong dash upon the surging flank. Another instant and, with crash and shock that hurls many a
rider from the saddle among the grinding hoofs be-

low and overthrows a dozen plunging steeds, Kearny and his swordsmen are hewing their way into the very heart of Hampton's legion and making straight for the flag. There is a moment of fierce, thrilling battle, of vehement struggling, of yells and curses and resounding blows and clashing steel and sputtering pistol-shots ; a moment of mad excitement wherein he sees, but for a second of time, bearded, grimy, sweat-covered faces, lit up with battle-fire, that live in his memory for years ; a moment when every sense seems intensified and every nerve and sinew braced to fivefold force, and in the midst of it all, just as he spurs his charger to the standard-bearer's side and his sabre is raised to cut him down, and all around him is one wild yell and clamor, there springs between him and his prize a face and form he well remembers ; a bearded knight in gray and gold, whose gleaming steel dashes to one side the blow he aims at the standard-bearer's skull, and before he can parry in return has gashed his cheek from ear to chin. Kearny reels from the force of the blow, but firmly keeps his seat ; and though he is half stunned, his practised hand whirls his blade to the point, and sends it straight at the bared and brawny throat before him. An agile twist is all that saves the jugular; but it is a well-nigh fatal move, unbalancing the horseman just as he is struck in flank by a stalwart sergeant of Kearny's little troop, and down he goes, horse and rider crashing to earth in the centre of the struggling mass. Almost at this supreme moment, too, Kearny's buzzing ears are conscious of a tremendous cheer and thundering shock behind him. He hears Dayton's ex-

ultant yell of welcome to Hart and his charging squadron, and then he hardly knows what happens. He
feels that the crowded mass about him is disintegrat-
ing, slipping away, edging back up the field. He finds
that he is borne helplessly with them. He is dizzy,
faint, bleeding, and exhausted, and can only drift
along; and he hardly knows how to account for it
when, a few minutes later, he is leaning, breathless,
against the shoulder of his panting horse, and Dayton, panting too, is at his side bathing and bandaging
his mutilated face.

"Have we driven them?" he gasps.

"Driven them? Look!" is the answer as Dayton
points exultingly up the field. A cloud of dust is
settling back to earth, shrouding many a group of
prostrate, stiffening, or struggling men and horses;
but, surging up the slopes down which they swept so
gallantly but a little time before, goes a disordered
mass of fugitives, with Custer and McIntosh, Michigan, Pennsylvania, and Jersey cheering, hacking, hewing at their backs. The great cavalry fight is over,
and Stuart is foiled. Even as Pickett's torn and
cruelly shattered lines are drifting back from the assault on Hancock's stubborn front, their daring breth-
ren were breaking before the sabres of Gregg's division—they had been sacrificed in a vain attempt.

That night, late, Frank Kearny is seated with bandaged face by the bedside of the man whose sabre dealt
the blow. Stunned and bleeding, Wayne Falconer
had been dragged from under his dying horse and
carried, just after the return of the troopers from their

successful pursuit, to the lines of Jersey battalions ;
and men wondered why on earth Major Kearny should
insist on giving to the Confederate officer the rude cot
they had brought from Lott's farmhouse for him.
Not only that, but he would not rest until he had
found a surgeon who could spare a moment in which
to attend the suffering man thus thrown a second time
a prisoner in his hands.   Thanks to both of them, and
to Dayton, too, Captain Falconer is so much better
by the hour the trumpets are pealing tattoo that he is
propped up on his rough pillow of overcoat and blankets and enjoying a bite of something to eat—the first
he has had for twenty-four hours—and a big tin cup
of coffee—the first he has tasted since they raided the
trains down by Rockville.   Then he grows communicative.

"Whom do you suppose we had the pleasure of
hanging just before we crossed the Potomac ?" he
asks the major, for Kearny had been speaking of the
destruction of the Armistead homestead.

"Tierney, I hope," suggests Captain Dayton.

"Tierney it was," is the reply.   "As thorough-
paced a villain as we ever had to deal with.   It was
he who really got Henry Armistead into that awk-
ward scrape.   It was he who succeeded in clouding
your name with a charge of murder, so we heard, Major Kearny.   And he bragged prodigiously when he
first got back to us of having shot the captain in a
duel.   He told a whining story of self-defence afterwards.   Stuart found out his double-dealing and had
him kicked out of camp.   Then he joined some guer-

illas, and out of sheer drunken wantonness burned the old homestead. Then he was caught at Leesburg in some more dirty work, and the next thing I heard he was strung up in front of the house he had robbed."

"I may as well tell those fellows of Mullane's old regiment, Kearny," says Dayton, after a moment's silence. "It will interest them to know the fellow confessed to the shooting."

But Kearny makes no reply. His heart is dwelling on a far different matter.

"You knew the Armisteads well, did you not?" he presently asks his captive guest.

"Yes. Our people have been their friends and neighbors for three generations."

"Can you form any idea where Miss Armistead has gone, or whether she has remained under Dr. Loring's care?"

"Indeed I cannot, major. I did not hear of either of them while we were at White Plains. Has Henry been exchanged yet, or that brother of mine? If not, and I am sent to join them, very possibly I can find out and get word to you. Either one of them would be more apt to know than I. Scott has always been an adorer of hers."

"I heard as much," answers Kearny, averting his bandaged face and looking gloomily away. "It is an engagement, I presume."

"It may be, I suppose, if we ever get through with this—unpleasantness."

XXVII.

Once more the guidons are fluttering along the familiar roadways under the shadows of the Bull Run range. Once more the echoed trumpet-calls float musically on the breeze, and long columns of horsemen in jaunty blue jackets, yellow-trimmed, come trotting down from the gaps and join the lines below. Southward push the long, dusty ranks of infantry—brigade after brigade trudging cheerily along, with the guns of the batteries "clinking" behind them. Lee is beaten back from Pennsylvania and is returning to his old line below the Rapidan; and from many a Virginia homestead whence issued stalwart, soldierly forms to join the gray columns on their northward march, and at whose doors and windows stood enthusiastic women waving God-speed and loving farewell and wildly-hopeful encouragement, there is heard now only the wail of mourners for whom there seems no earthly comfort. Pickett's grand assault, Stuart's headlong charge, have left no lasting impress on the Union cause, but have desolated half the homesteads in their native state.

And Warrenton is saddest hamlet of them all. Not a household here that wears not the badge of mourning. Husbands, lovers, sons, and brothers, who so buoyantly set forth on the march of invasion, are missing by hundreds when the thinned and sad-faced columns reappear ; and though she, too, wears such mourning-garb as the situation affords, Lucy Armistead, loving-ly welcomed and tenderly cared for in the family of good old Dr. Loring, is the only woman in this sore-stricken community to whom Gettysburg has not brought new and grievous disaster.

Once more she is in Warrenton—not the social pet she was before the cruel war-days, for in most exagger-ated form the story of her deeds at Hopeville has gone from mouth to mouth, and there are many among her former intimates and "schoolgirl" friends who coldly avoid her now. To this she appears to give no heed. Ever since her dear old father's death she has seemed crushed and hopeless. Loring took her to his home, with faithful Hannah to serve her, and then, finding it impossible to subsist in the western valley, and urged by many friends to come and cast his lot with theirs in the lovely old town among the wooded hills, he moved into Warrenton, and now is living there, doing what he can to alleviate the want and suffering, the pitiful sorrows, of the bereaved ones all around him. From the window of her lonely cham-ber, where she sits most of the livelong autumn day, Lucy Armistead looks out over the peaceful church-yard where, side by side, are resting the father and mother whom she loved so well ; and neither Loring's efforts, the tender pleadings of his kind-hearted wife, nor Hannah's spirited sallies seem potent to rouse her from the apathy into which she is fallen. The neigh-

bors run in every now and then to see Mrs. Loring, or
to beg for some advice from the doctor, but they do
not ask for Lucy. She does not walk abroad; for
that matter, no one among the women cares to, except
the few who are so unterrified as to rejoice in the possibility of being spoken to by the hated Yankees, or
so ill-favored as to repel the most determined and ruth-
less of the invaders. The streets are given up to the
swarming soldiery, and communication from house to
house is mainly through the backyards. Some few
among Lucy's old friends have called and expressed a
desire to help her in her trouble, but they are *very* few,
and the reception she accords them is not encouraging. She has heard the grievous exaggerations that
have been current as to her father's life at the old
homestead, and she can be roused from her apathy
only by mention of this subject. Then she is one
blaze of indignation, and will hear no explanation, no
extenuation. That her honored father could have
lived in this community nearly seventy years only to
be branded in his declining days as a traitor, a spy, a
consorter with the enemy, an open and defiant har-
borer of men who sought the lives of his oldest friends,
a double-faced villain, giving information to both
sides, and living in comfort on their pay and bounty,
while his neighbors were starving — such were the
statements told and believed in Warrenton in those
days when the coolest heads and most logical minds
were apt to be warped in their judgments by the end-
less tales at the expense of any man or woman who
dared show less than hatred at sight of the Union

blue — that her father should have been so cruelly
slandered is something Lucy Armistead can forgive in
none of her townsfolk, and so stands aloof from all.

And yet, poor girl, even while she hardens her heart
against them, she is oppressed with sore anxiety, and
is most in need of comfort. The story that is going
the rounds among the Warrentonians is that Henry
Armistead—the one real, loyal Virginian of the family—the gallant Confederate soldier and gentleman—
the only one now left in the beloved gray uniform since
his heroic kinsman fell dead among Cushing's guns,
foremost in Pickett's memorable charge — that this
brave, true Harry, whom they all loved and honored,
is now being tried for his life by a military commission of bloodthirsty Yanks, and will doubtless be
hanged as a spy. The trial was ordered in Washington, and his case is well-nigh hopeless. Such has been
Colonel Van Duzen's sense of what was due the nation under the circumstances, that, leaving to Lieutenant-Colonel Westerlo the command of the regiment
and the rescue from Stuart's raiders of his constitu-
ents along the Susquehanna, the late district commander has turned up in Washington with his side of
the story, and, all other witnesses and persons interested being battling at the front, or defenceless under
guard, the colonel has enjoyed the inestimable advantage of having the field to himself. The campaign
over, the opposing lines once more facing each other
down along the Rapidan, a military court has indeed
been organized to try poor Armistead, who stands
charged with entering the Union lines in disguise,

with fraudulent papers and felonious intent—in plain words, with being a spy.

Reluctantly enough has Dr. Loring confessed these details to her in answer to repeated inquiry. He dreaded the effect, believing that the news would only augment her wretchedness and plunge her deeper in this deplorably apathetic condition; but doctors are sometimes as much surprised in their patients as in the result of their prescriptions. If he had told her of some great victory, and Harry's release from durance, he could hardly have roused her to more instant and energetic action. For the first time since the Union troops reoccupied the town she appears on the little veranda, and, to Loring's amaze, walks straight down through the shrubbery to the front gate, faithful Hannah following, and there in the twilight stands eagerly gazing up and down the quaint old village street. Soldiers are sauntering along across the way; a train of army-wagons is slowly trundling by; several officers, some in cavalry, some in infantry dress, are lounging near the corner, and these she studies closely a moment, "shading her eyes with a slender white hand," just as she stood that battle-eve at Hopeville. Loring anxiously follows, and takes his place at her side.

"What do you mean to do, Lucy, child?" he asks her, noting the flush that has mantled her white cheek and the feverish excitement in her eyes.

"Doctor!" she exclaims, turning impulsively, almost imploringly, towards him, "do not hinder—do not blame me! *Here* I have no friends but you and

19

your loving ones, and you cannot help me now. There, in that uniform, I can find one whose friendship is tried, one who can and will aid me.   He is here somewhere, for I heard his voice but yesterday."

Even as she is speaking, and before the doctor can reply, Hannah comes scurrying along the walk, followed by a sauntering young cavalryman, who looks back at the group of curious and watchful comrades as though he half expects to be made the victim of some practical joke and the butt of their ridicule. But at sight of Lucy Armistead's face he promptly throws away the cigar at which he was vigorously puffing, hastily buttons his natty shell-jacket, and raises the forage-cap, with its embroidered sabres.

"You—wished to see me?" he asks, with mingled hesitancy and incredulity.

"I wish very much to see Colonel Westerlo, and ventured to ask your assistance in finding him.   Is he not here?"

"He was here, but I think he left for Washington this morning. He is summoned as a witness at an important trial."

"Oh, do not tell me he is gone !   I must see him. It is—it is my brother whose life is at stake."

"Captain Armistead !" exclaims the lieutenant. "Is this—pardon me—*Miss* Armistead ?—the young lady who lived at Hopeville Gap ?"

"This is Miss Armistead," answers Dr. Loring, for she has turned away, overcome with emotion.

"And wants to see Colonel Westerlo at once," is the cavalryman's response.   " I'll fetch him if I have to follow him to Washington, and you shall know in ten minutes whether or not he has gone." Away goes the young cavalier down the village street, brushing through the inquisitive throng at the corner with impetuosity they can no more resist than account for. In less than ten minutes he is seen returning, and with him comes striding along in glistening top-boots and gleaming spurs and spotless gauntlets, a stout, sturdy, ruddy-faced, gray-mustached old trooper, with the silver-leaves of a lieutenant-colonel on his shoulders —a man at sight of whom the loungers respectfully straighten up and touch their caps—at sight of whom Lucy Armistead, who has retired with the doctor to the veranda of the little house, comes fluttering down to the gate once more, and in another moment is clinging to his arm—clinging to an arm encased in the hateful Union blue, and sobbing as though her heart would break. Loring thanks God for the sight of her tears.

Later that day they are seated in the simply furnished parlor listening to Westerlo, who has been back to his camp, and now reappears with a number of letters and papers. She is crouching on a low stool, looking up in his face in breathless attention as he begins. It is true, he tells them, that he had arrived in Warrenton but the morning previous, and received his orders to go to Washington as a witness for the defence in Henry's case; but a later telegram notified him that he would not be examined until the end of the week. The mail of the previous evening brought him letters forwarded from the Shenandoah, and this very morning came a telegram from Washington telling him Miss Armistead was living with Dr. Loring's family, and to be sure and find her.

"From Henry?" she inquires, eagerly.

"No, my child," answers Westerlo, gravely. "From your quondam patient and prisoner, Colonel Kearny. He is in Washington conducting your brother's defence with the best legal talent of the North to back him." And as the old soldier turns again to his letter, he fails to see the flood of rich color that instantly sweeps over the uplifted face and weighs it quickly down. He never hears or even imagines the fervency of the whispered prayer, "God in heaven bless him!" He reads on, never looking up from the page to note the effect of his words.

"Armistead is in excellent health, thanks to the attentions lavished on him with the consent of the authorities during his illness, and continued without interference during his convalescence, and until he was brought to this point for his trial. He is so serene and calm that I feel convinced that every soldier on the court is warmly disposed towards him—the only trouble lies with two or three vehement patriots of the Van Duzen type, who are death on rebels anywhere except at the front. We still believe that with your evidence and mine, and that of one or two men whom he encountered, it will be possible to disprove all charges of being a spy despite the disguise, but it is taking hard work. If that scoundrel, Tierney, had not been hanged, something might have been wrung from him to exculpate Armistead. Was it not odd that one of the Falconers should have been present at the hanging? *Is* it not odd—" But here the colonel abruptly stops. The next few words are, "That the other Falconer contentedly remains a prisoner, and his Virginia friends as contentedly permit it? Have they no use for him? Armistead does not like him—yet seems aware of the situation of affairs regarding which you once spoke to me." These words old Westerlo skips entirely and comes down to the following paragraph:

"Of course he was deeply affected by the news of his father's death and the wanton destruction of the old homestead. Anxiety as to Miss Armistead's future also seemed to weigh heavily upon him until he got the news that she was under Dr. Loring's roof; but all this occurred before my arrival. When you see her it might be well to assure her that nothing will be left undone to save her brother, but there is every reason why she should accept the earnest invitation of Mrs. Alexander to come to her here. Mrs. Alexander is her mother's younger sister, and has been devoted to Henry since he reached Washington."

"You will go with me, my child?" asks Westerlo. "You have read her letter?"

"It was for that I begged you to come to me. I would have gone to Washington—to Henry—if I had had to ride there alone."

And that night, at Warrenton Junction, Dr. Loring sees her safely ensconced in a queer old wreck of a passenger car, tacked to the end of a long train of empty brown boxes going back to Washington for supplies. It is full of soldiers, guards, invalids, fur-

loughed officers and men ; but songs and laughter
cease when the slender, girlish form in the garb of
deepest mourning is ushered in by bluff old Colonel
Westerlo.   Pipes and cigars are tossed aside.   There
is only low-toned talk as the train jolts slowly and
painfully away over a road-bed patched out of all re-
semblance to its original self, destroyed and rebuilt
time after time in place after place, and yet a blessed
thoroughfare to Lucy Armistead, since it leads to
Henry's side.

XXVIII.

ANOTHER month has rolled away. Wintry skies are lowering over the tented slopes of Arlington. Deep with mud are all the roads converging on the causeway that leads from the "sacred soil" to the Long Bridge. Gloom and depression seem prevalent everywhere throughout the capital, and increasing testiness becomes observable at the War Department. Nothing of consequence is going on at the front, yet officers who stand in need of brief leaves of absence find them hard to get, and others who had been summoned to Washington to testify before, or serve upon, the court which tried Henry Armistead, were sent to the right about the instant their duties were completed. A hard-fought case was that. Kearny had early taken the precaution to secure from the President himself authority to remain until its termination, and so, despite Van Duzen's efforts, he could not be sent away. But the judge-advocate developed unexpected traits as prosecutor, and had called a score of witnesses who, before the case for the government was allowed to rest, had succeeded, despite themselves, in convincing most hearers that there was little hope for the accused. Poor Lucy, who at first had occupied a seat close to his, was made so wretched by the appar-

ent complaisance with which Henry's counsel permitted this accumulation of evidence that her brother
begged her not to return to the court-room until the
defense began. "Wait until Westerlo and Kearny
are summoned," he had said. "Then they will hear
and see the other side."

Womanlike, however, she chafed at the idea of
waiting until the adversary was utterly talked out
before opening fire in return. But Mrs. Alexander
gently added her arguments to those of her brother;
old Westerlo, who daily escorted them to and from
the court-room, gravely pleaded with her to remain
at home or to drive in the open air each day for the
week to come, by which time, he promised her, there
should be something worth hearing. As for Kearny,
he never left the court an instant, and when not engaged in consultation with the prisoner and his counsel, or in taking notes of the testimony, he was around
among Van Duzen's people questioning. Only to greet
her with grave and courteous welcome, and a few words
of sympathy and cheer, had he been near her since
her coming, and—it was not quite what she had hoped
or expected.

"I am ordered to return to Warrenton by first
train," said old Westerlo, coming suddenly in upon
them the day after her reluctant acceptance of the
new arrangement. "They will summon me by telegraph when I am needed. You ask me *why* this order.
Ah, how can I say? Fear not, little one. All goes
well. That Kearny—he is a wonderful fellow! He
is more than a match for them; he will overturn

them — overwhelm them. The lawyer, he is very well; but Colonel Kearny is the *soldier*. He knows what will best tell with soldier judges, and every time he writes a question they say the judge - advocate scowls and refuses to put it, and then the court is cleared for discussion; and when it is reopened and they go in again, the question *is* put, and our lawyer smiles. Fear not, my child. All will come right. Ah, you little thought a year ago that you had nursed back the life that was to save your brother's!"

At last the case for the defence began, and once more she took her place by Henry's side, and stout old Westerlo—the picture of the "square" and solid soldier—gave his testimony, and stood unshaken by the cross-fire of the judge-advocate. It was a matter of some hours' work, and Lucy's tearful eyes and flushing cheeks bore witness to the emotion with which she listened. Time and again that morning she found it impossible to resist the longing to steal her hand into Henry's as he sat there, so calm and serene. More than once she found her eyes glancing furtively at Kearny, seated as usual close by the lawyer's side. How pale, how worn he looked! How red and deep seemed the scar of that sabre stroke upon his cheek! Then *he* was called to the witness stand, and all through the evidence that he gave she was conscious that the eyes of the judge-advocate—a sandy-haired, sharp-featured New England lawyer—were wandering from her face to that of the witness and back again. Then he began writing his questions, and presently they were read, one at a time. They related to Kearny's sojourn at the Armistead place; to his reception there; to his wounds, illness, suffering; then to the fact that she had been mainly instrumental in nursing him back to health. She saw that Kearny's pale features were becoming flushed, and that his eyes were beginning to glow under their heavy brows. It was apparent to him, then, that the purpose in asking these questions was to convince the court that a sense of gratitude impelled him to testify in behalf of the prisoner. She saw that so long as the judge-advocate looked towards the witness, Kearny's eyes never flinched from their stern, set gaze into his adversary's face—for as adversaries the events of the trial had caused them to regard each other; but when, presently, the military exponent of the law glanced down to look over his memoranda, Kearny quickly turned: one instant he gazed at her, their eyes meeting fully as he did so, and then he looked, rather than gave, a signal to the counsel for the defence. At the next question asked by the judge-advocate there was prompt objection; brief, animated discussion; a protest on part of the defence that the question was irrelevant and trenching upon new matter; a vehement rejoinder, and, in the midst of the war of words, the brief, stern order from the lips of the presiding officer, "The court will be cleared!" A moment afterwards, as she stood in the corridor without, gazing up in Henry's face and clinging to his arm, she was conscious that Kearny was at her side.

"May I speak with you one moment, Miss Armistead?" he asked.

It was the first interview he had asked since her coming, the only time he had sought to see or speak with her alone; but she never hesitated. She well knew the tone and tremor of his voice; she well knew that it was some urgent and imperative need. Smilingly Henry looked down as she turned away, and beckoned to Mrs. Alexander to come to him in her stead. Together they stood and watched the pair as they walked slowly towards a window at the end of the broad hall-way, Kearny bending over and speaking earnestly to the slender girl, whose face at first seemed looking up into his, then, all on a sudden, drooped from the search in his shining eyes.

"How I wish it could be !" said Mrs. Alexander, as she read the thought revealed in Armistead's frank face.

"And why shouldn't it ?" he asked, in some surprise at the doubt in her tone. "What man on earth is better worth her ?"

"I do not know. It isn't—him. Any one—any woman, at least, can see how he loves the very ground she moves on. There is something wrong; he has hardly come near her. I believe he *has* told her, and she has refused."

"Then I mean to know the reason why !" said Armistead, hastily.

"*Henry!* If you want to ruin the whole thing, just do it."

They were coming back now. Only a few words had been exchanged. He was very pale, and his face had a set, steadfast look, an expression of a knowledge

of an ordeal ahead which there was no dodging. Hers
was downcast, suffused. As they neared the waiting
pair, she seemed to quicken her pace, and, quitting her
escort's side, came straight forward without another
word to him, without even a glance of farewell.

Presently the doors were reopened; the prisoner,
and his counsel and friends, and the array of curious
spectators, filed quickly back into the close atmosphere
where sat in solemn dignity the blue-uniformed court.
Mrs. Alexander endeavored to move in with the rest,
but turned in surprise at Lucy's whispered "Wait!"
Amidst the rustling of dresses, the tramp of feet, the
moving of benches, and the crowding of lookers-on
at the door, the rasping voice of the judge-advocate
could be plainly distinguished.

"It is the decision of the court that the question is
relevant, and the objection of the defence is over-
ruled, The witness will therefore answer."

"Aunt Annie! Come away—anywhere! I can-
not stay!" was the astonishing plea that fell on Mrs.
Alexander's ears. Without a word she led her niece
out into the open air, out into the November sleet; but
even as they passed the portals, where sentries in belted
blue kept guard, the bell in a neighboring tower tolled
three o'clock. The court stood adjourned for the day.
When it met on the morrow she was not there, and the
question the judge-advocate meant to ask when she reappeared was not asked at all. He had reserved it as
a dramatic *coup*, but Kearny's quick wits had forestalled
him. "Miss Armistead," he had said to her, "in order
to convince this court that I am biassed in your broth-

er's favor, and so to discredit my evidence, it is the purpose of that man to ask questions which, except the court forbid, I must answer. It is not that I shrink from laying bare my heart, if good could come of it, but *here* it might do harm. To make its effect telling, he means to ask it in your presence. I beg you to remain away —not to re-enter that room until you are notified that I am no longer under examination. Will you promise?"

She could not look up. Down in the depths of her heart she knew—knew well—what he meant. The tenor of the questions already asked was but preparation for others yet to come. She *knew* now, after these few words of Kearny's, that he would be questioned as to his sentiments towards her—possibly, in plain words, whether he did or did not love the sister of the prisoner, the young lady now seated by the prisoner's side. Never would she subject him to that. And yet —and yet, still with drooping head and downcast eyes, she stood trembling, hesitant. *Could* it be she wished to hear from his lips once again the words she had forbidden when last they met? *Could* it be that even in this supreme moment there was in her sweet, frank, open nature a tiny spark of coquetry? Would she have been quite woman without it!

"What—what can he ask?" she murmured; and though her head bowed lower, though she could not look up in his face, she listened with eager ears and beating heart.

"He would ask that which would compel me to say again, and, this time, to the whole populace, that my heart and soul are bound up in the girl who sits there at the prisoner's side—the sister of this imperilled man. God knows it is not for myself I implore you to keep away. It is for Henry's sake. But for *that* the whole world might know that ever since your sweet face led me back to life and strength I have loved you—utterly."

The end of the dreary month is at hand. The court has adjourned, and its members have gone their ways to other spheres of duty. As to the verdict, no one of their number can reveal it. The "proceedings" are now under review at the War Department; but an old soldier who knew her father in the *ante-bellum* days calls and asks for Lucy before he leaves the city. "My dear young lady," he says to her, "you have made such a study of military law of late that you know we are sworn not to divulge the sentence of the court; but the first time I find myself in a scrape I shall beg that fine fellow, Kearny, to be *amicus curiæ* for me—though I shrewdly fancy it isn't money that inspires his efforts." And the veteran goes away thinking he has said something capital.

Everybody tells her Henry is triumphantly acquitted. Dozens of people—good Union-loving people among them, too—were fascinated by his dignity and noble bearing before the court, as well as by her sweet, pallid face and pathetic mourning garb. Old Westerlo telegraphs from Warrenton words of hearty congratulation the very day after the adjournment of the court, though he is careful to make no allusion to Henry or Henry's case in doing so. But how could he know the result? Who could tell him? Mrs. Alexander's cosey home has many callers just now—people who are full of sympathy and loving-kindness, and whom Lucy thanks with tears in her eyes; but the one whom she longs to see and thank, the one for whom her heart prays night and day, never comes near her. It is with a shock of bitter sorrow, of almost incredulous grief, she hears in answer to the timid question that for two days has trembled on her lips that Colonel Kearny has returned to take command of his regiment at the front. Gone without a look or a word! Gone without giving her opportunity to say, "God bless you for all you've done for me and mine"! Gone when now, at last, she fully realizes that, except the love she bears her soldier brother, all the maiden wealth, all the girlish worship, all the woman's honor and reverence of her heart of hearts, is centred in him, her knight, her hero, her brother's savior.

Henry has been escorted back to his guarded casemate in a distant harbor, and as letters from the prisoners have to be scrutinized by the authorities, he has warned her to look for no line from him until after the promulgation of the orders in his case. Then he expects prompt exchange, and Mrs. Alexander is to take her to see him once more before he goes back to rejoin his gallant troop in Stuart's lines. Wayne Falconer and he are planning to go in the same "batch" of prisoners, he has told her, and she recalls the fact that of the other Falconer he has avoided all mention. She used to wonder at Henry's evident dislike for "poor Scott," as the elder brother once spoke of him.

Now she shares it, and one day when Mrs. Alexander, narrowly watching her as she does so, reads aloud that this officer has given his parole and expects to go abroad, she at once amazes and delights her warm-hearted relative by springing to her feet, her face flushing with indignation and vividly contrasting with the pallor of the past week, and with all her old spirit, exclaiming, "Given his parole! Going abroad! Oh, the shame of it! I hope he may never set foot in America again!"

"And yet," said Mrs. Alexander to herself, "they thought it was he who stood in Colonel Kearny's way."

Two days more and there comes sudden telegram to Mrs. Alexander that fills them with surprise. It is dated New York.

"Come at once. Captain Armistead leaves for Fortress Monroe to-morrow—for exchange.   GERARD B. PAULDING."

"Who is Gerard B. Paulding?" asks Mrs. Alexander, after a moment of rapid calculation as to time and train.

"He is a relative of Colonel Kearny's," answers Lucy, slowly. "Henry knew him when he was at college, at least he knew his daughter."

Early the next day they are in New York, and a little steamer plying down the bay conveys them to the island fortification under whose guns is already moored the big black transport that is to carry the swarm of prisoners "back to Dixie." Aboard the boat with them are numerous people, men and women,

who are mainly silent and apparently distrustful of
one another. They are friends or relatives, hoping
for a word or two with the Southerners before they
go. As the gang-plank is thrown out, a young officer
springs briskly aboard, followed by two or three non-
commissioned officers and men. The guard at the
sally-port is paraded under arms. A number of pas-
sengers press forward and attempt to go ashore, but
are promptly checked. None may land who are un-
provided with passes from the general commanding in
the city. There has been no time to think of such a
thing, and Lucy, in despair, turns her brimming eyes
to her aunt. " Oh, what can we do?" she asks. Mrs.
Alexander appeals to the officer. He is courteous,
but firm. The orders are imperative. But at this
instant there appears upon the scene a tall, distinguished-looking man, somewhat elderly, but with alert
movements and observant eyes. " Mrs. Alexander ?
—Miss Armistead ?" he inquires, lifting his hat as he
bows with courtly grace. " They hardly dared expect
you until the noon boat, but I came out to see, and
was assured the instant my eyes fell on this young
lady's face. Take my arm, Mrs. Alexander. Captain
Cutting, will you escort Miss Armistead ?"

And so they are led ashore past sentries, who salute
in silence instead of opposing glittering arms. A
moment's walk brings them to the quarters of the commanding officer, and there another sentry " presents "
to the officer of the day, and a corporal reports that
" the gentleman is in the colonel's parlor." Wonderingly, Lucy ascends the wooden stairs. Who may

20

"they" be? she asks herself as the party enters. Opposite the doorway to the bright army parlor Mr. Paulding pauses with Mrs. Alexander at his side, and smilingly beckons Lucy to lead. She does so, silently, and stands just inside the portals, looking around in surprise and disappointment. No Henry there to welcome her! Beyond, there is another room, a library and a study combined, and its door is open. Stepping lightly thither, Lucy Armistead pauses in astonishment. Yonder stands Henry, oblivious of her presence, and by his side, gazing up into his eyes, clinging to his arm, encircled by the other, is the explanation of his oblivion—a beautiful, dark-eyed, dark-haired girl. Even in her stupefaction, Miss Armistead cannot but notice how admirably she is dressed, and, womanlike, feels herself at disadvantage; but in the next instant the absorbed pair have suddenly looked up and seen her.

"Lulie!" cries the captain, as he springs forward and clasps her in his arms. Then, with pride and mirth and gladness mingling in his heart, he raises her tearful face, kisses tenderly the moistened eyes. "Come!" he says, laughing in delight, holding her with his left arm and stretching forth the other hand for the tall stranger standing there with such a happy blush upon her face. "Come! It's high time you knew each other, you sisters that are to be, despite the fact we are Rebs to the very marrow. Lucy, this is my promised wife, Kate Paulding."

She comes forward smilingly, and bends with glistening eyes and mantling cheeks to greet the girl who still hovers there wonderingly, encircled by Henry's arm. There is an instant only of silence and hesitation on Lucy's part; then her voice obeys her.

"Oh, forgive me !" she cries. "I—I'm so glad; but—I thought—all along— Why, Henry! You told me so yourself !"

And Kate Paulding's lips are pressed to her wet cheek before she answers, laughing low amid her blushes.

"That was all *my* fault. A school-girl romance, all my own, and long since forgotten."

Mine Run, that bloodless contest wherein for the last time Lee's science prevailed over the Army of the Potomac, is over and done with. The nation has dismally resigned itself to the inevitable winter of masterly inactivity in the East, but looks hopefully to the generals rising, fight after fight, to eminence in the West. Thither enterprising young soldiers are eagerly turning. Thither Colonel Frank Kearny has determined to make his way, and is once again in Washington seeking service in the distant field. Lucy Armistead listens with bated breath and wildly fluttering heart to her aunt's cool announcement of her casual meeting with him near Willard's, his kind inquiries after her, and his regrets that he would probably be unable to see her, as he expected to start for Chattanooga on the morrow. But cool as is Mrs. Alexander's manner, her eyes are observant as ever, and that evening he comes.

How he looks, what he says, what she replies—these

are matters that for ten minutes or more Lucy Armistead knows nothing of. She is seated there in the armchair, listening to the grave, courteous tones in which he is telling Mrs. Alexander of some friends of hers in the cavalry corps. For a quarter of an hour she herself hardly speaks a word. Then Mrs. Alexander rises.

"I know your time is precious, colonel, and so I will go and write the letter at once. You are sure it won't be a trouble to you? No doubt the mails would eventually carry it to Cousin Harry."

"But I shall see the captain in less than four days. Don't fear to burden me. Make it as long as you like." And in another moment she is gone. Lucy glances timidly, tremblingly, up at the tall, stalwart soldier who opens the door for the departing lady. Then the room seems to whirl as he slowly returns and stands there by the mantel. He will not speak, and at last she *has* to.

"I am so glad you came—to see us, colonel. There would have been no way to tell you how I thanked you," she begins.

But he raises his hand, interposing.

"There was no need," he answers, gently. "What have I done compared with what you and yours have done and suffered on my account?—though you lost no opportunity, Miss Armistead," he adds, with rather a dreary smile, "to assure me it was all on Henry's account. Have you heard from him at all?"

"Not since his return; that is, not directly." And now she is tingling all over. How can she speak of Kate Paulding?

"Through my Cousin Kate?" he unhesitatingly asks. "That reminds me. We can congratulate each other on being *in futuro* second cousins-in-law, can we not? I am really delighted with that engagement, though they tell me it is not to be spoken of until the war is over—rather an indefinite time. By the way—*now* may I see the letter Henry wrote to insure my welcome at the homestead? How the conceit is taken out of one as he advances in years! Henry demands my safety and nursing and concealment solely, I find, on account of my fair cousin, with whom he was in love, and who, with the ruthlessness of her sex, exacted the promise from him that if ever I fell into his hands he would do his best to save me. Being an Armistead, he had to keep his word. Then *you* nurse and guard me—all on Henry's account; and I—ah, well! I've paid for it heavily. Once I was absurd enough to hope it might have been a little on my own account. There — forgive me — I mean no reproach. I vowed not to speak of it. I even meant — not to see you; but your aunt sent an urgent message; she wished to see me. Let me have Henry's letter to read every now and then; it will cure this malady better than anything else perhaps."

But she has bowed her head and will make no answer. He comes a step or two towards her, wondering at her silence. Still she sits there bending forward now, her face hidden in her trembling hands.

"You need not hesitate, Lucy," he continues, gently. "She has written me the whole story—how she once fancied it was Cousin Frank she adored, and all that school-girl nonsense. It was all over with when a fellow like your Henry appeared as a lover, and I don't wonder. And so twice, it seems, am I forestalled by these incomparable Virginia wooers. I surrender my boy sweetheart to an Armistead. I yield the love, the queen, the wife of my heart and soul and strength—you, oh, my darling, to Scott Falconer."

She springs to her feet now, her eyes dilating, her little hands clasping tightly as she gazes full into his quivering face.

"Scott Falconer! Colonel Kearny, what *can* you mean? Scott Falconer! The man—the *Virginian*—who gave his parole and has fled to Europe to avoid further service—*that coward!*"

"They told me so—his own brother—you yourself—just after I saw you with him. If he is not 'that other' who stood between us, in God's name who is it?"

She cannot answer—she cannot speak. Her eyes are drooping again, her bosom heaving, her heart bounding. Oh, why cannot he see—why does not he understand? Suddenly there is a rustle of skirts in the upper hall—Aunt Annie's brisk and cheery voice. The letter is written and she is returning. It is now or never, and Lucy knows it. He springs to her side as the steps of the lady of the house, distinct and deliberate, are heard at the head of the stairs.

"Lucy, tell me," he implores.

And then quickly she turns, though even now her sweet eyes are hidden ; quickly her hand flutters into his throbbing palm, almost breathlessly she murmurs the longed-for answer,

"No man on earth."

What eccentric creatures some women are! Half-way down the stairs Mrs. Alexander discovers she has forgotten a postscript, and turns about to write it. There is a blessed quarter of an hour in which to recover from the semi-dazed condition in which the occupants of the parlor find themselves. A little later they are standing at the mantel, and she is looking shyly up into his glowing, soldierly face, a great joy illumining her violet eyes.

"And it was Wayne Falconer whose sabre did that—a Virginia sabre?"

"A Virginia sabre, indeed! You must thank your own neighbors for spoiling what good looks I had, Lucy," he replies, laughingly.

She is silent a moment, still looking up at the red scar on his cheek.

"I was thinking of a story I once read. A soldier who went to his king and begged his permission to challenge a brother officer who had struck him in the face. Nothing else, he said, would wash out the stain upon his honor or heal the smart. Did you ever hear it, or how the king made amends for the injury?"

"I do not remember it," he answers.

She hesitates a moment, the color deepening in her face. Her hands are clasped together but she raises and rests them timidly on his breast. Then looking up in his eyes she whispers,

"Bend down, just a little."

He does so, inclining his ear for the expected words.

Suddenly she rises on tiptoe, her arms are quickly thrown about his neck, his bronzed cheek is drawn still nearer, and then her soft lips rest upon the sabre's scar.

THE END.

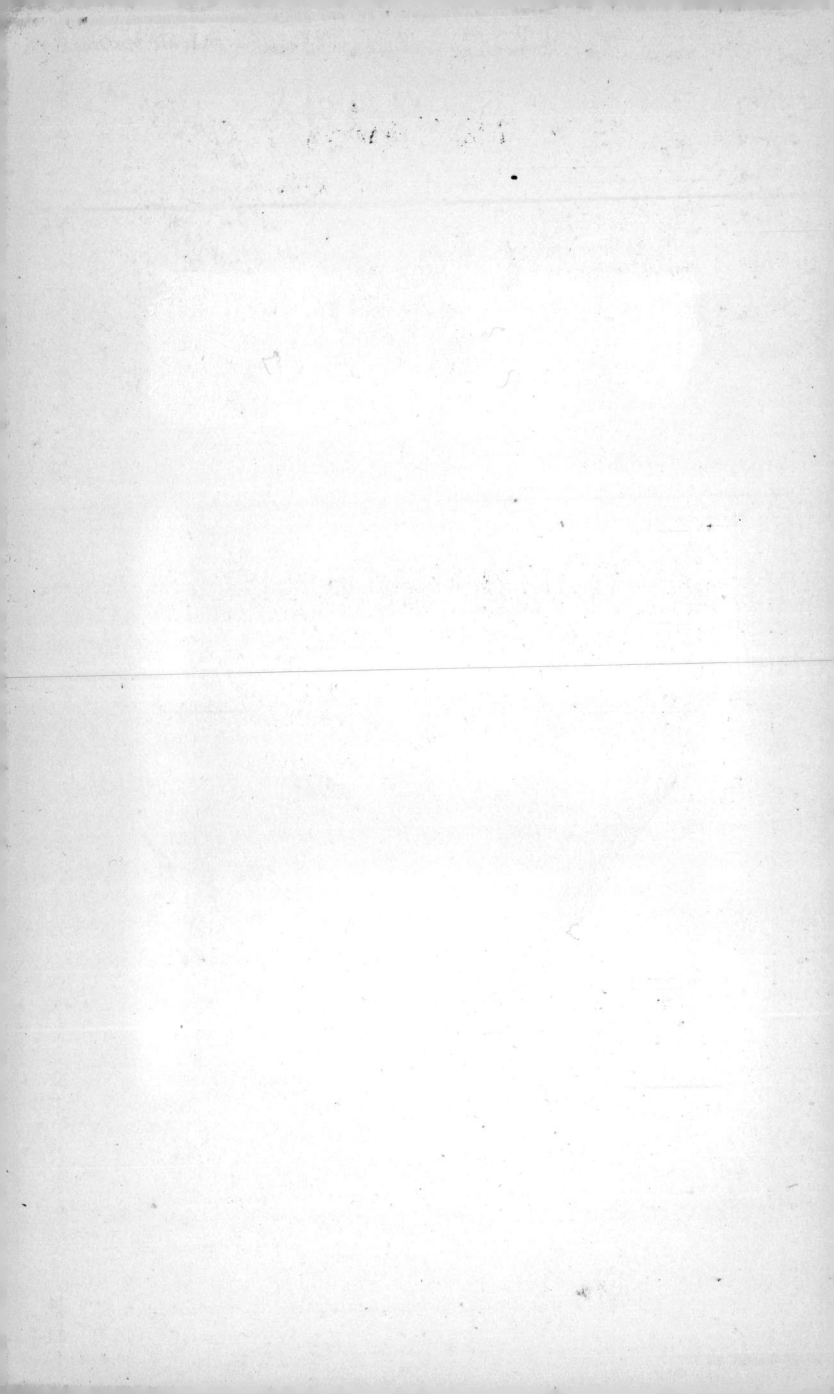